Understanding the Case against Shukden

Understanding the Case against Shukden

The History of a Contested Tibetan Practice

Compiled by
The Association of Geluk Masters
The Geluk International Foundation
and
The Association for the Preservation
of Geluk Monasticism

Translated by Gavin Kilty

Foreword by Lama Zopa Rinpoché

Wisdom Publications
199 Elm Street
Somerville, MA 02144 USA
wisdompubs.org

Library of Congress Cataloging-in-Publication Data
Names: Kilty, Gavin, translator. | Rgyal-spyii Dge-ldan Lhan-tshogs, author, issuing
  body.
Title: Understanding the case against Shukden: the history of a contested Tibetan
  practice / compiled by The Association of Geluk Masters, The Geluk International
  Foundation and The Association for the Preservation of Geluk Monasticism;
  translated by Gavin Kilty.
Other titles: Dol-rgyal gyi dçnos yod gnas tshul rab gsal legs nes bden rdzun rnam byed
  luçn rigs gser gyi lde mig ces bya ba bzugs so. English
Description: Somerville, MA, USA: Wisdom Publications, [2018] | Translation of: Dol-
  rgyal gyi dngos-yod gnas-tshul rab-gsal legs-nyes bden-rdzun rnam-vbyed lung-rigs
  gser gyi lde-mig. | Includes bibliographical references and index. |
Identifiers: LCCN 2018016976 (print) | LCCN 2018051384 (ebook) |
  ISBN 9781614295549 (ebook) | ISBN 9781614295358 (pbk.: alk. paper)
Subjects: LCSH: Rdo-rje-shugs-ldan-rtsal (Buddhist deity)—Cult—Tibet Region. |
  Dge-lugs-pa (Sect)—Tibet Region.
Classification: LCC BQ4890.R373 (ebook) | LCC BQ4890.R373 T5528213 2019
  (print) | DDC 294.3/4211—dc23
LC record available at https://lccn.loc.gov/2018016976

ISBN 978-1-61429-535-8   ebook ISBN 978-1-61429-554-9

23 22 21 20 19   4 3 2 1

Cover design by Graciela Galup. Interior design by Gopa&Ted2. Typesetting by Jordan Wannemacher. Set in Diacritical Garamond Pro 10.5/13.5.

MIX
Paper from
responsible sources
FSC
www.fsc.org   FSC® C011935

Please visit fscus.org.

Contents

Foreword by Lama Zopa Rinpoché

I AM VERY HAPPY that this compilation of advice from His Holiness the Dalai Lama combined with the results of extensive historical investigation into the question of Shukden, or Dölgyal, has been translated and made available in English. Much misinformation has been published on this topic, and so this book eliminates misconceptions and clarifies why His Holiness has spoken against the practice.

Several times, I have personally thanked His Holiness the Dalai Lama, who has with so much compassion and patience for us sentient beings, and Gelukpa practitioners in particular, persisted in explaining how Dölgyal is a harmful practice based on mistaken thinking. Some learned lamas with thousands of disciples criticize him, yet no matter how many critical books have been published, His Holiness continues to heroically advise us and guide us, showing how to avoid mistakes that not only destroy this life but destroy so many future lifetimes.

Even if we were to offer wish-granting jewels completely filling the whole sky, continuously in every second, still it is not possible to repay His Holiness's kindness. He is really saving us from falling into the extreme and dangerous wrong path that is more dangerous than falling into a fire. His Holiness the Dalai Lama is most unbelievably kind, inexpressibly kind.

Some people believe that before His Holiness began speaking out about the harm of Dölgyal practice, no Gelukpas had ever spoken out against Dölgyal practice, but this is not the case. Many Gelukpa masters who are like the sun eliminating darkness in this world, such as Yongzin Yeshé Gyaltsen, Thuken Chökyi Nyima, Phurchok Ngawang Jampa, Changkya Rölpai Dorjé, and Ngulchu Dharmabhadra, have advised stopping the practice of Dölgyal. His Holiness's own precious teacher His Eminence Ling Rinpoché was never a Dölgyal practitioner, despite being a student of Phabongkha Dorjé Chang. My own teacher Geshé Sopa, who was renowned in the three great Geluk monasteries and expert in Dharma and philosophy—he was there when His Eminence Song Rinpoché, who is also my teacher, was giving Dölgyal initiation in Geshé-la's room at 3:00 in the morning, but he did not receive it.

In this foreword, I want to address Gelukpa practitioners in particular, both those who favor the practice of Dölgyal and those who oppose it. For it is we Gelukpas who face the greatest risk for harm on this issue; our karma regarding Dölgyal is our great obstacle. The other sects do not have problems like this, but we Gelukpas, those living in the twenty-first century, have this karma. Whichever side we take on this issue, we face grave risk.

Many of those who now rely on Dölgyal have received teachings and initiations from His Holiness the Dalai Lama, taking him as their most kind guru. Similarly, many do not practice Dölgyal now but have been disciples of those who showed the aspect of following Dölgyal, gurus such as Kyabjé Phabongkha Dechen Nyingpo, Kyabjé Trijang Rinpoché, and Kyabjé Song Rinpoché. This is the case for me personally. Whatever the case, if you have received tantric initiations from a guru, it is essential that you protect your pure vision and do not come to see your guru as an enemy.

It is a great loss if you take someone as your guru and later err in your devotion to that guru. The *lamrim* text *Essential Nectar* explains that belittling your guru is the same as belittling all the buddhas of the past, present, and future. The buddhas manifest as gurus to help practitioners subdue their minds, and so disparaging one's guru creates incredibly heavy negative karma. The risk is not only to the happiness of one's future rebirths; it also makes it incredibly difficult to meet a guru or the Buddhadharma for eons to come.

If relying on Dölgyal causes you to denigrate the guru who tells you not to do so, such reliance is not only harmful to you yourself but also to other sentient beings, the teachings of the Buddha, and the world in general. Likewise, if rejecting Dölgyal causes you to denigrate your guru who relied on Dölgyal, then you also bring great harm to yourself and others.

As this book explains in great detail, Dölgyal is one who, in the past, broke his samaya—his sacred tantric bond—and made mistaken prayers harmful to the teachings of our founder, Śākyamuni Buddha. Although His Holiness the Dalai Lama did practice Dölgyal earlier in his life, he came to the clear conclusion, after years of examination, that this practice brings great harm to the Dharma and sentient beings. His Holiness's advice to not practice Dölgyal has been severely criticized and contradicted by some of the learned geshés of the main monasteries, some who have previously received teachings and initiations from His Holiness. This heavy negative karma brings the experience of unthinkable, inexpressible suffering for many eons, and this arises from the mistake of relying on Dölgyal practice.

Since renouncing one's guru is the worst of all negativities and the source of great suffering, I often wonder if reliance on Dölgyal—whether out of pure Dharma motivation or in hopes of financial gain—hasn't been even more harmful than the forceful annexation of Tibet by the Chinese government and its subsequent destruction of the teachings of the Buddha.

With respect to Phabongkha Rinpoché, the twentieth-century Gelukpa lama who promoted Dölgyal practice more than any other, many people think that it was because he practiced Dölgyal that he was able to spread the teaching and benefit beings, but this is a complete hallucination. We must examine the facts and not believe this out of blind faith. Earlier in his life, Kyabjé Phabongkha Dechen Nyingpo practiced Most Secret Hayagrīva, the Dharma cycle that springs from the pure appearance of the Fifth Dalai Lama, but later he stopped that practice. He had told his attendant one day, "Tomorrow a heavyset monk will come to see me. Don't permit him to enter my room." He said this explicitly, but the attendant forgot his instructions, and when the heavyset monk arrived the next day, the attendant allowed him into the lama's room. When the attendant entered the room subsequently, the lama looked cross and sort of possessed. All the paintings of Most Secret Hayagrīva and others had been removed from the walls, and the lama's behavior had changed.

But Kyabjé Trijang Rinpoché and Kyabjé Dechen Nyingpo are buddhas. Their practice of Dölgyal is the act of showing an ordinary aspect for us. Showing an "ordinary aspect" means displaying flaws. Without showing us this ordinary aspect, we cannot be rescued from saṃsāra. Showing the aspect of having flaws leads us to enlightenment. It is so extremely kind of the guru to show this; it is like the guru is giving us skies filled with wish-granting jewels. The guru shows the aspect of having flaws in many ways. Showing the aspect of being sick so that we can understand which foods harm and what not to eat, for example, or when the road is washed out or there is a precipice and we need to learn to avoid that route. There are many ways the guru manifests flaws.

When the appearance of flaws in the actions of the gurus arises, we should use that to perfect our devotion, for devotion is the cause that allows us to achieve full enlightenment. The *Vajra Tent Tantra* states,

> In the degenerate time, I, who am called Vajrasattva, will abide
> in the form of the spiritual master. With the aim of benefiting
> sentient beings, I will abide in ordinary form.

This is mentioned not only in the tantras but also in the sutras. The Buddha was once giving a teaching on a high mountain in the south, and at that time a bodhisattva thought, "The Buddha is teaching us now, but after he has passed into the sorrowless state, no one will be left to give us teachings." Guru Śākyamuni Buddha saw the bodhisattva's mind and proclaimed, "O bodhisattva, when the future comes I will abide in the body of the abbot, I will abide in the form of the master, and in order to ripen sentient beings, I will show birth, old age, sickness, and death."

Even if the guru is an actual buddha, if from our side we do not see him as enlightened, then as the Kadampa geshé Potowa said, "Should even Mañjuśrī and Avalokiteśvara descend before you, if you do not see them as buddhas, you'll receive no benefit at all. You will receive neither blessings nor profit, only loss."

And if, from the guru's side, he is not in fact a buddha, we receive only profit and no loss if we see him as one. We need only recall the story of the elderly mother who, convinced that a bone fragment from a dog skeleton given to her by her son was the Buddha's tooth, generated faith. The blessings of the Buddha's actual tooth entered the dog bone. In this way, truly, a disciple can attain the path and achieve enlightenment before the guru does and can then perform perfect works for sentient beings.

The Great Fifth Dalai Lama Ngawang Losang Gyatso mentions,

> To the hallucinated mind, the contrary mind, one's own flaws
> manifest in the guru's actions. Realize that this is one's own mistake and abandon it like poison.

So according to Lama Tsongkhapa's tradition, if the guru's actions appear to us as flaws, this becomes a support to develop guru devotion. Please think well on these quotations. We should see whatever the guru does as positive, in pure appearance. If we practice with faith and respect like this, everything we do will become Dharma. These are the profound, vital points.

If one guru says not to practice Dölgyal and another guru seems to be practicing, both are correct. The appearance of contradiction comes from our own mistaken mind. Whatever action the guru manifests has a specific purpose; we just can't discern what it is. In the *Sutra of the Meeting of Father and Son*, the Buddha says,

> The Buddha manifests in the costume of Indra or Brahma
> and sometimes in the costume of Māra
> to work for the benefit of sentient beings,
> but worldly people are unable to realize this.
> The Buddha also appears as a woman and as an animal.
> Free of attachment, the Buddha manifests having attachment;
> free of fear, the Buddha manifests fear;
> the Buddha is not ignorant but manifests ignorance;
> the Buddha is not crazy but can appear crazy;
> the Buddha is not lame but manifests a limp.
> In such transformations the Buddha works for sentient beings.

In other words, the Buddha manifests in all these guises to work for sentient beings. We must always recall this when thinking about how our gurus guide us. We can think that while not practicing Dölgyal, our guru manifests practicing Dölgyal. Either way, our guru's actions are unmistaken. This is the very important conclusion we need to reach.

This world contains many religions, but our founder, the great kind mighty one, Śākyamuni Buddha, said,

> O bhikṣus, examine my teachings well,
> as one would check gold by burning, cutting, and rubbing it.
> Accept them only then, not out of faith alone.

Whatever Buddhist practice we do, we must examine it well, just as Buddha has advised, and Buddha gave us the freedom to do this. This is what I am expressing; please understand this.

It is said that the subduer of the snow land of Tibet is Avalokiteśvara, who not only does the holy action of working for others and not himself but also has great bodhicitta and powerful compassion. He performs only the holy actions of guiding and saving the six types of sentient beings and showing compassion, like all the buddhas in the ten directions. This is the ārya supreme one, Avalokiteśvara, His Holiness the Dalai Lama. We should follow the advice of His Holiness. For there to be peace, happiness, harmony, and unity among the people of the world, for problems to stop, for ourselves and others to achieve liberation from saṃsāra and the state of omniscience, for the stainless teachings of the Buddha, especially the immaculate teachings of Tibetan Mahayana Buddhism, to spread throughout this world, His Holiness has advised that the practice of Dölgyal must stop.

Lama Thubten Zopa Rinpoché
Aptos, California
October 2018

Translator's Preface

TIBETAN RELIGIOUS CULTURE likely houses more protectors, or guardians, than any other religion. The pre-Buddhist Bön faith that flourished before the eighth century was well stocked with local deities and nature spirits to which supplications were made for protection, conducive circumstances, and so on. Some of these deities survived the Buddhist incursion, and even when they didn't, the tendency to rely upon such spirits prevailed in Tibetan culture. The great Indian tantric master Padmasambhava came to Tibet in the eighth century and proceeded to tame many local, unruly spirits, and made them pledge to work for Buddhism and the common good. But the pantheon of protector spirits in Tibet is not solely indigenous. The colonization of Tibet with Buddhist teachings brought from India a millennium ago also introduced Dharma protectors and other divine beings of Indic origin into Tibet.

Over time, as fledgling Buddhist traditions began to establish themselves all over Tibet, and sects divided and divided again and new monasteries sprang up, each adopted its own protectors. The result was a bewildering array of nonhuman guardians, some differing only by the number of arms, faces, implements, or color. In one book on Tibetan Buddhist deities, I count fifty-eight different forms of the protector Mahākāla alone. Later, many propitiatory rites and invocations of these spirits appeared, many of which Jamgön Kongtrul Lodrö Thayé (1813–99) includes in his renowned *Precious Treasure Collection* (*Rinchen Terzö*).

But what are these nonhuman beings and what is their purpose? As suggested above, some are spirits abiding in a specific locality and going about their business, occasionally making mischief, when a powerful tantric adept appears and forces them to pledge themselves to assist practitioners, protect the teachings, and clear away obstacles. Other protectors are themselves spiritually advanced beings who from their own volition work to provide assistance to genuine practitioners. Some are even said to be emanations of enlightened beings. A small subset are human practitioners in previous lives who vow to be reborn as protectors of the teachings.

Some protectors are associated with specific tantras and some with specific practices. Six-Armed Mahākāla is said to be an emanation of the enlightened deity of compassion and as such is relied upon by those meditating upon the altruistic mind of enlightenment (*bodhicitta*). Some are wrathful. Some are seers and announce their predictions via oracles. Nechung, the protector for the Tibetan government, is one of these. Some help with mundane considerations, such as the continuation of personal prosperity, the maintenance of health, and so on.

All this assistance afforded by these beings begs a question. A Buddhist practitioner who sincerely goes for refuge to the Buddha, Dharma, and Sangha and abides by the ethical precepts is protected from hindrances in this life, the intermediate state, and the next life. Why rely upon these beings when refuge grants protection? What need do Buddhists have for protectors? The answer is that protectors act on behalf of practitioners to help them attain spiritual goals and aims. Protection from sufferings and the obstacles of life is the goal of going for refuge to the Three Jewels of Buddha, Dharma, and Sangha, and this goal is facilitated by reliance upon protectors. The protectors themselves are not the refuge.

The renowned Tibetan Buddhist master Tsongkhapa (1357–1419) says that there are many oath-bound protectors found in the tantras and the Indian texts, all dedicating themselves to removing hindrances. However, reliance upon them should be in tune with the three scopes of practice described in the stages of the path literature. He says that practitioners focused on the lowest level of practice, for example, contemplate the transience of life together with the unfailing process of karma that determines the nature of the rebirth they will take after death. Protection from a miserable rebirth is afforded by going for refuge to the Three Jewels and following the ethical precepts. For such a person, the main practice is to distinguish virtuous acts from nonvirtuous acts, and to develop the former and reduce the latter. To those pursuing this path Tsongkhapa recommends reliance on the protector Dharmarāja, who is said to be like a king (*rāja*) or judge who is able to distinguish right from wrong, good from bad, or like a mirror that clearly reveals the karmic effects of our actions. In this way, Dharmarāja helps practitioners accomplish their spiritual goal of attaining refuge.

It is said that advanced practitioners "use protectors like servants," insomuch as they can order them about. The less advanced rely upon them as aids to their practice. There is a protector ritual in Tibetan Buddhism called a *life-entrustment rite*. While this may be seen as entrusting the protector to carry out the tasks allotted to them, some in Tibet have understood it to mean completely handing over one's life to one's protector, effectively placing it in their hands. His Holiness the Fourteenth Dalai Lama has condemned this and said it is the protectors who entrust themselves to us and not the other way around.

There is a saying in Tibet: "Where the Dharma is deep, so the hindrances run deep," and it is to deal with these hindrances that protectors come into their own. However, with so many protectors volunteering their services within the Tibetan pantheon, and because many of them are not free of their own worldly bondage, it is conceivable that not all will hold the best interests of the practitioner and the spiritual traditions at heart. It is the contention of the compilers of this work that Shukden, or Dölgyal, is one such being.

A Golden Key of Scripture and Reasoning

This book is a translation of a 2013 Tibetan work entitled *A Golden Key of Scripture and Reasoning Clarifying the Reality of Dölgyal: Distinguishing the Good from the Bad and Truth from Lies* (*Dol rgyal gyi dngos yod gnas tshul rab gsal legs nyes bden rdzun rnam 'byed lung rigs gser gyi lde mig*). Dölgyal refers to Dorjé Shukden, a nonhuman entity variously called a "religious protector," "a worldly spirit," or "a ghost," according to perspective.

The origins of this book lie in the issue of Shukden that has surfaced in the Tibetan religious community periodically over the past four hundred years, beginning from the time of the Fifth Dalai Lama, Losang Gyatso (1617–82). The nature of Shukden is a bone of contention. To some he is a fierce but loyal protector of the Tibetan Geluk tradition, or more specifically a guardian of the doctrine of Tsongkhapa Losang Drakpa, founder of the Geluk. To others he is a violent, worldly protector, useful for destroying hindrances and obstructions to religious goals, and to some, including the present Dalai Lama, he is nothing more than a ghost, a reincarnated product of perverted prayers.

For many years, Shukden was propitiated by individuals within the Sakya and Geluk traditions. There was never much ritualistic propitiation in monastic assemblies, and consequently the practice remained low-key. It was only when the charismatic Geluk lama Phabongkha Rinpoché (1878–1941) enthusiastically adopted Shukden as the exclusive protector and guardian of Tsongkhapa's legacy in the form of the Geluk tradition that his name and practice became widespread. This attracted the criticism of the Thirteenth Dalai Lama, Thupten Gyatso (1876–1933), who attempted to put a stop to it.

Later in the 1960s, Tibetan religious and secular communities in exile in India were busy rebuilding their society as refugees, and it seems that the controversial nature of Shukden had slipped the collective memory. This was owing to the cultural destruction caused by the Chinese Communist invasion and occupation in the 1950s, and also because Tibetan history is patchily recorded and not well studied. This changed in the 1970s when certain events, recorded in this book, resulted in the Fourteenth Dalai Lama researching the history of Shukden and ultimately denouncing him as a threat to the unity of the Tibetan people in exile in precarious times, when their very identity was threatened.

Over the next two decades the controversy rumbled and, at times, erupted unpleasantly. Most Geluk monks at that time had received teachings from either Phabongkha Rinpoché or his illustrious disciple Trijang Rinpoché (1901–81) and therefore were actively propitiating Shukden. His Holiness stated publicly that those who wanted to attend his teachings should give up the Shukden practice. There arose a polarized division between those who supported the stance of the Dalai Lama and a minority who felt he was restricting the freedom to worship as they pleased.

The issue received attention in Western countries and in China. Organized and disruptive protests against the Dalai Lama were held by Shukden supporters whenever he traveled abroad, and it became evident that the Chinese regime was attempting to use the controversy to its advantage both in Tibet and in India.

Finally, in 2008, the increasing seriousness of the situation and the simmering discontent around the Shukden issue in the monasteries prompted the Dalai Lama to conclude that the matter had to be clarified, and he proposed employing a remedy prescribed in the Vinaya for the resolution of disputes in the monastic community. He suggested that the six main Geluk monasteries in exile hold a referendum to decide once and for all the Geluk approach to Shukden and his followers and that he would be bound by the outcome. The result of the referendum was overwhelmingly in favor of excluding Shukden and his followers. This decree was written into Geluk monastic law and became the official position on Shukden and its practice.

Because of this referendum and because of the many books written in Tibetan that were appearing at that time on the issue of Shukden, some well researched, some not, the Geluk hierarchy believed it was time to produce a definitive account of the history of Shukden, its practices, and its followers. To that end, three authoritative Geluk organizations—the Association of Geluk Masters, the Geluk International Foundation, and the Association for the Preservation of Geluk Monasticism—collaborated to produce the Tibetan work of which this is a translation.

This work is not an inquiry that begins from a neutral stance, only to arrive at firm conclusions after comprehensive research and a review of the evidence. The compiler and publisher of this book are from the Geluk tradition, whose official position, verified by the referendum, is one of complete support for the present Dalai Lama. It is therefore a presentation of the case against Shukden being a genuine protector for the Geluk tradition. Though it marshals extensive research, reasoning, and citations, the purpose of the book is clear from the outset.

Although it was expressly hoped that a translation into English would be made for Westerners, who were relatively uninformed on the reality of the Shukden issue, the Tibetan edition is clearly aimed at a Tibetan audience. The Tibetan text carries a polemical tone not uncommon in Tibetan works where criticism and argument form the basic motive for the composition. It disparages opponents and praises its own side. The monastic debate courtyard is often witness to enthusiastic and animated argument, often resulting in the exultation of forcing the opponent into contradiction. However, it was felt that such passion would not enhance Western appraisal of the arguments in this book and might even serve as a distraction. Therefore, with the compilers' knowledge, we have toned down the rhetorical elements—the excessive praise and the invective. Some repetition has also been eliminated. Such editing has not altered the arguments presented in the book.

Acknowledgments

Among those who assisted me in resolving queries in the book, foremost was Ven. Tsultrim Öser of Ganden Shartsé Monastery. He is the main compiler and author of the Tibetan edition. He kindly traveled from his monastery in the south of India to Dharamsala in the north specifically in answer to my request for help with some parts of the book. He spent three days here with me in Dharamsala, and his assistance was invaluable.

I would like to thank David Kittelstrom, senior editor at Wisdom Publications, for skillfully editing the text, as well as his suggestions for some rearrangement of the chapter order, condensing the introduction, removing repetition, helping with the bibliography and glossary, and so on.

Introduction

THE GREAT BODHISATTVA Śāntideva said:

> The sole medicine for the suffering of living beings,
> the true source of every happiness:
> may the teachings, together with material support and devotion,
> remain for a long time.

This snowy, northern Dharma land of Tibet was praised again and again in authentic scripture by the fourth fully enlightened Buddha of this auspicious eon, the incomparable Lord of the Śākya clan. Our kings, such as the three early ancestral Dharma kings,[1] our ministers, translators, and learned pandits, with no regard for their own welfare—their lives or material wealth—and with considerable effort, established the complete and flawless precious Buddhist teachings of sutra and tantra combined. Successive generations worked hard to preserve and pass these teachings on. Through their kindness, the teachings of the Buddha appeared like the rising sun throughout the land of Tibet.

However, owing to a number of causes and circumstances, even the precious teachings have suffered a mix of fortunes of late. In particular, in 1949 the Chinese Communist Party was victorious in mainland China and announced the formation of the People's Republic of China. The Red Chinese army immediately began their violent incursions into its neighboring country, the Dharma land of Tibet. Finally, in 1959, the Chinese government swallowed up the whole of Tibet and its occupants, destroying more than six thousand monasteries and causing the deaths of more than a million people.

Faced with this critical situation, this frightening invasion that threatened to wipe out our religion, culture, and noble traditions, as if sky and earth had been rent from their places, the precious Fourteenth Dalai Lama, glorious leader of the religious and secular traditions in the Dharma realm of Tibet, the Noble One Who Holds the Lotus, left for the noble land of India together with his government ministers. His intent was to restore independence for his country in the future and to ensure that the truth of the Tibetan struggle prevailed.

In India, he transformed the Tibetan administration into one that embraced the three pillars of democracy and gradually established seven central departments within it. He founded settlements for those Tibetans who had fled into exile, unable to bear the yoke of Chinese oppression, schools for the education of children, residences for the elderly to live out their lives in peace, medical centers for the health of the people, craft and other factories for communities to have a livelihood and increase their wealth, centers of teaching and practice for monastic communities to pursue their studies regardless of tradition, and so much more. By willingly taking on countless hardships to achieve all this, he has brought the Tibetan people and their culture back from the brink of death and imbued them with the power of life.

This has been an act of singular compassionate kindness, and unbiased observers in the world have said that though "there are countless refugees in this world, the Tibetan refugees stand out with their incredible organization and progress." Thus we have become objects of praise, "admired by others and happy in ourselves."

For many years His Holiness the Fourteenth Dalai Lama has worked tirelessly to ensure that the religious traditions of the world, as well as the Tibetan Buddhist traditions—the Sakya, Geluk, Kagyü and Nyingma—who practice the teachings of the Buddha, source of all happiness for all living beings, and who specifically follow the flawless Dharma lineage of the glorious Nālandā monastic tradition, as well as Tibet's Bön tradition, are all united in harmony through pure ethics and, by using stainless reasoning, ensuring that they regard each other through the light of the jewel of pure perception. The Buddha's precious teachings of scripture and insight that have flourished within the exile community today spread throughout the whole world. Those who study Buddhism and develop faith are increasing daily.

In 2011 His Holiness graciously handed over to the people of Tibet his political power in governing Tibet and his administration, which had been in the hands of the Dalai Lamas from the time of the Great Fifth in the seventeenth century. With his connection to the Ganden Phodrang[2] in the past, and in the manner of those Dalai Lamas who preceded the Great Fifth, he has now taken on the extraordinary responsibility of working to spread the teachings, bringing happiness to living beings, working for harmony among religious traditions, promoting democracy, improving the conduct of the people, and so on, all with the aim of bringing peace and happiness both temporary and permanent to the world at large.

Shukden

Almost four hundred years have passed since the spirit known as Shukden, or Dölgyal, entered our society. In the beginning no one questioned that Dölgyal was a malicious oath-breaking spirit born from perverse prayers who brought harm and hindrance to living beings. However, as time passed, the accounts of Dölgyal's origins strayed. Some say that Dölgyal was sworn into the services of Padmasambhava and Hayagrīva and so on, or that Dölgyal was recognized by Nechung himself. Others say that in the presence of the great and venerable Tsongkhapa himself, master of the doctrine, Dölgyal offered himself as the protector of his teachings, or that Dölgyal is the exclusive guardian of the doctrine of Mañjunātha Tsongkhapa, the second Buddha. All manner of fabricated assertions have appeared.

The Fourteenth Dalai Lama relied on Dölgyal when he was young, but later, over a period of several years, he carried out thorough investigations using logical reasoning focused on both past and present. As a result, he recognized that Dölgyal was undermining the unity and harmony that existed among the religious traditions of Tibet and was damaging the pure ethical code and accord within the Geluk tradition. He saw that individuals and institutions that rely on Dölgyal turn good into bad, profit into loss. Because of this, he saw that the practice of Shukden had been and was continuing to be a hindrance to the preservation, development, and propagation of the teachings of the Buddha across all traditions, a task accomplished by study, contemplation, and meditation of the vast ocean of scripture without regard to sectarian divide. It was also damaging the unity of the Tibetan community.

He also recognized that the claim that Dölgyal was the exclusive protector of the doctrine of Mañjunātha Tsongkhapa, the second Buddha, was completely at odds with reality. To not hold in great esteem the teachings on basic phenomena, paths, and resultant states, the complete presentations on philosophy, meditation, and conduct found in the Great and Lesser Vehicle and the tantric systems of Tibet, of which we can be justly proud, but to rely instead upon propitiation of gods, nāgas, and malevolent spirits would be a huge detriment to the teachings and to living beings.

In short, he realized that by performing devotions to Dölgyal, the followers of Dölgyal, whether as institutions or individuals, were turning good into bad and profit into loss for everyone. He has again and again given sound guidance on this matter, and because of this kindness, most of those who used to practice Dölgyal, both within and outside Tibet, set aside their practice in good faith. They have understood the good and bad in this whole affair and have pursued study and contemplation of the great works of scripture without regard to sectarian division. Within a brief period, the pure perception and respect as well as the bond among the religious traditions of Tibet have increased and continue to do so. That this has arisen solely from the kindness of this great refuge and protector can be clearly seen. Anyone with any awareness can see that the entire Tibetan community, both in Tibet and in exile, can never repay just this one act of kindness for as long as they remain on this earth.

However, as the saying goes, "Where the Dharma is deep, so the hindrances run deep." A few Dölgyal practitioners, in collusion with the Chinese Communist Party, who are enemies of the teaching and see Dharma as poison, have abused the saying "One's faith is one's own choice" and make serious and baseless accusations about the Fourteenth Dalai Lama. They say that his advice regarding Dölgyal is not to be taken literally and that in reality he still practices Dölgyal. They have attacked and beaten those within the Tibetan refugee community who have worked hard with sincere motivation for the betterment of their country and their people. They have even killed and shed blood. Up to the present day, those who follow Dölgyal have exploited time and place, showing not the slightest intention of refraining from these acts against the Tibetan administration and the people.

Those in Tibet under the oppression of the Chinese Communists have no opportunity to meet the Dalai Lama and drink the nectar of his words. Knowing this, some who follow Dölgyal are bent on deceiving devoted communities across Tibet. They say that Dölgyal is a genuine Dharma protector, how it is necessary to continue to rely upon Dölgyal, and so on, using CDs and DVDs to propagate lies and nonsense among the people of Tibet, who are prevented from knowing the reality of the situation or face great difficulties in doing so. One clearly sees this happening these days.

In Western countries too, where the true nature of Dölgyal is not widely known, followers of Dölgyal have exploited the situation to deceive people, investing in effort to propagate this malevolent spirit.

Ensuring that those who are unaware of the reality of this matter do not fall prey to the deceptions and guile of others, and exposing to the whole Tibetan community the bare truth concerning the history of Gyalpo Shukden, or Dölgyal, ranks among the greatest responsibilities of the Tibetan people, in general, and of the Geluk tradition in particular.

Compilation of the Book

In response to overwhelming kindness of His Holiness the Dalai Lama in giving us a huge amount of profound and clear guidance, and with the aim of ensuring that those of us who wish for the best never again fall under the control of deceptive, oath-breaking spirits, it was commonly recognized that a book establishing the reality of Dölgyal, and the final and overall position of the Riwo Genden tradition,[3] was now a necessity. And as the Tibetan tradition of Buddhism continues to spread in lands where previously not even its name was heard, it was realized that clarification by way of honest research on the reality of Dölgyal was important so that Western devotees, too, would not confuse earth and stones for gold.

Three associations, namely (1) the Association of Geluk Masters, consisting primarily of the Great Vajradhara Ganden Throneholder, regent of Mañjunātha Tsongkhapa, as chair, alongside the unparalleled Sharpa Chöjé and Jangtsé Chöjé, (2) the Geluk International Foundation, whose permanent members consist of the Ganden Throneholder as chair, the Sharpa Chöjé and Jangtsé Chöjé, the abbots of the eleven main Geluk monasteries and colleges—namely, the six major colleges of Sera, Drepung, and Ganden monasteries, Gyütö and Gyümé tantric colleges, Tashi Lhunpo Monastery, Ratö Monastery, and Namgyal Monastery—as well as a general secretary, and (3) the Association for the Preservation of Geluk Monasticism, consisting of the precious abbots of the above eleven Geluk monasteries and colleges, met and engaged in lengthy discussions on this topic. In particular, during the great Kālacakra initiation kindly bestowed for the thirty-first time by His Holiness the Fourteenth Dalai Lama, in the sacred Indian place of Bodhgaya, from December 31, 2011, to January 10, 2012, members of the Association for the Preservation of Geluk Monasticism held their conference, during which they discussed the compilation of an authentically sourced and reliable history of Dölgyal to be produced by the Geluk tradition. Once they had come to an agreement, they reported to the Association of Geluk Tradition Masters, where the Ganden Throneholder and the Sharpa Chöjé and Jangtsé Chöjé gave it their approval and offered words of advice in support.

Immediately, an editorial committee was formed. It gathered from the individual colleges rough drafts of documents written on the history of Dölgyal. Using these as a foundation, the three Geluk associations worked together to research the facts of almost four hundred years of Dölgyal-related history up to the present day. They extracted important and relevant citations from the various discourses His Holiness the Fourteenth Dalai Lama had given on Dölgyal and chronicled the facts concerning recent· events connected with Dölgyal. In this way they began the compilation of the new work.

Many meetings were organized to examine and discuss the work completed by the editorial committee. For example, on March 23, 2012, at Ganden Monastery, the monastic seat of Tsongkhapa, in the upper story of the Ganden governing council's quarters, the Association for the Preservation of Geluk Monasticism held its conference. On August 26, 2012, the Geluk International Foundation held its conference in the Drepung governing council's quarters at Drepung Monastery. And on September 10, 2012, the Association for the Preservation of Geluk Monasticism held a meeting at Ganden Monastery. At each of these meetings, the assemblies examined the work and offered valuable opinions and advice.

Finally, on December 12, 2012, while His Holiness the Fourteenth Dalai Lama was kindly giving profound and extensive teachings on the stages of the path, the Ganden Throneholder, the Sharpa Chöjé and Jangtsé Chöjé, as well as the abbots of the six major colleges of Sera, Drepung, and Ganden monasteries, Gyütö and Gyümé Tantric colleges, Tashi Lhunpo Monastery, Ratö Monastery, Namgyal Monastery, Dzongkar Chödé, and others met in the Ganden Palace reception hall of Drepung Monastery. After the plenary discussions, it was decided that a copy of *A Golden Key of Scripture and Reasoning* would be offered to the great Vajradhara Ganden Throneholder, the Sharpa Chöjé and Jangtsé Chöjé, the precious abbots of the above monasteries, and to the colleges themselves, for their perusal.

It was also decided that the colleges of the monastic seats should set up their own research committees and thoroughly examine the work and offer suggestions for improvement, and that this task should be completed within a month. Consequently, each college carried out a review of the text and returned the texts with invaluable advice and suggestions. The editorial committee spent considerable time considering each amendment and suggestion.

Finally, during the seventh annual conference of the Geluk International Foundation held August 25–27, 2013, at Ganden Monastery in South India, the three Geluk associations conferred, and once more the whole assembly discussed the wording, the layout, and so on of the text. A final determination was made, and *A Golden Key of Scripture and Reasoning* was successfully completed. The conference assembly decided that the work should be quickly published by the Geluk International Foundation.

In December 2013, when His Holiness the Dalai Lama was again giving profound and extensive teachings on the stages of the path at Sera Thekchen Chöling Monastery, the Geluk International Foundation took advantage of such an excellent occasion, and on an auspicious day, together with the book's launch, distributed to the general public *A Golden Key of Scripture and Reasoning Clarifying the Reality of Dölgyal: Distinguishing the Good from the Bad and Truth from Lies*, which is a title given by Rizong Tulku Thupten Nyima Lungtok Tenzin Norbu, the venerable 102nd Ganden Throneholder Vajradhara, regent of Mañjunātha Tsongkhapa. Thus the project was successfully completed.

The Geluk International Foundation was aided in its publication efforts by gifts from generous sponsors.

Overview of the Book

The main purpose of this book is to clarify through reasoning the true nature of Dölgyal. The first person to subdue Dölgyal was the Great Fifth Dalai Lama (1617–82), whose kindness with regard to the religious and secular traditions of Tibet and her people was immeasurable. The most thorough and detailed descriptions of unquestionable scholarship from the time of Dölgyal's first appearance are found in the Great Fifth's autobiography, *Heavenly Raiment*, as well as in his *Secret Sealed Teachings on Pure Perception* and other works. Therefore here too we used these as an indispensable reference.

In the year 1656, the Great Fifth Dalai Lama built a new protector spirit chapel in a place called Döl White Springs in order to house this spirit, placing within the chapel various precious items and possessions. According to Tibetan reckoning, he spent about eighteen years ensuring that this spirit remained in a peaceful state and caused no harm to the teachings and the people, but his efforts did not bear the desired fruit. Therefore, following seven days of wrathful ritual, a fire ritual was performed, and from that day for about forty years, no more was heard of the spirit.

Dölgyal arose because of the figure of Tulku Drakpa Gyaltsen. Therefore accounts of Drakpa Gyaltsen's life, the situation of the Tibetan society at that time, Drakpa Gyaltsen's view of the Geluk tradition, the harm or good he may have done, how he came to be included among the candidates for recognition as the Fifth Dalai Lama, how he was recognized as the Upper Residence incarnation, and so on are explained based on *Dreams at a Young Age* found in Drakpa Gyaltsen's autobiography, *Jewel Casket: A Special Life-Story*, and on other passages in his autobiography and other works. To clarify understanding, we have reproduced some passages of Drakpa Gyaltsen's works that have been questionably interpreted.

In later centuries, the Eighth Dalai Lama (1758–1804) Jampal Gyatso, the great conqueror; the Thirteenth Dalai Lama (1876–1933), refuge and protector and guide of gods and humans; and many great and noble beings, like the sky covering the earth, from the Sakya, Geluk, Kagyü, and Nyingma traditions have imposed restrictions on Dölgyal. We have tracked down their dates and the years they imposed their restrictions as best we could.

The first tradition to call on Dölgyal was a faction of the glorious Sakya, but we will show that these were not devotions made from faith and trust but from fear, a response to Dölgyal stirring up supernatural omens. To learn how Dölgyal first appeared within the Sakya tradition, and to determine what status those who relied on Dölgyal as a protector attributed to him at that time, we have studied the works and biographies of those Sakya lamas and others associated with them.

Later generations of Dölgyal followers invented many exaggerated qualities for him, completely at variance with the original and authentic accounts of his origins. As the saying goes, "Food carried in the hands diminishes, but words carried in the mouth grow larger." Within the Geluk tradition, Kyabjé Phabongkha Dechen Nyingpo propagated the practice of Dölgyal far and wide, greatly praising him as "Dorjé Shukden Tsal, exclusive protector of the doctrine of Mañjunātha Tsongkhapa, the second Buddha." To discover the reasons behind this claim, we have pored through the collected works of this master. His student, Tutor Kyabjé Trijang Vajradhara, also composed works on the origins of Dölgyal as well as *Commentary on the Praise of Shukden* and so on. We have carefully reviewed each of these in their own context to determine the reasoning behind them, and we present the findings accordingly.

These devotees composed invocations and so on of Dölgyal, and we have investigated to see whether the praises to Dölgyal in these works accord with the reality of Dölgyal. We have also researched the reasons cited for naming Dölgyal the exclusive protector of the doctrine of Tsongkhapa and whether or not he is actually such a protector.

Over the years the precious Fourteenth Dalai Lama has given much advice on the practice of Dölgyal, all based on scrupulous research. To make this accessible, we have distilled the essential sections that convey the precise meaning, along with details of the time, place, and audience.

During the time it took for us to compile this work, a few libraries unstintingly lent us ancient and precious research material, such as the collected works of the Great Fifth Dalai Lama and Panchen Losang Chögyen, and offered us their complete support. To these and all those individuals and organizations that offered guidance and support throughout this undertaking, we express our boundless and sincere gratitude.

To determine the reality of anything, one must work to correct and refine, wherever necessary, one's understanding of that phenomenon by meticulous research carried out with faultless reasoning. This is indispensable in the tradition of the peerless Lion of the Śākyas [i.e., the Buddha] in general, and specifically in the tradition of the second conqueror, Mañjunātha Tsongkhapa. In his *Essence of Excellent Explanation: Differentiating the Definitive and the Provisional*, Tsongkhapa says:

> Ultimately, it must be determined by faultless reasoning, because a proponent who holds a tenet that contradicts reason cannot be a reliable witness. Also, the reality of a phenomenon will supply a proof establishing its own validity. Seeing the significance of this, the Buddha said:
>
> > Monks and scholars should accept my words
> > not out of respect but by investigating,
> > like smelting, cutting, and rubbing gold.

The mandate to accept even the words of the Buddha, the founder of the teachings, only after analysis and investigation has as its source the Buddha himself.

Even though certain works of great masters of the past contain elements that do not stand up to reasoning or are mistaken, it is wrong to regard those great scholars and practitioners as mistaken in everything. The practice of the great masters of all traditions is to "regard the person with pure perception and analyze the doctrine." It would be a mistake to regard those past masters who relied on Dölgyal as nothing more than a body of faults simply because of this practice. Their minds were enriched by the nine great qualities.[4] Therefore, with our intelligence that distinguishes what should be done from what should not, we separate the good from the bad, as clearly as the tips of *kuśa* grass, and without regarding their practice of Dölgyal as a good quality, we train ourselves in the good qualities. This has been the pure way of great masters of the past. If we subscribe to this, we will become a source of good for all, both now and in future times. In his *Discourses on Dölgyal*, His Holiness the Dalai Lama says (2:62):

> In terms of their practice of Dölgyal, Kyabjé Phabongkha Rinpoché was mistaken and Kyabjé Trijang Rinpoché was likewise mistaken. It was not merely a mistake; it also harmed their life and work. But to cast Kyabjé Phabongkha Rinpoché and Kyabjé Trijang Rinpoché into the category of mistaken lamas on the basis of their error is completely wrong. They were inconceivable lamas. To cite their inconceivable qualities as a reason to revere whatever they did as good, however, goes against the teachings in general.

Homage and Commitment to Compose

Namo Guru Śākyamuniye

To bring to the place of **truth** those living beings in this era of the five
    degenerations
who wander on wrong paths in matters of **truth** and falsehood,
you completed the noble path of the four **truths** and spoke **truth** to others.
A **truth**-speaking spring rain of nectar, source of infallible truth,
Lion of the Śākya clan, teacher of the four **truths**,
you are, therefore, in all ways, the supreme refuge of **truth**.

Your **body**, ablaze with the marks and signs of enlightenment,
vermillion in color, a **body** adorned with scripture and sword;
your **speech**, powerful and rich with the sixty qualities of voice,
captivating to the mind, beautiful to hear, **speech** without compare;
your **mind**, whether in meditation or not, a **mind** that simultaneously
    knows
the great ocean-like treasures of method and wisdom;
Mañjuśrī, composite of all three **refuges**,
sole father of every Buddha, constant **refuge**.

The supreme deity and wisdom of every **conqueror**
performing the dance of the saffron robe,
having considered how the sun of the **Conqueror's** teachings
was being hidden by the dust of the five degenerations;
treasure of wisdom truthfully revealing the noble paths
of sutra and tantra, the profound intent of the **Conqueror**;
care for us, Mañjuśrī and second Buddha
known as the mighty **conqueror** Tsongkhapa.

Arising in the form of the vajra **holder**, possessed of the three vows;
mighty Avalokiteśvara, embodiment of compassion of every conqueror,
guide and refuge for the **teachings** and living beings,
your deeds as deep as an **ocean** that **rules over** the glories
of peace and happiness in the **three realms**;
beneficial to all, treasure of compassion, wisdom and ability
in the **realm of the unparalleled**, constant guide and refuge,
to the root guru we bow.[5]

Building on the foundation of the assertions based in **reality**
of those wise masters of the past whose **Dharma** eyes were open wide,
and for those beings who walk only errant paths not in accord with
    Dharma,
we will present in accordance with **reality**, the outcome of the research
the true nature of **reality**, carried out by way of **Dharma** and science
by the **Dharma** king and great conqueror, the precious wish-granting
    jewel
who grants the hopes of the **Dharma** and secular traditions.

PART 1
Seventeenth Century:
Drakpa Gyaltsen and
the Fifth Dalai Lama

1. The Rise of Tulku Drakpa Gyaltsen

The Upper and Lower Residences of Drepung Monastery

As is well known to us all, Drakpa Gyaltsen (1619–56), or Tulku Drakgyen, the Drepung Monastery Upper Residence incarnation, was said after his death to have been reborn as a worldly spirit known as the oath-breaking Dölgyal, or Gyalpo Shukden. To start, we need to identify the Drepung Upper Residence.

The Upper Residence (Simkhang Gongma) was the first residence of the refuge, protector, and great conqueror Gendun Gyatso, the Second Dalai Lama (1475–1542). Later, he moved to the Blue Stone House of Drepung, known as the Lower Residence, which was offered to him by the ruler of Nedong.[6] These two residences are so called because of the features of the land on which they were built. The conqueror Gendun Gyatso offered the Upper Residence to his disciple Panchen Sönam Drakpa (1478–1554).[7] From then on the Drepung Upper Residence was the residence, or *labrang*, of the incarnations of Panchen Sönam Drakpa.

The Lower Residence of Drepung, Blue Stone House, was given the name Drepung Ganden Phodrang and, from the time of Gendun Gyatso onward, became the residence and labrang of the successive incarnations of the precious Dalai Lamas.

Birthplace and Parents of Drakpa Gyaltsen

Tulku Drakpa Gyaltsen was born in the Tibetan earth-sheep year of 1619. His father was Namsé Norbu from the Gekhasa aristocratic family of Lhasa Tölung, and his mother was Lak Agyal of Gekhasa district. He was the third of five children.

It was said that his parents described many extraordinary signs seen at his birth and that, when the child was two years old, Panchen Losang Chögyen,[8] who was traveling to Lhasa, was invited to their house. They requested him to perform a hand blessing and to give the child a name. He bestowed the name Chösang Gyaltsen on him. These accounts are described in Tulku Drakpa Gyaltsen's autobiography, *Jewel Casket: A Special Life-Story* (2b1), handwritten and in long format:

> On the fifteenth day of the month of miracles
> in the wood-rabbit year, Tulku Gelek Palsangpo[9]
> was invited to Trülnang Jampa Shingta,
> where at the age of twenty-two he passed away.

> Then, it is said, in a place known as Nup,
> he entered a womb and was born,
> but he did not reach a significant age
> and again passed away.

> Then I entered the womb, and at that time,
> to the minds of the sacred objects of refuge,
> rays of light like the sun appeared
> emerging from the heart of the statue
> of that tulku in Ganden and entering my home.

> In particular, in the dreams of my mother
> many signs of purification were seen,
> such as a crystal shrine falling to her lap
> and a saffron-robed monk calling from within.

> In reality also, the form of Palden Lhamo
> was seen to appear upon a rock,
> and syllables miraculously formed on her body.
> Many such amazing signs were seen, it is said.

> Then in the *siddhārtha* female earth-sheep year,
> at sunrise on the eighth day of the *vaiśākha* month,[10]
> when the *puṣya*[11] lunar mansion and Jupiter were conjoined,
> I emerged from the womb with ease.

The general name of the area was Goser,
and my parents' estate was Gekhasa.
My father was Namsé Norbu of aristocratic descent,
while my mother's name was Lak Agyal.

Of five brothers and sisters, I was the third.
As soon as I was born I looked at my mother,
smiled, and even spoke some words, it is said.
These and other extraordinary actions pleased my parents.

Also, in the same work (3a3), it says:

When I was two, the omniscient Panchen
came to the vajra seat of this land of Tibet.
My parents invited him to their home,
and with both hands he bestowed on me a blessing.

He gave me the name Chösang Gyaltsen,
and because of pure prayers and pure karma,
my undying faith in him increased.

I received the nectar of his words
in the form of a long-life initiation and so on.
To my parents he gave much advice
on how this boy was no ordinary child.

The Political Situation in Tibet at That Time

The accuracy of any historical account, whether of an individual or a community, depends upon knowing the situation of the society at that time. Therefore, in order to understand the story of Drakpa Gyaltsen, the Drepung Upper Residence incarnation, we will present an overview of the situation of the Tibetan people at that time.

When Drakpa Gyaltsen was born, political rule in Tibet had been in the control of three generations of the kings known as the Tsangpa Desi.[12] The generations of Tsang rulers were avid patrons of the Karmapa and his disciples, but toward other religious traditions, especially the Geluk, they were hostile and caused them much harm.

The Fourth Dalai Lama, the conqueror Yönten Gyatso (1589–1616), was invited to Central Tibet in the iron-ox year of 1601,[13] where he was installed on the Ganden Phodrang throne. Panchen Losang Chögyen bestowed on him the vows of the novice monk and later those of the fully ordained monk. He immersed himself in the study and contemplation of the vast ocean of scriptures, both sutra and tantra. However, his lifetime was plagued by fierce territorial disputes between Tsang and Central Tibet. From the beginning, the Tsangpa Desi and his sons regarded the Geluk tradition as bitter enemies and suppressed them ruthlessly.

For example, in the wood-snake year of 1605, the Tsangpa ruler in collaboration with the head of the Drigungpas[14] attacked and destroyed the ruling family of Kyishö,[15] who were financial patrons of the Geluk. Also, around the water-ox year of 1613, the Tsangpa Desi attacked the Ngari king and marched into Phenyül, Shika Neu, and elsewhere and brought them under his control. He built a new monastery called Tashi Silnön[16] between Tashi Lhunpo Monastery and Shigatsé town, thereby pursuing a policy of weakening the Geluk tradition, which was exemplified by Panchen Losang Chögyen of Tashi Lhunpo, and bringing the Geluk doctrine close to extinction.

At this point, the Tsangpa king was struck down with illness, and people said this was a sign that the conqueror Yönten Gyatso had performed a wrathful destruction ritual, sent as a warning to the Tsangpa king. From then on the great conqueror was also known as Thutop Gyatso.[17] During this time, Mongolian armies initiated repeated military action in support of the Geluk tradition. However, the conqueror Yönten Gyatso would not accept their help and made efforts to turn them back. This is stated by the Great Fifth Dalai Lama in the *Precious Garland: The Life of the Lord of the World, the All-Knowing and Glorious Yönten Gyatso* (50a1):

> During the time that this great master planted his lotus feet on this earth, the elder and younger sons of Lord Qoloci[18] set out many times with their armies, preparing to wage great battles against those such as the Tsang Kur. However, as they approached Tibet, he sent out special messengers to them, and with wise words designed to restrain them, he restrained any proliferation of the conflict. Therefore, during the time his lotus feet were on this earth, no foreign army ever caused harm in Tibet.

Thus, during the lifetime of the conqueror Yönten Gyatso, no great damage was inflicted by the Mongolians in Tibet. However, in the fire-dragon year, on January 20, 1617, the conqueror Yönten Gyatso passed away suddenly at the age of twenty-eight. The Tsangpa Desi had blamed the conqueror Yönten Gyatso for casting a curse upon him earlier and so issued a proclamation forbidding the recognition of his reincarnation. Nevertheless, in the following year, the Great Fifth Dalai Lama, conqueror and guide of gods and humans, was born in Taktsé Chingwa in Chongyé of the Lhokha region. His father was Hor Düdul Dorjé of the line of the Sahor[19] kings, and his mother was the noblewoman Tricham Kunga Lhadzé. However, under the suppression of the Tsangpa Desi, there was no easy way to identify him.

As mentioned, the Tsangpa had from its inception carried out disgraceful and abusive actions against the Geluk. In the fire-snake year of 1617, when a large group of Chokhur Mongolian pilgrims arrived in Central Tibet, they chased away some yak thieves belonging to the Tsangpa Desi, Karma Phuntsok Namgyal.[20] In revenge, in the early autumn of 1618, he led a large military force to Central Tibet, where he wrought grave destruction upon Geluk religious establishments, particularly the great monasteries of Sera and Drepung. Many thousands of monks and laypeople were killed. As a period of continuous conflict had commenced between Tsang and Central Tibet, the monks of Sera and Drepung, who were powerless to do anything, fled to Phenyul, Taklung in the north, and elsewhere. Even Panchen Rinpoché had to seek refuge in Ngari. The Tsangpas had seized the whole of the Kyishö rulers' estate, and the Kyishö family fled to Kokonor. Many of the Geluk philosophical systems were forcibly changed.

At this time, the Dharma master of Taklung Monastery sought a truce. The Sera and Drepung monks were allowed to live in their monasteries as before, but Drepung was levied with a fine of two hundred gold coins and Sera a hundred gold coins. Neither monastery could produce such an amount. Therefore Shalngo Sönam Chöphel[21] of the Ganden Phodrang said he had to travel to Chökhor Gyal,[22] to a treasury belonging to the former Dalai Lama, in order to fetch the gold. On the road to Chökhor Gyal, accompanied by a representative of the Tsang ruler, Sönam Chöphel fled and made his way to Mongolia by Nyangkong.

At first the Tsangpa Desi protected Hor Düdul Dorjé, the father of the Great Fifth. However, the Desi was completely hostile to the nobles of Yarlung and other districts, and soon strong resentment developed between the Tsangpa Desi and the Yarlung governor Kurap Namgyal. Hor Düdul Dorjé was thought to favor Kurap Namgyal, and in the earth-sheep year of 1619, the Desi seized the administrative district of Taktsé Chingwa from Hor Düdul Dorjé and handed it over to the Mukpo Né governors.

Düdul Dorjé was taken to Tsang and put in prison, where it was reported he was harshly treated, and ultimately he died there. Following the seizure of Taktsé Chingwa, the mother had been given Lhashong in Chushur as her inheritance, and so she had no choice but to go to Chushur. Later, the Desi ordered the mother and son back to Tsang. However, the governor of Nakartsé appealed to Tsang, offering to take responsibility for mother and son, and she was permitted to stay in her homeland of Nakartsé instead.

In the iron-bird year of 1621, a Mongolian force of two thousand soldiers led by the Mongolian Lhatsun Losang Tenzin Gyatso and Guru Khong Taiyiji and accompanied by Treasurer Sönam Rabten and the Kyishö ruler Tsokyé Dorjé, arrived in Lhasa to support the beleaguered Geluk. The Tsang army was camped on Mulé Plain, and there on August 27, during a break in the hot weather, the Mongolian cavalry attacked, and many hundreds were killed. Panchen Losang Chögyen was in retreat in Drepung at the time, and as soon as he heard this news he set out to negotiate a truce. This is described in his autobiography, *Precious Garland: A Clear Account of the Deeds of the Dharma Proponent the Monk Losang Chögyen* (66a5):

> For a while I was in strict retreat. At the beginning of the seventh month the entire Tibetan army had camped on Mulé Plain. On the eleventh day, in a break from the heat, the Mongolian horsemen suddenly attacked the camp, and it was reported that many hundreds were killed. When this news reached my ears, I was unable to bear it and immediately left my retreat. Walking as far as the Denbak[23] boundary, I hurried on and saw that the Tibetan soldiers had congregated at Chakpori Hill. I arrived as the Mongolian horsemen were preparing to launch a second attack, and gunfire and arrows were raining down. With many offerings I implored Lhatsun, and with the benefit that Tibetan trickery had not yet spread to Mongolia, the attack was halted. The precious lives of close to a hundred thousand soldiers were saved, and the Tsangpas and the Mongolians presented Lhasa to me as a general offering for the benefit of the people.

The Tsang rulers accepted the condition that the many estates and monasteries that had fallen into the hands of the Tsangpa were to be returned.

Amid the fighting between Tsang and the Mongolians, the home of Chösang Gyaltsen—that is, the young Drakgyen—was destroyed by the Mongolian army, and it seems that the three-year-old Drakgyen may have been kept by the Mongolian army as security or taken from his parents forcibly. *In Dreams at a Young Age* (6b3) he says:

> When I was three I had to stay for a long time in the Mongolian encampment. For food I only had meat broth made from freshly killed sheep, and I had to share a bowl with the soldiers. As a result, the contaminated food caused a black growth, the size of a bean, to appear on my tongue. My tongue was in pain....

At that time, as will be made clear later, Chösang Gyaltsen, or Drakgyen, was included in the list of candidates for the reincarnation of the conqueror Yönten Gyatso. It might have been owing to this fact that Panchen Losang Chögyen skillfully retrieved him from the Mongolians. Drakgyen's autobiography, *Jewel Casket* (3a6), describes this event:

> Then, in the bird year at the age of three,
> much conflict ensued when I and others
> were taken away from my parents,
> and bad circumstance became my friend.
>
> Not long into the conflict, an official document
> from the Panchen himself brought by a messenger,
> nephew Sönam Paljor, and others
> skillfully released me to return to my home.
>
> After that, I could not remain at home,
> and my mother took me to Sangphu.[24]
> On the road....

This is saying that even after Panchen Losang Chögyen delivered him from the clutches of the Mongolians, he was unable to remain at home and that his mother took him to Sangphu Neuthok Monastery. However, it makes no sense to say that he still had to seek refuge from the dangers of the

Mongolian army and so could not remain at home. We are to understand that Drakgyen himself developed a kind of renunciation that meant he no longer wanted to remain in his father's home, and so his mother took him to Sangphu Neuthok.

Prospective Reincarnations of the Conqueror Yönten Gyatso

The way in which Chösang Gyaltsen came to be considered a candidate for the reincarnation of the conqueror Yönten Gyatso through the manipulations of his mother, Lak Agyal, is described in the Great Fifth's autobiography, *Heavenly Raiment* (1:126b6):

> Shalngo Sönam Rabten had settled in the Ganden Phodrang. Although he was keen to identify the incarnation of the all-knowing Yönten Gyatso, nothing could be clearly decided. For Chongyé was part of Yarlung but not of Serma Shung,[25] and the great protector at Samyé had mentioned Yarlung Serma Shung. It was said, therefore, that someone the same age as me called Yishin Norbu from Yarlung Chögyal Phodrang might be the one referred to.
>
> Lak Agyal of Gekhasa said that her young son, when he was conceived, had said to her in a dream, "The all-knowing Yönten Gyatso has come. Give him a home to live in." Using this as proof she approached Jamyang Könchok Chöphel[26] and many others. A father from a household in the region of Nyang said that there were many trustworthy reasons for recognizing his son as the incarnation. The two most senior Geluk lamas at that time were the Panchen Rinpoché of Tashi Lhunpo and Shabdrung Jamyang Könchok Chöphel of Lower Ling. They discussed what was to be done and decided to travel to Radreng Monastery in the north. There in the presence of the Jowo Jampal Dorjé image,[27] they performed the doughball divination. The result pointed to me, and so the matter was decided.

This clearly describes how the son of Lak Agyal of Gekhasa came to be one of the four candidates for the incarnation of the conqueror Yönten Gyatso and how, at this time in 1621, the decision on the incarnation of the conqueror Yönten Gyatso was made. At that time the great incarnation of the conqueror was five years old in the Tibetan system of calculation,[28] and Chösang Gyaltsen was three.

Recognized as the Upper Residence Incarnation

The first incarnation of the great proponent of sutra and tantra Panchen Sönam Drakpa was Sönam Yeshé Wangpo (1556–92), followed by Sönam Gelek Palsang (1594–1615). After the hopes for Chösang Gyaltsen to become the incarnation of the conqueror Yönten Gyatso were not fulfilled, those close to him used various ways to try and get him recognized as the incarnation of Sönam Gelek Palsang. Finally, Panchen Losang Chögyen recognized him as the incarnation. This is described in the Panchen Lama's autobiography, *Precious Garland* (66b6):

> Then, in the Great Drum year, the great incarnation of the all-knowing Yönten Gyatso was invited to Drepung. There I performed the hair-cutting ritual and gave him the name Losang Gyatso. In the Mars year I acted as the preceptor in bestowing the preliminary monastic vows, and at the same time I recognized the Upper Residence incarnation and performed the crown-hair offering ritual. I gave him the name Drakpa Gyaltsen.

The Great Drum year is the male water-dog year of 1622. Therefore, in that year, the precious incarnation of the conqueror was invited to Drepung, and Panchen Rinpoché performed the hair-cutting ceremony. He was six years old at the time.

The Mars year is the male wood-rat year of 1624. Therefore, in that year, when Panchen Rinpoché acted as his preceptor in the preliminary monastic-vow ceremony, the precious conqueror was eight years old. At the same time, he recognized Chösang Gyaltsen as the Upper Residence incarnation. At that time Chösang Gyaltsen, or Drakpa Gyaltsen, must have been six years old.

However, in the Great Fifth's autobiography, *Heavenly Raiment* (1:30a1), it says:

> In the latter half of the third Hor month, on the first *bhadrā* day,[29] when Mercury and the lunar mansion *anurādhā* were conjoined, in the Highest Bliss Room, in the presence of Panchen

> Rinpoché Losang Chökyi Gyaltsen, I underwent the crown-hair offering ceremony, and he bestowed on me the name Losang Gyatso.

And so on up to:

> Nangso Drolhuk[30] of Gekhasa also came that day, having been proclaimed the incarnation of Sönam Gelek Palsang by Rapjampa Chakdik and others. He had undergone the crown-hair offering ceremony previously it seems.

Thus, in the third month of the water-dog year of 1622, the precious incarnation underwent the crown-hair offering ceremony, and on that day Drakpa Gyaltsen also came. He also mentions that Drakpa Gyaltsen had apparently already undergone the crown-hair offering ceremony. In 1622 Tulku Drakpa Gyaltsen would have been four, and if so, then because the crown-hair offering ceremony occurs within a year following recognition, it must be that the recognition also occurred before the above event.

However, Panchen Losang Chögyen makes explicit that when the crown-hair offering ceremony was performed by way of recognition, Drakgyen must have been six. Therefore there is a discrepancy between the biographies of the Panchen and Dalai Lamas over the year Tulku Drakgyen underwent the crown-hair offering ceremony.

The question remains, however: Why did the four-year old Chösang Gyaltsen, or Drakgyen, come to the place of the crown-hair offering ceremony for the precious incarnation? Moreover, in his *Jewel Casket* autobiography (3b5), Tulku Drakpa Gyaltsen says:

> Again, the supreme refuge, Panchen Vajradhara,
> came to Drepung, and in the Ganden Phodrang,
> he accepted the crown hair from the head
> of the lord of Tibet, Losang Gyatso.
>
> At the same time, he bestowed on me
> the name Drakpa Gyaltsen, and with his own hand
> that venerable master cut the hair from my head.

Here Tulku Drakgyen makes it clear that at the same time that Panchen

Losang Chögyen accepted the crown-hair of the precious incarnation, he also recognized Chösang Gyaltsen as an incarnation, giving him the name Drakpa Gyaltsen and performing his crown-hair ceremony. This agrees with neither Panchen Rinpoché's nor the Great Fifth's account.

In any case, Panchen Losang Chögyen did not recognize Chösang Gyaltsen as the incarnation of Tulku Sönam Gelek Palsang at that time through any investigation by way of exalted wisdom.[31] It was a response to various claims made by those close to Drakgyen. As the Great Fifth says above, "Nangso Drolhuk of Gekhasa also came that day, having been proclaimed the incarnation of Sönam Gelek Palsang by Rapjampa Chakdik and others."

In particular, Tulku Drakgyen in his *Jewel Casket* autobiography (3b2) says:

> After that, I could not remain at home,
> and my mother took me to Sangphu.
> On the way my mother carried a stone
> that I had reshaped in my grip.
>
> Not wanting to stay in Neuthok,
> I said we should go to Drepung Monastery,
> and we arrived at the small mud dwellings.
> Not long after, the Dharma master Chökyong Losangpa
> also arrived from Ölga in the east.
>
> When I went to the Upper Residence,
> I recognized the Dharma master,
> the shrine housing the clay statue of Panchen Śākyaśrī,[32]
> and the *rakṣa*-bead rosary and other items in the Kalok Room.
> Everyone, it is said, was filled with faith.

His mother, Lak Agyal, had a stone she claimed had been reshaped by the child's grip, and this was something to show others. The boy did not want to go Sangphu Neuthok and insisted on going to Drepung instead. When he arrived at Drepung Upper Residence, he recognized various items in the Kalok Room, as well as the Dharma master Chökyong Losangpa, and as a result everyone was filled with faith. In this way, it is clear that his status was "proclaimed."

Afterward, Panchen Losang Chögyen also said, "I think this is Tulku Gelek Palsang," thus having to recognize him. However, there was much talk in the community at that time that there had been no authentic recognition. Drakgyen says in his *Jewel Casket* autobiography (2a2):

> The all-knowing mighty Panchen looked on me
> with a mind of great compassion
> and announced with words from his own mouth,
> "I think this is Tulku Gelek Palsang."
>
> However, some doubted these words,
> and from the flames of their anger and wrong views
> shot forth the sparks of various pronouncements.
> With them all karmic connection is lost.
> How did it come to this?
>
> This is a brief account to generate trust,
> and now is the time to elaborate a little.

It is clear from this that Drakgyen was initially pushed onto the list of candidates for the incarnation of the precious conqueror. When that did not succeed, he was again proclaimed, with much persistence and effort, to be the Upper Residence incarnation. Panchen Losang Chögyen considered the situation with a mind filled solely with compassion and declared him to be the incarnation, saying, "I think this is Tulku Gelek Palsang." That it was this kind of recognition will become clearer if the story is researched thoroughly. Whether Panchen Rinpoche recognized Drakgyen as a result of direct or indirect communal and political pressure is something those with open minds must continue to investigate.

Within the community, and especially in the Geluk tradition, there was a lot of talk in those times that Drakgyen was not the genuine incarnation of Tulku Gelek Palsang. In an apparent attempt to put an end to that, the Great Fifth was requested twice to compose a prayer based on the previous lives of Drakgyen, which included the Kashmiri Panchen, Butön Rinchen Drup[33] and others. The Great Fifth explains how he did not comply with these requests in *Heavenly Raiment*, his autobiography (1:91b4):

The chant master of the Great Assembly Hall, Tashi Gyatso,

asked me to compose a supplication prayer based on the past lives of the Upper Residence incarnation, which included, among others, the Kashmiri pandit and Butön Rinpoché. Shalngo said that this would be unsuitable because Panchen Rinpoché and the Shabdrung of Lower Ling had declared that the mention of Butön Rinpoché in the colophon of a work by Panchen Sönam Drakpa was a mistake.[34] Therefore I compiled something in a very general way. He waved the unwanted scroll around like a stick!

Thus the Fifth Dalai Lama did not compose the prayer as requested but composed something that was generally acceptable, and the chant master waved the unwanted scroll around like a stick. The phrase "compiled something in a very general way" is of great significance. At that time, the conqueror was twenty-two years old, it being the summer of 1638, the fifth month of the earth-rabbit year.

Also, in the same woodblock autobiography he says (226b3), "Requested by the monk Drakgyen, I composed verses of visualization of the *Three Essential Points*.[35] Knowing the reason, and being moved by great faith in the all-knowing Butön, I also wrote verses of praise." At that time, late summer of 1654, the conqueror was thirty-eight years old.

Panchen Losang Chögyen also composed *Supplication Prayer to the Past Incarnations of Tulku Drakpa Gyaltsen*, and the lamas supplicated in the verses included Butön. However, Panchen Losang Chögyen did not compose this work on his own initiative but at the insistence of those close to Tulku Drakgyen. This can be seen in the colophon of this work (35a2):

> This prayer request to the great incarnation Drakpa Gyaltsen, made by way of a succession of his past lives, was composed by the monk Losang Chökyi Gyaltsen in the monastery of the great Dharma institution of Tashi Lhunpo at the insistence of many of his retinue, such as the monk Lekpa Gyatso.

The Great Fifth's composition *Spontaneous Evocation of the Four Actions* (148a6) states:

> The false incarnation of Tulku Sönam Gelek Palsang, who was successful because of the manipulations of Lak Agyal of

Gekhasa, became a malicious oath-breaking spirit born from perverse prayers and brought much harm to living beings.

It continues in the same vein.

Also, Desi Sangyé Gyatso[36] in his *Yellow Vaidūrya history* (81) says:

> The Fifteenth Ganden Throneholder was Panchen Sönam
> Drakpa. His incarnation was Sönam Yeshé Wangpo, born in
> Tölung. His incarnation in turn was Ngawang Sönam Gelek.
> After him came Nangso Drolhuk. At first it had been hoped
> he would become the incarnation of the all-knowing Yönten
> Gyatso. However, by later becoming the incarnation of Ngawang
> Gelek, his rebirth was also unfavorable.

Thus Nangso Drolhuk is Chösang Gyaltsen, or Drakgyen. The phrase, "it
had been hoped..." is followed by the contrasting particle "however," indicating that the hopes were not realized. The phrase "his rebirth was also
unfavorable" contains the inclusive particle "also," meaning that the unfavor-
ability was not simply that he was not an incarnation. The phrase "by later
becoming the incarnation" contains the causal particle "by," indicating that
it was a nonincarnation falsely proclaimed as an incarnation that caused his
rebirth to be unfavorable.

Conflict with the Mongolians

Around the wood-pig year of 1635, a succession of calamities occurred that
threatened the teachings of the Buddha, and the teachings of the Geluk in
particular. For example, the Inner Khalka[37] had joined forces with Choghtu[38]
and arrived in Kokonor, where for a time they were very powerful and controlled Tibet and Mongolia from the Amdo region. Choghtu was a follower
of the Chinese Daoist religion and was hostile to the lamas and monks of
Tibet and Mongolia. The Beri chieftain Dönyö in Kham was a follower
of the Bön religion and was very hostile to the Sakya, Geluk, Kagyü, and
Nyingma traditions. The Tsangpa Desi ruled over Central Tibet and Tsang.
He professed to be a follower of the Karmapa and his disciples and had a
strong dislike of the Geluk.

These three joined forces and, by blocking trade routes and connections
to Central Tibet and so on, brought about much hardship in Kham, Tsang,

and Central Tibet. At that time, a letter from Beri Dönyö of Denchö Khor in Kham was sent to the Tsangpa Desi Tenkyong Wangpo[39] by way of the merchant Dralha Chen. It read, "Next year I am coming with my army to Central Tibet and Tsang. We two should join forces. The copper statue of the so-called Jowo Rinpoché is the guide of their army; we will cast it into the river. After we have destroyed Sera, Drepung, and Ganden monasteries, we will build a shrine worthy of veneration for the Bönpos[40] of Amdo, Kham, and Central Tibet." [41]

The Tsangpa was also preparing for war. In order to combat this and other related events, the Mongolian Gushri Tenzin Chögyal[42] amassed a huge army. In the first month of the fire-ox year of 1637, Gushri Khan and his army of ten thousand men defeated the Choghtu army of thirty thousand. In the earth-ox year of 1639, the army of Gushri Khan marched to the stronghold of Beri Dönyö, and in the iron-dragon year of 1640, he seized the entire territory of Beri Dönyö, who was also captured and thrown in prison in Chamdo.

In the iron-snake year of 1641, the army of Gushri Khan arrived in Tsang, and the Desi and his ministers were taken prisoner. At this time Panchen Rinpoché hurried there to meet with Gushri Khan and to plead for the safety of the Tsang ruler and his ministers. This is described in Panchen Losang Chögyen's *Precious Rosary* autobiography (114a5):

> I discussed my intention to be of service to the Desi Rinpoché, but this was prevented by a previous pledge, and beyond protecting his life, I was not able to be of much help. As he did not wear the garland of his fortunes around his neck, he did not have even a day's provisions. I offered him good food, tea, butter, and so on....

On May 4, 1642, in the assembly hall of Shika Samdrüp Tsé (Shigatsé) Palace, filled to capacity with countless lamas and noblemen of Tibet and Mongolia, the Dalai Lama Ngawang Losang Gyatso Palsang, guide of gods and humans, refuge and protector, sat upon a high golden throne supported by lions, where he was offered as his dominion the land, domains, and people from China and the Tibetan borderlands to Ladakh in the west. Gushri Khan also pledged himself and his descendants as an unending ceremonial offering.

Shalngo Sönam Chöphel, a.k.a. Treasurer Sönam Rabten, was offered the position of Desi in the service of the government of the Great Fifth, and this was announced to the whole of Tibet. The new government was founded at the Ganden Phodrang.

In the preceding conflict between the Mongolians and Tsang, Tulku Drakpa Gyaltsen had secretly employed wrathful rituals against the Mongolians. This was exposed, and Gushri Khan's army had killed many of Drakgyen's family. As a result, his parents told him he had to now take responsibility for the household. This is described in his *Dreams at a Young Age* (1ob1):

> Later, when I was nineteen and staying at Gekhasa, our secret rituals had been exposed and the Mongolians had killed our people. From my perspective I understood that death was the inevitable result of being born, and in the face of the teaching that the world was transient by nature, sorrow was of little use. However, my parents were grieving the loss of a son. Wondering what was best to do, I went to them. They told me I had to take over the household.

In 1637 Tulku Drakgen would have been nineteen by Tibetan calculations. This was the year that Gushri Khan defeated Choghtu at Kokonor and tallies with the time that Gushri Khan came straight to Central Tibet. Therefore Tulku Drakgyen engaged in secret rituals at that time. However, the existence of these rituals became known later. The Mongolians, displeased, killed some of his people in retaliation.

The object of these secret rituals of Drakgyen was a supporter of the Geluk tradition, Gushri Khan. Therefore, by engaging in secret rituals to thwart Gushri Khan, he was undermining a protector for the Geluk, who for a long time had suffered, through no fault of their own, mistreatment and contempt under the yoke of the Tsangpa Desi.

Furthermore, in a work composed by Drakgyen called *Prophecies* he says:

> The king of the wild animals will come to this snowy land,
> and most of the deer and antelope who roam this land
> will be persecuted by hunters and snared in traps.
> Not being able to escape from the forests,
> for some time they will be burdened thus.

Thus, at a time when the Riwo Genden tradition had been ravaged and almost laid to waste, he utters these disparaging words to Gushri Khan, who had come specially to help the Gelukpas. It is clear from this just what sort of attitude Tulku Drakgyen held toward the doctrine of the Riwo Genden tradition and its patrons. Therefore, in 1642, when the administration of the country was offered to the Ganden Phodrang, Panchen Losang Chögyen lowered the throne of Upper Residence Tulku Drakpa Gyaltsen to about the height of a square seat cushion. This was doubtlessly a response to Drakgyen's having engaged in rituals to repel the Mongolians, but it also reflects the way many in the Geluk tradition regarded him. As the Great Fifth's *Heavenly Raiment* autobiography says (1:105a6):

> For a while the Upper Residence Tulku had been coming to the Lesser Prayer Festival as the presiding lama. However, the venerable master Panchen Rinpoché had said to Shalngo, "The Prayer Festival is not the time for setting up thrones for many lamas. What is the difference between his venerable red decree and that of someone like Tashing Chöjé traveling as far as Tsokha, and having returned, receiving a red seal?"
>
> Therefore Panchen Rinpoché sent Tardongpa from Tsang to say, "You venerable masters should only have square cushions, and there should be no thrones." Because of this, Drakgyen did not want to attend the Prayer Festival and asked permission not to attend. He was embarrassed, and so I had to preside over both the Great and Lesser Prayer Festivals.

Therefore, while he was alive, Drakgyen had very little loyalty toward the Riwo Genden tradition. To say that after he died, he arose in the form of an exclusive protector of the Geluk doctrine is absurd.

2. Two Works by Drakpa Gyaltsen

IN THIS SECTION of the work we are investigating Dölgyal's origins, and to do that we must look not only at the life of Drakpa Gyaltsen but also at the works he composed. An examination of his compositions shows that much of what he wrote is difficult to corroborate. His *Precious Garland Life Story: Taking Birth as the Youth Nayanotsava in Ancient India*, on his birth as the scion of a king, is a particularly puzzling composition. His work on the origins of written language in Tibet called *Vaidūrya Garland: A History of the Written Word*, which is completely at odds with contemporary historical research, is another perplexing composition.

We present these compositions to the open-minded as subjects for examination, asking those of wide intellect who delight in historical research to investigate them. Both texts have spelling mistakes.[43]

The first composition is found in the second volume of his collected works (12b1ff.):

PRECIOUS GARLAND LIFE STORY: TAKING BIRTH AS THE YOUTH NAYANOTSAVA IN ANCIENT INDIA

Namo Guru Mañjughoṣāya.

> I prostrate to the Three Jewels, the lama,
> and the meditation deity, united as one.
> I will recount the precious life story
> of the youth Nayanotsava in ancient times.

Long ago there was a place in India south of Rivihila known as the Forest of the Dancing Peacocks, and it contained 108 different types of trees, such as sandalwood, juniper, and aloe. In its center was Mahābhadrā Ratna City, with half a million households.

Amid the city stood the king's palace, built of nine precious materials. It was three hundred armspans wide and topped with a three-story golden pagoda. It had ninety rooms, and in the central room, upon a golden throne sat the great universal king and emperor, Dharmapāla. He had a thousand queens, the chief of whom was Dharmatārā. He had five hundred sons and five thousand ministers. His subjects were beyond number.

To the east of his kingdom was the bright white town called Growing Crystal. To the south was the deep blue town called Singing Parrots. To the west was the copper-red mountain town called Place of Birds. To the north lay the town called Mound of Sapphires. All four were beautiful to gaze upon.

In the southeast was a pure snow mountain where the snow lion sat. In the southwest was a sandalwood mountain where the tigress roared. In the northwest was the lotus mountain where the yakṣa demons played. In the northeast was the *patrasarka*[44] mountain where the elephants roamed. From these four mountains, four rivers gently flowed into the center of the city.

The senior queen had three sons. The youngest was born on the eighth day of the month when the queen was observing the eight daylong vows of a householder. As soon as he was born, he began speaking fluent Sanskrit. He became skilled and unparalleled in the sixty-four arts of love. His form and youth were glorious, like the new petals of a lotus unsullied by the mud. He became skilled in every field of knowledge, and in the world he was unrivaled.

For fifteen days following his birth, the people of the city were treated to a grand festival, when even the word "poverty" no longer existed. At that time the king called together all those brahmans skilled in reading the signs. As they prepared to examine the signs, a *garuḍa* bird appeared in the sky and proclaimed:

> In this world the wish-granting jewel is rare,
> but rarer still is to gain a human birth
> endowed with leisure and opportunity.
> This youth endowed with glory of body and mind
> will one day be praised as the supreme guide of all.

As a result the child was called Ratna.[45] It was not necessary to examine the child for special signs. Nevertheless, he showed great faith in the Buddha and his followers. He enjoyed the renunciate life and wandering alone in the forest and did not like a large entourage or the company of ministers. He saw the affairs of the kingdom as being without essence. Every day, to relieve his sadness, he would go to play in the parks with about thirty young friends of the same royal caste.

One day, while his friends were enjoying themselves among the *udumbara* flowers,[46] the prince fell asleep and had a dream. In it a senior śrāvaka monk of Buddha Śākyamuni appeared at the entrance to the park begging for alms. His body was the color of pure gold, and the mass of light that radiated from it suffused the entire kingdom. He wore the three saffron robes, carried a staff and a begging bowl, and the crown of his head was endowed with a protuberance. He thrust the staff into the prince's heart and said:

> This place of samsara is surrounded by the snares of
>   suffering.
> Why then, Prince, do you spend your time in the unaware-
>   ness of sleep?
> Even for the bodhisattvas this is not the time for
>   indifference.
> And so strive, Prince, to achieve great things.
>
> The lady friends of Māra with their moist disturbing emo-
>   tions are manifold.
> And so prince, with your handsome body, will you not
>   take care?
> It is not right that you remain alone in the forest.
> It is proper that you take your friends to an isolated place.

As soon as the monk had said these words, the prince awoke, rose from his seat, and washed. As he walked past a flower, a small tiger-bee who was circling it sang:

This flower has such a beautiful color,
but come the autumn, when touched by frost, it will fade.
Likewise, the youth of this prince is a thing of beauty,
but the time will come when it will be destroyed
by the frost-like lord of death.

Therefore, keeping in mind that all things are transient,
live peacefully in the forest, and you will be content.

The bee drank much nectar from the flower, and circling the
prince it sang:

This nectar gathered by this turquoise bee
is full of flavor but will be used by man.
Your wealth, prince, is just the same.
Therefore take the essence from that without essence.

The prince saw that his handsome young body may be outwardly beautiful, but like the flower, it was just a signal that
beckoned the bees of Māra. Inside it was nothing but unclean
substances and prone to the sufferings of illness and old age. It
would be destroyed quickly by the frost of the lord of death, and
dogs and jackals would leave not even bones behind. Therefore it
had no essence whatsoever.

As he was a child of a royal family, he feared that his father the
king would not give him permission to live in a place of solitude.
He became disillusioned with the ways of samsara. The hairs on
his body stood up, and tears welled in his eyes. Suddenly, a young
child of eight with a body as pure as crystal, carrying a bouquet
of lotuses, appeared among the flowers. Smiling, he said to the
prince:

Prince and young bodhisattva, do not be sad.
Go in peace back to the palace.
The confines of samsara are very difficult to cut.
It would be better for you to live in solitude.
I will eliminate all obstacles on the path.
Your parents will without doubt allow you to go.

The prince was reassured by these words. The day was drawing in, and he returned to the palace.

His mother and father thought to themselves, "Previously, this child always wore a cheerful expression. He would play with his friends and return early. Today his expression is somber, and he has returned late. Why is that?"

They questioned the prince, who immediately prostrated three times before his mother and father. Going on one knee and placing his hands together, he pleaded:

My dear kind parents, hear me with your great compassion.
Today in the park of flowers this wretched child
heard Dharma words on the transience of all things.
Even this great kingdom is of no essence.

If I do not practice the Dharma,
this short human life of mine will have no purpose.
The ways of samsara are now hard to bear,
and so I wish to go and live in the remote forest.
Mother and father, I ask that you allow me to go.

His parents did not dare grant his request. Going to the forests meant great danger from wild animals. Besides, they loved their son very much. Not knowing what to do, both fainted and fell to the floor. At that time, the same white child appeared in the sky sitting on a cloud, and a rain of white flowers fell. The king and his queen recovered their senses. Although they tried to delay the prince, he would not be persuaded from his course of action.

Therefore, on an auspicious day, he set out for the thick forests on the sandalwood mountain. His mother and father on the roof of the palace watched him leave, tears in their eyes. The other princes, ministers, and people of the city had gathered. Some took hold of his hand. Others gazed at his face, and wailing and grieving for three days, they followed him into the forest. When they reached the edge of a kuśa grass plain, the prince said, "From here on the way is frightening. Those who wish to practice for enlightenment may accompany me. The rest should return home."

Everyone, with longing for this wish-fulfilling jewel of a prince, sadly returned home. The prince accompanied by two companions of a similar age ventured into the lonely forest. At this, the palace of the king became desolate. The houses of the city fell into ruin, and the people passed their days in sadness.

The prince and his two companions traveled into the jungle, where they made efforts in their meditation. Meanwhile, Buddha[47] was in the summer retreat in the Upananda enclosure near the city of Sukha. When the Bhagavan Buddha was walking close to the jungle, the prince saw him. As soon as he saw his form, the hairs of faith stood on end, and he begged the Buddha for ordination. The Buddha agreed and he became a monk. The prince and his two companions immediately attained the stage of an arhat.

My father, King Dharmapāla at that time, is now in India on Otrala Mountain, and having attained the tantric knowledge of longevity, he emanates endlessly for the sake of living beings. My mother, Dharmatārā, now abides in the ḍākiṇī realm. The prince at that time is now me. The śrāvaka monk of the Bhagavan who urged me to the Dharma is now the precious abbot, Panchen Losang Chökyi Gyaltsen. The young child whose body was like crystal is now my kind root guru and peerless refuge, Ngawang Losang Gyatso:

On that occasion, at that time,
the Panchen, emanation of Amitābha,
and the all-knowing conqueror, holder of the white lotus,
kindly placed me on the true path.

The bee that was circling the flower is now the precious master Könchok Chöphel. At that time he was in a pandit dwelling in the Sukhasaṃpatti Temple, and in order to teach me impermanence he took the form of a bee.

Of the two companions who came with me into the sandalwood forest, one was to become the bodhisattva Śāntideva, and the other became Gyalsé Sherap Phel. At that time there were two ministers to the senior queen who with perverse views spoke unpleasantly about my abandoning the responsibilities of the kingdom and going to live in solitude, and who slanderously reported this to the king. The one called Gupta was born inside a metal house in the Hell of Wailing. The other minister, Prajñā was reborn as a creature in the outer ocean. When they leave those places, they will be reborn close by, where they will hold wrong views toward all holy beings. When they die they will again be reborn in hell, where they will have to climb and fall upon the sword-leafed *śālmalī* tree as the ripening experience of their wrong deeds.

Of the other ministers and entourage, some are beginning on the path. Others are in my circle. Some are relatives, and some are people of the area.

This has been the chapter *Precious Garland Life Story: Taking Birth as the Youth Nayanotsava in Ancient India.* Sealed, sealed against being seen by an impure vessel!

> This precious life story,
> requested by the one called Buddha,
> was composed by Kīrtidhvaja[48]
> in the monastery of Kyormolung.

By this too, may the teachings of the Buddha remain long. The text has been revised once.

The second composition is found in the third volume of Tulku Drakpa Gyaltsen's collected works (2b2):

VAIDŪRYA GARLAND: A HISTORY OF THE WRITTEN WORD

There were over 364 written languages in the noble land of India, and I will tell of how written language came to this northern snowy land.

During the time of Nyatri Tsenpo,[49] ruler of the central kingdom of Tibet, it is well known that Tibet had no written language. It was 338 years after the fully enlightened one, Buddha Śākyamuni, passed away that Emperor Nyatri Tsenpo appeared in Tibet. Five generations after Nyatri Tsenpo's appearance, Songtsen Gampo (609–49 CE), the son of Namri Songtsen, was born. He was the Great Compassionate One, Lokeśvara, appearing in the form of a king, and for the sake of nurturing living beings, a mere fraction of his thousandfold light rays of wisdom dispelled and illuminated any darkness cast by the hidden aspects of any existing phenomenon.

However, in keeping with the perception of ordinary disciples, he held with pure ethics the system combining religious and secular rule. To accomplish that, he realized that a written language, which was like the foundation of all qualities, would be necessary.

Sambhota was the son of Thönmi from Nyal and a great minister. His heart had been touched by the fresh drops of camphor that was the blessing of Protector Mañjuśrī, and so he was free from any anguish of ignorance and confusion. Therefore the king gave him a full measure of gold powder and gold bars to please the Vedic teachers and others, commanding him and his servants to go to India to study language. He traveled to India without mishap. There he met the brahman Lijinkara, offered him the gold, and requested him to teach the 364 languages.

The text continues, but realizing that to include the whole work would produce excessive text, we have just presented this small portion.

Points of Doubt in These Works

Now those with wide eyes of wisdom, please look carefully. Drakgyen says, "It was 338 years after the fully enlightened one, Buddha Śākyamuni, passed away that Emperor Nyatri Tsenpo appeared in Tibet." We are still searching for reliable verification that will settle the dates of Emperor Nyatri Tsenpo. However, according to what is commonly accepted these days, this year (2012) is year 2131 of the Tibetan royal calendar, and thus for the purposes of our investigation we can say that it has been 2,131 years since Emperor Nyatri Tsenpo appeared in Tibet.[50]

When it comes to the matter of the year the Buddha passed away, there are many schools of thought. (1) According to the literary corpus of the Abhidharma and the Vinaya, as well as the system accepted by Butön, the master Tsongkhapa, and Khedrup Gelek Palsang, 2,880 years have passed since the Buddha passed away (if we take 2012 as the present). (2) According to the Phuk system,[51] the Buddha passed away 2,680 years ago. (3) According to the system of Jowo Atiśa (982–1054), the Buddha passed away 2,860 years ago. (4) According to the system of Sakya Paṇḍita (1182–1251), the Buddha passed away 4,131 years ago. And (5) according to the present-day Theravāda tradition, the Buddha passed away 2,556 years ago.[52]

Therefore, when Drakgyen says that "It was 338 years after the fully enlightened one, Buddha Śākyamuni, passed away that emperor Nyatri Tsenpo appeared in Tibet," should we presume that this comes from his clairvoyance? We do not know whether he based his calculation on one of these five different systems of calculations, or whether he used a calculation system other than these five. Knowing which system he used is an important consideration. Neither do we know what historical source he relied on for his account of Emperor Nyatri Tsenpo's appearance. These issues require more research to be resolved.

Furthermore, for Drakgyen to say, "Five generations after Nyatri Tsenpo's appearance, Songtsen Gampo, the son of Namri Songtsen, was born" does not agree with widely accepted works on the history of Tibet. According to those, the fifth in the line of descent after Nyatri Tsenpo was Metri Tsenpo. Sixth was Daktri Tsenpo. His son was Siptri Tsenpo. These were the seven Tri emperors of the upper realm. Next came the two emperors named Teng of the intermediate realm, followed by the six emperors named Lek of the earthly realm, the eight emperors named Dé of the earthy realm, and the four emperors of the underworld. Then came Lha Thothori Nyentsen, Drongnyen Deu, and Takri Nyensik. The thirty-first in line was Namri Songtsen, and the thirty-second was Songtsen Gampo.

Why did Drakgyen posit something so completely at odds with this chronology? Did he have valid sources? This should be investigated. Alternatively, should we conclude that Drakgyen was mistaken? If such things—spoken by someone who claims the ability to remember past lives, who confidently asserts what birth living beings took in previous lives and in which of the six realms they have taken birth in now—are indeed true, then what is the purpose of our mistaken histories, preserved in written documents?[53]

3. The Great Fifth and Drakpa Gyaltsen

IN HIS *Heavenly Raiment* autobiography (1:155a3), the Great Fifth says:

> In the crowded assembly hall, with the initiation rows occupied by almost a thousand monks, headed by the Nenying Shabdrung throneholder,[54] the Upper Residence Tulku, Jamyang Tulku, the Lingtö Shabdrung, the Radreng abbot, the masters of Sera and Drepung, and about one hundred chieftains headed by the Mongolian Khalka Bāthur Khong Taiyiji and others, I offered, for the benefit of the continuation of the teachings, the Mañjuvajra Guhyasamāja initiation, with the preparation on the seventh day of the fifth month and the actual initiation on the eighth, continuing until the three mandalas for good fortune[55] on the twenty-fifth day, with every detail of practice included and no shortcuts taken.

Also (175a4):

> Headed by Neudong Shabdrung Rinpoché, the Upper Residence Tulku, Lhari Rinpoché, the Gyari and Kyishö nobles, and masters from Sera and Drepung monasteries, most of the escort returned home.

Also (221a6):

> The Upper Residence Tulku arrived from Powo Chumdo, and on the third of the twelfth month came to meet me, bringing gifts of tea and armor.

And (226b3):

Requested by the monk Drakgyen, I composed verses of visualization of the *Three Essential Points*. Knowing the reason, and being moved by great faith in the all-knowing Butön, I also wrote verses of praise.

And (231b3):

I conferred the Hundred Long-Life Initiations on the Upper Residence Tulku and the Tsawa incarnation, and the Four Initiation blessings of Six-Armed Mahākāla on the Gungru incarnation.

And (236a6):

The Upper Residence Tulku and the Tsurphu Drungpa arranged many dedication items around the Mandal Rawa for the benefit of the deceased king.[56] The Upper Residence Tulku distributed silk, Lhapa distributed butter, and the Kyishöpa distributed fresh barley.

And (247a2):

From the twelfth to the twenty-third, I offered each day after the midday meal one session of the transmission of the collected works of the all-knowing Gendun Gyatso to about a hundred monks headed by the Upper Residence Tulku, the abbot of Palkhor Chödé, and masters of Drepung Monastery headed by former throneholders.

On the fourth line of the same page:

On the twenty-fifth I was invited to the Upper Residence for tea.

On the sixth line:

For two days beginning from the first of the fourth month, I concluded a teaching, held over from before, to an audience headed by the Upper Residence Tulku.

Further (248a2):

> On the twenty-fifth the Upper Residence Tulku became ill with serious fever, and a message was received saying that an obstacle-removing permission initiation was needed. Therefore I gathered provisions for the torma and intended to go there.

And (248b3):

> Concerning the illness of the Upper Residence Tulku...

Up to:

> I broke my retreat and went to the Upper Residence, where I gave the Mahākāla permission initiation Dispelling All Obstacles. However, he had been adversely affected by a spirit, and his mind was unable to receive it. It was no use.

And (250a5):

> The great protector divined, "At the time of the cremation of the tulku, you should not be in the vicinity. Return to the Potala."
>
> Therefore, on the twenty-second, for seven days, I applied myself to virtuous deeds, such as saying prayers, making offerings, and mantra repetitions in front of the Ārya Brothers.[57]

And (251a5):

> I composed verses for the following: The rebirth of the Upper Residence Tulku, as requested by Jampa Kunsang; the speedy rebirth of Sempa Chenpo, as requested by Trewo Tulku and Pönpo Gyatso; the clear rebirth of Baso Tulku, as requested by several monks; praises to the past lives of Gyalsé Sherap Phel, as requested by the monk Drak Ö; and verses on the first imprint of the seal offered to Lokeśvara by the ruler Sönam Rabten.

From these and other extracts, it is clear that the Great Fifth regarded Drakgyen as a chief disciple and imparted to him much profound Dharma instruction. When Drakgyen was close to death, the Great Fifth specially performed life-sustaining rituals, such as the Mahākāla permission initiation known as Dispelling All Obstacles. Also, at the time of the cremation, he deliberately spent a week applying himself to virtuous deeds such as reciting prayers and making special offerings. Finally, he composed a prayer requesting for the speedy return of his incarnation. This is a narrative of how the Great Fifth cared for him with great compassion in the early, middle, and later part of their relationship.

Likewise, in the *Precious Garland Life Story* (12b1), Drakgyen says, "The young child whose body was like crystal is now my kind root guru and peerless refuge, Ngawang Losang Gyatso." Thus he praises the Great Fifth with words like "my kind root guru and peerless refuge."

These accounts confirm that while they lived, the Great Fifth and Drakgyen had a relationship of guru and disciple that was deep, firm, and authentic.

4. The Death of Drakpa Gyaltsen

THE GREAT FIFTH says in his *Heavenly Raiment* autobiography (1:248a2):

> On the twenty-fifth the Upper Residence Tulku became ill with serious fever, and a message was received saying that an obstacle-removing permission initiation was needed. Therefore I gathered provisions for the torma and intended to go there. However, in Lhasa the Depa did not approve, saying the illness was contagious and it was not suitable to go there at that time; he conveyed this to the Upper Residence as well. Confronted with an infectious illness, postponement was therefore unavoidable. Accordingly, from the twenty-sixth, even though the Tulku was ill, I completed the teachings on *Origins of the Kadampa* by Lechen Kunga Gyaltsen for the masters from the monasteries and others and began the overview of the Kālacakra tantra commentary by Khedrup Norsang Gyatso before the break.

The "twenty-fifth" mentioned above is the twenty-fifth of the fourth Tibetan month in the fire-monkey year, or June 17, 1656. On that day the Upper Residence Tulku had suddenly become ill with an acute fever, and the Great Fifth had been requested to come and bestow an obstacle-removing initiation. Accordingly, he gathered the torma provisions and was about to leave. Desi Sönam Rabten asked him to postpone the visit, saying that the illness was infectious and that it would be better if the Great Fifth did not go. He also told this to the Upper Residence. From the twenty-sixth, even though Drakgyen was ill, he gave teachings in which he completed *Origins of the Kadampa* and began the overview of Kālacakra. This extract makes explicit the circumstances and dates for the onset of Tulku Drakpa Gyaltsen's illness.

Also in the *Heavenly Raiment* (1:248b2), the Great Fifth says:

In keeping with the forthcoming eclipse on the fifteenth, I had planned to perform the wrathful *masha*[58] ritual. So on the eleventh I entered a strict retreat and began chanting the White Mañjuśrī mantra. In the middle of the morning I was helplessly overcome by sleep. I put aside the session for a while and tried to refresh myself. I sent word to Jaisang Depa[59] saying that in the afternoon, unless such an occurrence disappeared, no genuine practice will be accomplished.

Concerning the fever of the Upper Residence Tulku, he had been cared for by both Lingtö Chöjé and Jang Ngö[60] and was in good health. The venerable Depa sent Depa Norbu to inquire after his health, and at that time there was no problem. However, he suddenly worsened in the late morning. Tea was offered in the great assembly, and in the Pehar Chok temple[61] the protector entered the oracle. The Depa was informed of his pronouncement, and he came from Lhasa at the end of day. Through Jaisang Depa he said that the other day he had postponed the initiation out of concern. But now by all means I should go. I broke my retreat and went to the Upper Residence, where I gave the Mahākāla permission initiation Dispelling All Obstacles. However, he had been adversely affected by a spirit, and his mind was unable to receive it. It was no use. On mid-morning of the thirteenth he passed away. My unprecedented sleepiness that morning indicated a demonic obstruction to my plan to bestow the initiation that evening. I had postponed the White Mañjuśrī retreat under the sway of a hindrance.[62]

Thus he says, "So on the eleventh I entered a strict retreat." This "eleventh" is the eleventh of the fifth Tibetan month, July 2, 1656. On that day the Great Fifth hastily left his retreat and went to the Upper Residence, where he offered to Tulku Drakgyen the Mahākāla permission initiation Dispelling All Obstacles. However, a spirit had adversely affected the consciousness of Drakgyen, and his mind was unreceptive. He passed away before noon two days later. This account is a precise record of the actual events at that time, written down clearly by the Great Fifth himself, exactly as he witnessed them.

The Alleged "Purpose" of Drakgyen's Death

Although there is no evidence for it in any authentic works contemporaneous with the first appearance of Dölgyal, it is now claimed with inflated eulogy more than three hundred years later that Drakgyen died intentionally because Nechung, the great Dharma protector, had repeatedly urged him to arise in the form of an imperious spirit to protect the Geluk doctrine. This account is described in Trijang Vajradhara's *Commentary on the Praise of Shukden* (47b6):

> Praise to you who generated the mind of wrathful courage
> when, repeatedly urged by Dorjé Drakden, lord of the
>   imperious,
> you arose in the form of a protector solely of the Geluk
>   tradition,
> thereby fulfilling your pledge.

During the breaks in the teachings given by Mañjunātha Tsongkhapa in Riwo Genden Monastery, a young boy dressed in white would come into his presence, asking again and again, "Please help me."

Gyaltsap Jé and Khedrup Chöjé understood that the child was an emanation of Pehar[63] but said nothing. Dulzin Drakpa Gyaltsen[64] was sitting as the senior monk in the teachings of Tsongkhapa at that time, and so one day he approached the child and said, "When the venerable lama is giving teachings, it is very tiring for him. It is not right for you to approach him like that. If you need help, I will give it."

The child replied, "Perfect! I too have been waiting for you as a companion. Now, among the great disciples assembled here, you have accepted." With that the child disappeared.

Later Dorjé Drakden, lord of all imperious deities in the world, came to Panchen Sönam Drakpa, who was the reincarnation of Dulzin, and urged, "The great master Jamyang Gawai Lodrö[65] insisted that I must chiefly protect the Geluk teachings, but previously in the presence of the great Ācārya Padmasambhava, I pledged to protect the Buddha's teachings in general. Therefore there is no way for me to look after the Geluk teachings exclusively. Panchen, these days among the ranks of the Geluk doctrine holders, you are the one who possesses the highest qualities of learning and insight. Moreover, in keeping with your previous promise to do this, you must arise in the form of an imperious protector of the Geluk teachings."

Panchen only replied, "I will consider it later," and made no commitment at that time.

Then Tulku Drakpa Gyaltsen, who was later in the same lineage of incarnations, was urged by the great protector Nechung to remember his previous promise. Drakgyen seemed not to remember, replying, "What promise?"

Pehar handed him something, saying, "Eat this and enter retreat. It will become clear." Accordingly, he ate what was offered and entered a strict retreat. After a short time, he recalled it, and in keeping with that previous promise, he became undaunted in generating the wrathful courage to arise in the form of a powerful, fierce, and swift protector in order to guard exclusively the doctrine of the Geluk tradition. The verse offers praise to that act.

The account of the great protector Nechung Dorjé Drakden urging Panchen Sönam Drakpa to arise in the form of a fierce protector of the Geluk doctrine can be found in the Drepung Monastery edition of his biography. Moreover, all this can be known if you study the previous composition,[66] written on the third day of the third month, just before he suddenly died at the age of thirty-eight in the fifth month of the fire-monkey year. Read from the lines "Arhat Upagupta, guide of gods and men" up to "the significance of these pledges are important to ascertain in one's mind."

The great Ācārya Padmasambhava exhorted:

It is like this. Listen, great king, possessed of faith.
He was Upāli when the Buddha was alive in the world.
After passing away, he became Upagupta.
In some cities he was known as Bhavabhadra.
In the east, in a place near the land of China,
he will become the Buddhist monk Losang.

In the vision, not only does Drakpa Gyaltsen take to the crown of his head the commitments and instructions of his actual and lineage lamas, such as the master Tsongkhapa, who was of one continuum with Arhat Upagupta, but also the exhorting words of Nechung Dharmarāja, guardian of the land, dissolve into his mind. He arises as the overlord of the imperious spirits, with an entourage of bodiless imperious spirits accompanied by many wrathful offerings, and emanates to become the guardian of the teachings of the master Tsongkhapa. Owing to circumstances, the Great Fifth and Drakgyen himself, two great beings who were like the sun and moon, had not had the opportunity to meet for a while, but in a short while the pledges would merge as one, and he would be enthroned as the powerful and fierce protector of the Geluk teachings. This is all clearly presented, and so it can be trusted.[67]

To see whether the above is factual, let's examine it part by part.

Many short, middle-length, and extensive biographies of the venerable Tsongkhapa were composed by his disciples, such as that by actual disciple Khedrup Gelek Palsang, and their disciples in turn. In none of them is there any reference whatsoever to an emanation of Dharma protector Nechung urging Dulzin Drakpa Gyaltsen to become a protector of Tsongkhapa's teachings. Moreover, there is no mention of it even in the biography of Dulzin Drakpa Gyaltsen himself.

The account of Dharma protector Nechung coming to Panchen Sönam Drakpa and urging that he should arise in the form of an imperious spirit protector of the Geluk tradition in keeping with his previous promise is stated clearly above. However, in the verse biography written by Pal Nyima Sangpo, an actual disciple of Panchen Sönam Drakpa, master expositor of myriad sutras and tantras, and in the biography composed by Jadral Lhawang Gyatso, another direct disciple, and so on, there is no mention of Nechung urging him in this way. And in the several authentic biographies of Panchen Sönam Drakpa composed by later disciples, there is no such reference.

Up to the present day, even the Shukden Society cannot find a biography of Panchen Sönam Drakpa anywhere in the *Shukden Compendium*[68] in which Nechung urges him in this way.

The account of Dharma protector Nechung urging Drakgyen to become a protector exclusively of the Geluk doctrine is something concocted in the twentieth century by Dölgyal followers in their praises of him. It appears only in those works, and prior to that, no authentic historians from the masters of the Sakya, Geluk, Kagyü, and Nyingma traditions have written anything like that.

It was stated that if we examine the composition by Drakgyen, beginning from the line "Arhat Upagupta, guide of gods and men," we can understand how Drakgyen deliberately arose in the form of an imperious spirit protector of Geluk doctrine. However, nowhere in those verses does he state that he will actually arise in the form of an imperious spirit protector of the Geluk doctrine. And even if he did actually make such a pledge, and we are able to accept the authenticity of what he says, we must also accept as true what he says in a previous chapter, "Two Works by Drakpa Gyaltsen."

Claims Surrounding the Circumstances of Drakgyen's Death

The circumstances around Drakgyen's death and how he died, as cited previously, are as described in *Heavenly Raiment* composed by the Great Fifth himself. However, more than three hundred years after that time there are still wild and fabricated claims that attendants from the Ganden Phodrang, or some such, murdered Tulku Drakgyen out of envy. For example, in *Commentary on the Praise of Shukden*, Kyabjé Trijang Vajradhara says (49a5):

> Praise to you, who arose as lord of the imperious spirits,
> through the power of your bodhicitta intention,
> when those of perverted prayer bound your throat with a
>   scarf,
> and day and night you terrified even the brave
> with your harrowing manifestations.[69]

When he had recalled his previous promise, he went to Pehar Chok temple, where he addressed Nechung Dharmarāja, "Now I have remembered my previous promise. What should I do?"

The Dharma protector replied, "The necessary deeds, I will do."

Soon, as a result of the magical workings of Nechung Dharmarāja, many travelers from Mongolia and Kham began arriving in Lhasa from all directions, and it seemed as if the audiences and offerings for the Upper Residence Tulku Drakgyen were greater than those for the Fifth Dalai Lama. The Ganden Phodrang of the Dalai Lama was called the Lower Residence, and the living quarters of Drakgyen were known as the Upper Residence. At that time the people were saying that the Upper and Lower Residences were of equal status. Moreover, at the head of the rows of the Offering Prayer at the Great Prayer Festival, his throne had the status of being next to the throne of the Great Fifth. Because of this and other incidents, the Ganden Phodrang attendants, headed by Desi Sönam Chöphel, became consumed with envy and they sought for a time to kill him.

This coincided with Drakgyen knowing that the time to fulfill his pledge had arrived, and so at the age of thirty-eight, on the twenty-fifth of the fourth month of the fire-monkey year, he suddenly displayed becoming ill with an acute fever. Depa Norbu, or Nangso Norbu, had married into the Gekhasa family into which Drakgyen was born and was also a relative of Desi Sönam Chöphel. In collaboration with the Desi, he had secretly planned use the illness as a pretext to visit Drakgyen and kill him. On the thirteenth of the fifth month, he tried to stab him, but the knives would not penetrate his body. Therefore he killed him by stuffing a ceremonial scarf down his throat.

In this connection, the Great Fifth in his autobiography, *Heavenly Raiment*, states:

> In keeping with the forthcoming eclipse on the fifteenth, I had planned to perform the wrathful masha ritual. So on the eleventh I entered a strict retreat and began chanting the White Mañjuśrī mantra. In the middle of the morning I was helplessly overcome by sleep. I put aside the session for a while and tried to refresh myself. I sent word to Jaisang Depa saying that in the afternoon, unless such an occurrence disappeared, no genuine practice will be accomplished.
>
> Concerning the fever of the Upper Residence Tulku, he had been cared for by both Lingtö Chöjé and Jang Ngö and was in good health. The venerable Depa sent Depa Norbu to inquire of his health, and at that time

there was no problem. However, he suddenly worsened in the late morning. Tea was offered in the great assembly, and in the Pehar Chok temple the protector entered the oracle. The Depa was informed of his pronouncement, and he came from Lhasa at the end of day. Through Jaisang Depa he said that the other day he had postponed the initiation out of concern. But now by all means I should go. I broke my retreat and went to the Upper Residence, where I gave the Mahākāla permission initiation Dispelling All Obstacles. However, he had been adversely affected by a spirit, and his mind was unable to receive it. It was no use. On mid-morning of the thirteenth he passed away.

Thus the Great Fifth speaks as if Drakgyen died of an illness. It is simply not possible that the Great Fifth would lie knowingly. It is clear that this was written by relying upon reports presented to him by Desi and others, who deceived him with their clever lies.

Regarding a secret plot carried out by [Depa] Nangso Norbu, the *Heavenly Raiment* autobiography of the Great Fifth says (1:87b):

The young men of Gekhasa had been killed by the Mongolians, and so the Gekhasa household was thinking of taking on another son-in-law. They could have found another, but with an attitude of wanting to cause harm, they took on Nangso Norbu.

If you think about the phrase "wanting to cause harm," much can be understood.[70]

The events described here include Nechung telling Drakgyen that he must arise in the form of an imperious spirit protector, many pilgrims coming from Kham and Mongolia, all emanated by Nechung, to seek audience with and present offerings to Drakgyen in far greater numbers than to the Great Fifth, resulting in Desi Sönam Chöphel and the attendants of Ganden Phodrang becoming consumed with jealousy. Then on the thirteenth of the fifth month they try to stab him but the knife does not penetrate, so they kill him by pushing a scarf down his throat, and so on. These events are all described as if they were witnessed firsthand. But who saw these events? Did Drakgyen's servants see them? Were the attendants aware of them? Alternatively, if they were not witnessed, then did Depa or Nangso Norbu or Desi Sönam Chöphel somehow expose their secret plan to others?

Also, in the root text of the story of Gyalchen composed by Dakpo Kalsang Khedrup, which was quoted above in the commentary, it says, "When those of perverted prayer bound your throat with a scarf...," thereby suggesting that he was strangled. The commentary on that line, however, states that he was killed by a scarf stuffed down his throat. Here root text and commentary do not agree. What are these if not invented accounts with no sound documentation?

These days, merely following what others say and taking the words of this commentary as their sole basis, the Shukden Society, like the startled rabbit,[71] continues to broadcast through various media that Drakgyen was killed by a scarf being stuffed down his throat, even down to producing a drawing of it. However, answers to the questions posed above, together with any reference to relevant documents and so on from around the time of the death of Drakgyen that would be able to authenticate their reliability, are like hair on a tortoise or the sky flower.[72]

Therefore such baseless lies do not bear scrutiny and hold no value for the many unbiased scholars who gather in the marketplace of orators of scripture and reasoning. Moreover, in this twenty-first century of science and technology, how can such false accounts and lies hold up for even a moment?

The above extract contains a serious misunderstanding, one that eludes credibility. It concerns the line quoted from the Great Fifth's biography: "but with an attitude of wanting to cause harm, they took Nangso Norbu."

Using this as a reason, it is stated that Desi Sönam Chöphel, in league with Depa Nangso Norbu, killed Tulku Drakgyen. However, you with fresh and unbiased minds, open wide those eyes that discriminate between right and wrong and look carefully. In the Great Fifth's biography it says, "Those of the Gekhasa household took Nangso Norbu as a son-in-law." Nowhere does it say that Desi Sönam Chöphel sent Nangso Norbu to be a son-in-law.

We can therefore expose the untruth of this biased account as follows. The Great Fifth says in *Heavenly Raiment* (1:87b6):

> The Desi was a little displeased with Jaisang Depa and so sent him to gather the harvest at Ölga. The Desi considered making

Nangso Norbu his replacement but was not completely happy with the idea, and so Lopa Chözö was brought on as an aide. The young men of Gekhasa had been killed by the Mongolians, and so the Gekhasa household was thinking of taking on another son-in-law. They could have found another, but with an attitude of wanting to cause harm, they took on Nangso Norbu.

It did not sit well with Desi Sönam Chöphel that Nangso Norbu could be considered as a replacement for Jaisang Depa, and so he took Lopa Chözö instead. Gushri Tenzin Chögyal had defeated the Beri ruler Dönyö and had come to Central Tibet to support the Geluk in the earth-tiger year of 1638. At this time Tulku Drakgyen was nineteen, and as we have seen, he had at Gekhasa been secretly engaged in wrathful rituals targeting the Mongolians. As a result of this secret being exposed, the Mongolians slaughtered the young men of Gekhasa. If the Gekhasa family had taken on another son-in-law who was clever at getting along with the Ganden Phodrang officials headed by Desi Sönam Rabten (a.k.a. Shalngo Sönam Chöphel) and the Mongolians who acted as their allies, then a hundred doors of opportunity would open in every direction. However, those of the Gekhasa family, "with the wish to cause harm" toward Desi Sönam Chöphel and so forth, took Nangso Norbu as a son-in-law, someone whose views diverged completely from the Ganden Phodrang headed by Desi Sönam Chöphel.

If this is taken as being the meaning of the above citation, it cannot be interpreted in another way.

Refuting the Claim that Desi Sönam Chöphel and Nangso Norbu Killed Drakgyen

We can see now how the claim that Desi Sönam Chöphel in league with Depa Nangso Norbu killed Drakgyen is nonsense. This can be established with valid reasons, which will be reiterated here.

The first reason is the authentic account in the Great Fifth's autobiography, in which he describes how he visited Drakgyen on his deathbed and performed a ritual, which was unsuccessful as Drakgyen had been adversely affected by a spirit and his mind was unable to receive it. Also, the Great Fifth describes how Drakgyen passed away on the morning of the thirteenth and so forth.

Moreover, as stated above, Desi Sönam Chöphel did not trust Nangso

Norbu even to be a replacement for Jaisang Depa. Depa Nangso Norbu was someone who only did things that displeased the Great Fifth and Desi Sönam Chöphel. We can show how they regarded him with just a few examples. It says in *Heavenly Raiment* (1:103b2):

> Nangso Norbu did not accept his duties, and when the weapon store was lost, he was said to be the first to flee.

This occurred in 1641, the iron-snake year. Also (1:114b2):

> The situation in Tsang was out of control, as illustrated by Nangso abandoning the Gyantsé Fort and fleeing. However, the Shokha army repelling the Dzingchi coincided with Gushri Khan and Depa Sönam Chöphel[73] arriving, and so the army of about five or six thousand men, including Shokha Nangso himself, were left like burnt straw.

This occurred in the water-horse year of 1642. Also (1:178b2):

> In particular, for the lord chamberlain, Darkhen Nangso, and others of a sensitive nature, their eyes became filled with tears, and they buried their faces in their robes. Depa Norbu had a huge smile on his face, unlike any he had before. Like the confidence of being sure that because fever and other illnesses were widespread in China, those who traveled there would not return, this was an outward expression of inner joy, as is said in the *Hevajra Tantra,* "The thought remains inside, but the expression cannot be hidden." However, as the Tsang people say, "The Angyikpa does not attain enlightenment, but the attendant does."[74]

This was in the water-dragon year of 1652, when the Great Fifth left for China. Also (1:226b5):

> As these people were fond of longevity initiations, I thought I would bestow a general initiation and mentioned this to Depa. Accordingly, Depa Norbu began to create a list of offerings that had to be made for the initiation by the official residences of the Nangso, each according to its status. Becoming apprehensive

about the possible gossip about this being some kind of extortionate tax, I postponed the initiation.

This was in the wood-horse year of 1654, when Tulku Drakpa Gyaltsen was still alive. Also (1:276a4):

> At the turn of the month Depa Norbu arrived. He had the glow of some spontaneously manifested official. These were the outer signs of Lhachö, the new governor of Shundrong, and Lhagyal, among others, showing their powers with their eyes closing from below.[75]

This is from the earth-pig year of 1659. Also (1:278b2):

> The great Nöjin[76] said, "If you do not take care with Depa Norbu, the goats will not be used for threshing[77] while in their enclosure and this will be like the musk deer fleeing to the mountain without being caught." This was in keeping with the prophecy from the protector One-Eyed Jatri of Tsongdü, who said that in early summer, water will burst forth from under your knee.
>
> The Gona Shak household needed permission to go together to Tsang under the pretext of visiting the hot springs. Considering the thoughts and deeds of the son, I was a little hesitant. However, people, not knowing the reasons, would develop a wrong view, and who's to say the uncle and nephew would not reveal their true colors. If they did, the frost of people's minds would be cleared away, I thought, and so I gave permission.

Also (1:277a2):

> The masters of Gyütö and Gyümé tantric colleges and Sera and Drepung monasteries and the Taklung Monastery treasurer gathered informally at the palace to give guidance to the Gekhasa household. The lamas and geshés were learned in Dharma but not versed in the duplicitous ways of the world. The Taklung treasurer displayed differing personalities in different contexts,[78] and so except for conforming and agreeing with the lamas, he exhibited no self-conviction. This led to Depa Norbu engaging

in self-centered interruptions like water being sloshed around from a pot. Because of this, nothing was accomplished, and the whole day was wasted in that way.

This was also written in 1659. Also (1:281a3):

> The great protector said, "Make immediate praise to the warrior deity." Accordingly, that day I went to the Nechung (Pehar) Chok temple and on the thirteenth offered praises at the Potala. That instruction from the protector was in connection with the flight of Depa Norbu, I think.

Also (1:284a1):

> These thirteen regions of Tibet were given to me by Tenzin Chögyal and were not given to be shared by the uncle and nephew. We discussed whether the occurrences of this year amounted to a people's uprising.

This was also in the earth-pig year of 1659. Therefore Drakgyen had been dead for three years. At that time Depa Nangso Norbu, a son-in-law of the Gekhasa family, and Depa Gona Shak, a nephew in the same family, conspired together and organized an uprising against the Ganden Phodrang, which became known as the earth-pig troubles, or the Gekhasa Gona Shak uncle-and-nephew troubles.

There is still a lot on this topic in the Great Fifth's biography, but the point is clearly made with the above extracts. Like the saying goes, "Knowing one, frees all." Also presenting every relevant extract would make the text excessively long.

Therefore, while Tulku Drakgyen was alive, and even after his death, Depa Nangso Norbu was unappealing to Desi Sönam Chöphel and the Great Fifth in all he did. They in turn did not trust him. However, in the Gekhasa camp not a single disparagement can be found in any literature of that time. If Nangso Norbu, urged on by Desi Sönam Chöphel, had killed Tulku Drakgyen, the Gekhasa people would have held Nangso Norbu as an enemy with unconcealed vengeance. However, the very opposite was true. The Gekhasa family aligned themselves with Nangso Norbu with full trust and confidence.

Moreover, he turned against the very government of Desi Sönam Chöphel and brought about the earth-pig troubles. With that in mind, saying that under the encouragement of the Desi, Nangso Norbu killed Drakgyen is clearly baseless.

Therefore the Great Fifth's autobiography *Heavenly Raiment* says (1:273b3):

> Depa underwent many hardships for the Geluk tradition. Moreover, his far-reaching deeds subsequently became known to everyone and were of great practical benefit. By this alone, I do not grieve greatly over his death.

Thus, when Desi Sönam Rabten, a.k.a. Desi Sönam Chöphel, died in 1658, the Great Fifth himself spoke of the hardships that the Desi underwent for the sake of the Geluk tradition and goes on to write of the immense gratitude that the Geluk owed to him. These days we should all likewise recall the kindness of people like Desi Sönam Rabten and think very carefully about the unwelcome consequences of the unbearable karma we would have to experience from repaying the kindness of others with serious and baseless accusations, and from gossip that blames others wrongly, completely at odds with actual historical events.

5. Cremation and Other Postmortem Matters

HEAVENLY RAIMENT STATES (1:250a5):

The great protector divined, "At the time of the cremation of the tulku, you should not be in the vicinity. Return to the Potala."

Therefore, on the twenty-second, for seven days, I applied myself to virtuous deeds, such as saying prayers, making offerings, and mantra repetitions in front of the Ārya Brothers. I had hoped for a good sign that the karmic obstacles were being removed, but one night I dreamed of a monk holding a length of rolled dough as thick as a finger and as long as a handspan. He placed it before me saying, "This is Depa Kyiruwa." The dough wriggled off like an insect. I also dreamed that the horse track outside a fort was crowded with soldiers, and together with the Depa I had to flee in the rain and darkness through the back gate, without any boots. This and other bad signs I dreamed.

The above constitutes reliable testimony for the cremation of Drakgyen's body, a contemporaneous account of the events. The great protector Nechung advises that it would not be right for the Great Fifth to be in the vicinity at the time of the cremation. Therefore, on the twenty-second of the sixth month, he retires to the Potala and performs virtuous practices for a week, culminating in a description of various bad signs he experienced during that time. The above citation from the *Heavenly Raiment* autobiography is the clearest statement on the cremation. It is the authentic composition of the unbiased and unquestionably learned scholar, refuge, and guide, the Great Fifth Dalai Lama.

However, an account from 1920, a full 264 years after the death of Drakgyen, states there still existed a mummified right arm from the corpse of Drakgyen at Döl White Springs in Lhokha district. Kyabjé Phabongkha offered a Guru Puja there and composed a new Guru Puja ritual for Dölgyal. This account is in a later chapter describing how the venerable Phabongkha began his connection with Dölgyal. Also, in *Heavenly Raiment* (1:264b4) it says:

> The great protector said, "Last year when the Depa was at the Tölung hot springs, I advised, through two monastic proctors, that the shrines of the Upper Residence be moved elsewhere because he had been attacked by a demon. The silver reliquary was dismantled and left, but nothing was moved to another place. It is because of this that the Depa is ill. Now the situation is serious, and so you must move the Upper Residence."
>
> There was much talk about whether it was actually necessary to dismantle the building or whether it would suffice to just banish the spirit. However, it was said that while the eight shrines remained intact, voices and groaning sounds could be heard coming from inside them. Whether this was true or not, the demon of superstition arose, and so there was no decision. The personal possessions were taken to Tölung, and the timber was taken to East River. In the remains of the residence the monastic college[79] performed several wrathful dances, and about a hundred monks from the three monasteries recited the scriptures.

Thus, in the preceding year the great protector Nechung said that Desi Sönam Chöphel, also known as Desi Sönam Rabten, had been afflicted by a demon, and that consequently the Upper Residence should be moved elsewhere. However, while the shrines were dismantled and left, nothing was moved. Now the Desi's illness worsened and the situation became acute. Therefore it was decided the Upper Residence should definitely be moved. However, there was much talk about whether destroying the residence were really necessary, and wouldn't it be enough to simply banish the spirit. Finally Drakgyen's possessions were transferred to Tölung and the timber hauled to the river. In the remains of the Upper Residence, the monastic college performed obstacle-removing rituals.

This is clearly stated. However, accounts of the body of Tulku Drakgyen refusing to be burned by the fire, of his body being mummified and placed as a sacred object in the principal shrine of the eight shrines, of that shrine being taken apart later, the body being placed in a wooden chest and taken to the Kyichu River, where it finally arrived at Döl White Springs, to be settled there, and so on, are not to be found at all in the *Heavenly Raiment* autobiography of the Great Fifth. Moreover, nothing resembling these accounts can be found in any of the religious and secular histories, biographies, and so on of those times.

Nevertheless, in later times followers of Dölgyal continued to offer him nothing but great praise. For example, it says in the *Commentary on the Praise of Shukden* (50b5):

> After he had died by way of these sudden circumstances, his body was cremated in the grounds of Drepung Tantric College. At that time the smoke from the fire offering rose up in three straight columns like three sticks of incense. The attendant said, "Still you act this way when others have committed such wicked acts of envy against you."
>
> With this he fanned the smoke with his upper robe. The columns of smoke split. Two continued up into the sky and the third whirled to earth near the village of Denbak and from there to Sangphu Monastery. This meant that the aspect of his exalted wisdom had gone to Sangphu, where he entrusted himself to the assistance of the protector Setrap and arose in wrathful form.
>
> At that time, the corpse refused to be burned by the fire and remained whole. It was placed as a sacred object within the main shrine of the eight constructed silver shrines. They were placed in the Upper Residence at Drepung, and for a while those attending the shrines heard unbearable cracking and pounding noises, and from within the shrines came the sounds of voices and groaning. In accordance with instructions from Nechung, the Desi dismantled the silver shrines, put the corpse in a wooden chest, and placed it in the Kyichu River. Finally it reached a valley in Döl, these days known as Döl White Springs.

These assertions are just imaginative fabrications presented as praise to Dölgyal. However, if you do no research at all and just wish to pass your days happily taking on stories that are solely those of the startled rabbit, then so be it. But when those of intelligence and impartiality conclude their research, they will find only a story that beguiles the minds of little children; they will never find an actual historical source for these accounts that is at once reliable and not embarrassing, even if they were to search for an eon.

For example, during the cremation of Drakgyen's body, the attendant says, "...when others have committed such wicked acts of envy against you." This certainly refers to the story of Nangso Norbu killing Drakgyen. In that case, the attendant would have known that Desi Sönam Rabten in league with Nangso Norbu killed Drakgyen, and so it could not be correct to say that the other attendants of Drakgyen and those of his household at Gekhasa would not have known. If they had all known this, then how to explain the fact that several years after his death, the influential people of the Gekhasa household put their trust in Nangso Norbu and associated with him, as described previously?

Also, the attendant fanned the smoke with his upper robe, and one column of smoke whirled its way to Sangphu Monastery by way of the village of Denbak. This is described as the aspect of Drakgyen's exalted wisdom traveling to Sangphu, where he entrusted himself to the assistance of the protector Setrap in order to arise in wrathful form. However, the distance between the Drepung Tantric College enclosure and Sangphu is over twenty-five kilometers. Therefore, did that single column of smoke travel like the vapor trail from a plane in a straight line from Drepung to Sangphu? Or did the smoke form into a ball and travel there? Did it billow there like an ordinary smoke cloud from a fire? When the smoke arrived at Sangphu, did it immediately enter the protector chapel of Setrap? Who at that time examined where that single column of smoke was going? And who followed it? Who had knowledge that the smoke traveled to Sangphu so that Drakgyen could arise in a wrathful form and could seek out the help of the Dharma protector Setrap?

Say that column of smoke at the cremation of Drakgyen's body had not traveled to Sangphu and had not sought the help of Setrap. Would Drakgyen then not have been able to arise in wrathful form? Why was it necessary to seek the support of Setrap in order to arise in wrathful form?

If the attendant of Drakgyen had not fanned the smoke with his robe, are you saying that the smoke would have not gone to Sangphu, in which case, instead of Drakgyen arising in wrathful form, his aspect of exalted wisdom would have risen into the sky together with the three columns of smoke and simply disappeared? Furthermore, regarding those two columns that rose into the sky, where did they go, and what was their purpose? If you say that you don't know, then it is illogical to say that you know about one column but not about the other two.

The stories of the body refusing to be burned at the cremation and remaining intact, of the body being placed as the sacred object in the main shrine of a set of eight shrines made of silver, and so on are not supported by any sourced historical accounts of that time whatsoever. Despite this lack of any valid source, it is being written down more than three hundred years later that these past events occurred in this way. Therefore, having examined these so-called facts in detail, we will be able to understand that the story of Dölgyal assuming the form of an imperious spirit protector of Tsongkhapa's teachings has no essence to it at all, like the story of the carpenter Ananda[80] who supposedly not only traveled to the god realms mounted on smoke but was able to return.

The Claim That the Great Fifth Enthroned Dölgyal as a Geluk Protector

In the extract from the *Commentary on the Praise of Shukden* it states, "Owing to the sudden arising of circumstances, the Great Fifth and Drakgyen himself, two great beings who were like the sun and moon, had not had the opportunity to meet for a while, but in a short while the pledges would merge as one, and he would be enthroned as the powerful and fierce protector of the Geluk teachings. This is all clearly presented, and so it can be trusted."

However, in the claim that "in a short while" the Great Fifth would enthrone Dölgyal as the great protector of the Geluk doctrine, does the phrase "in a short while" refer to a time following the death of Drakgyen? After Drakgyen died in 1656, the Great Fifth spent eighteen years, by Tibetan reckoning, attempting to placate Dölgyal but without success, and so finally, from the third month of the water-ox year, or April 1673, he had to employ only wrathful methods against Dölgyal. The Great Fifth wrote of this in *Heavenly Raiment,* details of which are presented below.

Furthermore, if the Great Fifth had enthroned Dölgyal as a protector of the Geluk doctrine, then Ganden Monastery, the main monastic seat of the entire Geluk tradition, as well as Sera and Drepung monasteries would have begun composing invocations of Dölgyal from that time onward. If that had happened, then how is it possible that Dölgyal would have had to stretch out his hand from the window into the chamber of Sönam Rinchen (1704–41), the head of the Sakya tradition, after he had been refused entry to Tashi Lhunpo?[81]

Similarly, if the Great Fifth had enthroned Dölgyal as protector of the Geluk doctrine, then without doubt it would have been written of in the Great Fifth's autobiography and in other authentic works of the time, but one finds no mention of it at all.

The Invention That the Great Fifth Composed an Invocation of Dölgyal

Present-day followers of Dölgyal possess an invocation of Dölgyal that ends with "composed by the Fifth Dalai Lama." To determine whether this is actually a composition by the Great Fifth, the great refuge and guide, the Fourteenth Dalai Lama conducted an exhaustive investigation of the outer, inner, and secret collected works of the Great Fifth. Instead of finding an invocation of Dölgyal, he came across this declaration:[82]

> This unholy Drakpa Gyaltsen, with pretensions of holiness,
> is an oath-breaking spirit born from perverse prayers.
> As he is harming the teachings and all living beings,
> do not help him or protect him but grind him to dust.

The Fourteenth Dalai Lama announced this in a talk on Dölgyal.

Therefore, if we examine the *Brief Invocation* included in the Shukden Compendium and declared by present-day followers of Dölgyal to be composed by the Great Fifth, we can find three reasons why this is a work composed by a later follower and wrongly ascribed to the Great Fifth:

1) As stated above, nowhere in the outer, inner, and secret collected works of the Great Fifth is there such an invocation to Dölgyal. In fact, only restrictions of Dölgyal can be found.

2) In the invocation is the verse:

> Praise to you, in the robes of a monk,
> summer-cloth hat adorning your head.
> In your right hand a club, in your left a human heart;
> astride various mounts, such as snake and garuḍa,
> taming the female demons of the charnel grounds.

Dölgyal, when this invocation was composed, was holding a human heart in his left hand. More than thirty years after the Great Fifth passed away, and more than sixty years after Drakgyen died, however, Dölgyal was said to have reached his hand through the chamber window of Sönam Rinchen, the head of the Sakya tradition, pleading, "Appoint me protector of the venerable Sakya master. Give me hand implements." The Sakya master rolled up a ball of dough left over from his meal and gave it to Dölgyal. As soon as he took it, it transformed into a human heart. This is described in *Commentary on the Praise of Shukden*, as will be presented below, and is universally related by present-day followers of Dölgyal. Therefore, while the Great Fifth was alive, Dölgyal did not hold a human heart as an implement, and when Dölgyal did hold such an implement, the Great Fifth was not alive. Therefore there is no way to justify the statement that this invocation was composed by the Great Fifth.

3) Drakgyen died in 1656, and for about eighteen years the Great Fifth tried several attempts to placate Dölgyal, but none were successful. Finally, in 1673, a group of great masters from the old and new traditions, headed by the Great Fifth, employed rituals to suppress and burn him. This is described in the Great Fifth's autobiography, *Heavenly Raiment*:

> There were many wonderful signs of the oath-breaking spirit and its entourage having been burned by this fire ritual. Moreover, the smell of burning flesh experienced by everyone there was convincing. Directly, this was the practice of granting freedom from fear by saving the lives of many living beings. Indirectly, those spirits were brought to happiness by being freed from accumulating even more bad actions and having to experience the unending suffering of bad states of rebirth.

These events will be described in more detail below. For about forty years after these events, nothing was heard from Dölgyal, and his whereabouts were uncertain, but after that period he first arrived at Sakya Monastery. Fearing that Dölgyal would cause harm, a few Sakya lamas wrote the first invocations to him. This is well known from authentic historical accounts. But as for an authentic historical record of an invocation of Dölgyal composed by the Great Fifth, this is simply not known to any valid perception.[83]

6. Rituals against Dölgyal

Attempts at a Peaceful Settlement

It says in *Heavenly Raiment* (2:257a1):

> There are reports that in Döl White Springs a particularly power-
> ful malevolent oath-breaking spirit, born from perverse prayers,
> has been causing harm to the people and the teachings, both
> generally and individually. Since the fire-bird year these have
> increased, and it has succeeded in many of its intrigues. However,
> because it did not concern them directly, few did anything about
> it. At the end of the earth-bird year, I had a dwelling constructed
> at Döl White Springs and moved some items there, hoping that
> it would become a base for the spirit. However...

Thus, in the fire-monkey year, 1656, Drakgyen died and became an
oath-breaking and harmful spirit. In the following year, the fire-bird year of
1657, reports of harm being caused to the people and the teachings increased.
Therefore, twelve years after the fire-bird year, in the earth-bird year of 1669,
the Great Fifth, from his great compassion, provided a building and possessions at Döl White Springs for this oath-breaking spirit born from perverse
prayers. Thus, from 1669, he hoped to pacify the spirit.

Signs That a Wrathful Ritual Was Needed

In *Secret Teachings Sealed by a Sword and a Skull*, the Great Fifth says (opening page, line 2):

> At the female earth-bird new year at Drepung, I saw a black
> woman, the size of a mountain, with her right foot on the Upper

Residence (*Khges gak khok*) and her left on Chökhor Ling Monastery (*Jor zgos khyik*), and by pressing down they became a haze of dust.

The earth-bird new year corresponds to February 1, 1669. The coded words *Khges gak khok* and *Jor zgos khyik* are annotated below the line as referring to the Upper Residence and Chökhor Ling Monastery, respectively.

Also in the old handwritten edition of *Secret Teachings Sealed by a Pot Marked by Hayagrīva and a Lotus* (8l2):

> Examine well, directly and in various ways,
> those who proffer respect with empty words.
> A vindictive demon is masquerading as a friend.
> Don't go along with others, but make efforts to tame him.

> Do not listen to well-intentioned words
> from those of inferior minds.
> The river at the mountaintop
> diverges where two valleys meet.

> The yellow flowers of the grassy meadow
> are in danger of being struck by frost.

> The tiger's stripes appear as the leopard's spots.
> The turquoise dragon has a golden mane.
> Its red tongue, lightning quick, flashes and is gone.

While listening to these words, the great Orgyen with *khaṭvāṅga* staff[84] in his right hand, a threatening mudrā gesture made with his left, and a ḍākiṇī on either side spoke:

> Between Avalokiteśvara and me, there is no difference.
> Without saying too much, put into practice
> what you have been shown previously.

To avert the hindrance, perform the thread-cross ritual[85] and the torma practices of Black Yamāntaka and Sitātapatrā,[86] perform the Ngak Gö Loktri.[87] In the ruins of the Drepung Upper Residence (*Khges gak khok*) perform the fire-offering ritual. Bind the horse of good fortune for the happiness of Tibet. Build a dwelling for nāgas.

Thus the great Orgyen Padmasambhava, by way of a vision, clearly tells the Great Fifth to perform a fire-offering ritual in the ruins of the Drepung Upper Residence and so on. Again, the words *Khges gak khok* below the line refer to the Upper Residence.

The Wrathful Ritual

For seventeen years, from the time that Drakgyen died, the Great Fifth strove repeatedly with great compassion to subdue Dölgyal in a peaceful way. However, his efforts did not bear the desired fruit. This is stated in his *Heavenly Raiment* (2:257a2):

> At the end of the earth-bird year, I had a dwelling constructed at Döl White Springs and moved some items there, hoping that it would become a base for the spirit. However, the harm increased.

The Great Fifth built a new dwelling for Dölgyal and placed various items and furnishings inside. However, regardless of these peaceful ways to subdue Dölgyal, the harms only increased. Therefore seventeen years after the death of Drakgyen, the Great Fifth announced in *Heavenly Raiment* (2:173b5) that there was no choice but to perform a wrathful ritual practice to safeguard the Tibetan people:

> The power of the spirit at Döl White Springs had risen greatly. Moreover, there had been various supernatural occurrences caused by a hostile force. Therefore, in the monastic college, specifically targeted practices were performed followed by a fire ritual, led by the vajra master Drakna Chöjé.[88]

This occurred in the third month of the water-ox year, 1673. During this period of time fire rituals and practices targeted at Dölgyal had to be performed continually.

Also, in his autobiography (239a1):

Because of disturbing omens brought on by a disembodied being, the monastic college, with the monk Lodrö Gyalwa as vajra master, performed ten million wrathful mantras, in the tradition of Rikzin Dorjé Drakpo Tsal,[89] targeting demonic forces in general and specifically the oath-breaking spirit at White Springs, after which a fire ritual was performed. This was done for the welfare of the Tibetan people.

Rinchen Gangpa Wangyal Dorjé said the initiation of Secret Hayagrīva was needed. I had hoped for a quick possession, but it was extensive. When the initiation had concluded, the torma fell from the table with no wind or other condition, and without breaking or cracking. At that time I did not think about it, but this strange occurrence I now see as the supernatural work of a powerful spirit.

This took place in the second month of the wood-rabbit year of 1675. At that time, for the welfare of the Tibetan people, it became necessary to perform a ritual practice directed at Dölgyal. Also, he had conducted most of a Secret Hayagrīva initiation, as requested by Rinchen Gangpa Wangyal Dorjé, when the magical display of a powerful spirit occurred.

In the Great Fifth's autobiography it says (257a3):

Many in the lay and monastic communities have recently been struck down by a contagious illness, and one or two monks had died. Therefore the monks of the college unanimously urged that a ritual be performed. Consequently, Ngakrampa Döndrup Gyatso as the vajra master of the Dorjé Drolö ritual, and Nangjung Ngakchang Losang Khyentsé as vajra master of the Most Secret Karma Drakpo ritual, headed two groups of ritual practitioners. Also, Rikzin Tulku of Dorjé Drak Monastery, Chögyal Terdak Lingpa, Ukja Lungpa, Drigung Tulku Rinpoché, Katsal Surpa Ngari Könchok Lhundrup, and Palri Tulku spent seven days performing the rituals of Wrathful Guru, Yama, Phurba, Loktri, and so on. This was followed by a fire ritual.

There were many wonderful signs of the oath-breaking spirit and its entourage having been burned by this fire ritual. Moreover, the smell of a burning corpse experienced by everyone there was convincing. Directly, this was the practice of giving freedom from fear by saving the lives of many living beings. Indirectly, those spirits were brought to happiness by being freed from accumulating even more bad actions and having to experience the unending suffering of bad states of rebirth.

At that time I composed a declaration that these spirits were without guide and protection. The college, Dorjé Drak Monastery, and Darding Monastery compiled the mantras.

Thus this malevolent spirit was not subdued by peaceful means, as was the wish of the Great Fifth in the beginning. The injuries it was inflicting on the people were multiplying, and hostile signs were also on the increase. Moreover, the great master Padmasambhava had urged the practice of a fire ritual in the ruins of the Upper Residence. Therefore, in the third month of the water-ox year of 1673, ritual practices and a fire ritual directed at Dölgyal had to be conducted, as is described clearly above.

At that time the monastic community unanimously urged that a wrathful ritual was now necessary. On this basis, in the sixth month of the wood-rabbit year of 1675, a group of great masters universally and unquestionably acknowledged to be endowed with the qualities of learning and practice, led by the Great Fifth, once more conducted a fire ritual preceded by seven days of ritual for the welfare of the people and teachings of the land of snow in general, and focused specifically, for the present and for all time, on that malevolent spirit and on others in that category.

Also, in *Heavenly Raiment* (2:257b5):

> For a while the precious tulku of Dorjé Drak Monastery performed the Mañjuśrī wind practice and the precious treasure revealer performed the destruction rite directed at some hostile spirits who resembled previously suppressed malevolent spirits. The monks of the college with Chöjé Silnön Dorjé as vajra master performed rites focused on spirits, and many auspicious signs were perceived. When Dorjé Drak Tulku performed the suppression ritual, the demonic nāgas actually appeared in the form of the eight oath-bound deities and seemed to take the offerings.

This also took place in the sixth month of that year. Thus, at that time the great Rikzin Pema Trinlé (1641–1717) of Dorjé Drak Monastery, the treasure revealer Terdak Lingpa Gyurmé Dorjé (1646–1714), and others performed suppression rites aimed at some hostile spirits, and many auspicious signs were observed.

Also, Minling Lochen Dharmaśrī says in his *Chariot of Faith: The Life Story of Terdak Lingpa Gyurmé Dorjé* (77):

> From the tenth of the sixth month onward, he performed the replenishing retreat of the Phurbu mantras, and by way of a fire ritual the malevolent spirit known as Dölgyal was burned until only his name remained. At that time of the summoning and placing, wailing sounds of someone dying were heard, and the foul smell of a burning corpse was experienced by everyone during the fire ritual. These and other signs were observed.

This records the same event described by the Great Fifth above.

The Declaration Issued by the Great Fifth

Above, the *Heavenly Raiment* states, "At that time I composed a declaration that these spirits were without guide and protection." That declaration can be found in his *Spontaneous Evocation of the Four Actions: The Insights, Offerings, Supplication, Praises, and So Forth of the Myriad Oath-Bound Dharma Protectors Possessed of Unimpeded and Wrathful Power* (148a6):

> The false incarnation of Tulku Sönam Gelek Palsang, who was successful because of the manipulations of Lak Agyal of Gekhasa, became an oath-breaking spirit born from perverse prayers and brought much harm to living beings. Consequently, seven groups of practitioners were assembled: Dorjé Drak Tulku Rinpoché, Chögyal Terdak Lingpa, Chöjé Ukja Lungpa, Ngari Ngakchang Könchok Lhundrup, Palri Tulku, and two groups from Phendé Lekshé Ling.[90] They destroyed this spirit by way of a fire ritual. At that time I wrote the following declaration.

> To the deities Six-Armed Mahākāla, Karmarāja, Palden Lhamo,
> to Four-Faced Mahākāla, Chamdral Bektsé,
> and other oath-bound protectors
> that we rely on, offer to, and practice,
> I offer to you this precious drink.

This unholy Drakpa Gyaltsen, with pretensions of holiness,
is an oath-breaking spirit born from perverse prayers.
As he is harming the teachings and all living beings,
do not help him or protect him but grind him to dust.

To the female guardians such as the yakṣa Yanghasa,
the Five Kings, Viṣṇu, and Dorjé Lekpa,
and in particular the Dharma king Nechung and entourage,
I offer to you this precious drink.

This unholy Drakpa Gyaltsen, with pretensions of holiness,
is an oath-breaking spirit born from perverse prayers.
As he is harming the teachings and all living beings,
do not help him or protect him but grind him to dust.

Tseu Marwa, the seven Barwa brothers,
the armored Setrap from Sangphu,
all fierce deity spirits in whom this spirit seeks refuge,
I offer to you this precious drink.

This unholy Drakpa Gyaltsen, with pretensions of holiness,
is an oath-breaking spirit born from perverse prayer.
As he is harming the teachings and all living beings,
do not help him or protect him but grind him to dust.

Having pledged to increase the well-being
of the doctrine and living beings
in the presence of mighty Vajradhara
and the root and lineage lamas,
if you now protect this oath breaker,
will your previous oath not weaken?

He causes human sickness, disease in cattle,
he brings frost, hail, famine, and drought,
and various unpleasant magical displays.
Grind to dust the power, body, speech, and mind
of this spirit and his cohorts.

PART 2
Eighteenth Century:
The Sakya Tradition

7. Dölgyal in the Sakya Tradition

AS DESCRIBED ABOVE, a group of great masters of unquestioned renown, headed by the Great Fifth, performed rituals to burn and destroy Dölgyal. From that time onward for about forty years, nothing was heard of him, and his whereabouts were not known. However, after those forty years he arrived at Sakya, and so the first to rely upon him as a protector were a few Sakya lamas. Only later did this practice spread to the Geluk tradition.

To research how Dölgyal first arrived in Sakya, we will examine the relevant and currently well-known works from the Geluk tradition, but we must mainly focus on the source material from the Sakya tradition. It is also necessary to research the differences in the ways Dölgyal is regarded between followers of the Sakya and Geluk traditions, their respective reasons for following this practice, any differences in the way Dölgyal is regarded by these two traditions in later times, and the actual reality in the time of the Great Fifth.

Position of "Commentary on the Praise of Shukden"

In *Commentary on the Praise of Shukden*, in the collected works of Kyabjé Trijang Vajradhara, it says (57b2):

> Praise to you, who arrived at Lhunpo Monastery in Tsang,
> but because of a somewhat inauspicious sign,
> went immediately with a display of anger to Sakya,
> where you were enthroned as a powerful doctrine protector.

In the past Drakgyen had received many profound teachings from Panchen Chögyen, and so after he had arisen in the form of an imperious spirit, he intended to go before the Panchen Dharma king in order to be made protector of Tashi Lhunpo

Monastery. When he arrived he saw Tashi Lhunpo was guarded by the eight horse-lords of Vaiśravaṇa,[91] their arms linked, surrounding the monastery's outer circumambulation route. Because of this somewhat inauspicious sign, anger arose, and recalling the imprints of having been born in the past as the venerable Sakya Paṇḍita, he immediately went to Sakya.

There, in the iron-ox year (1721), the seventeen-year-old Sakya hierarch Dakchen Vajradhara Sönam Rinchen was giving precious teachings on the path and its result (*lamdré*) to an assembly of over three hundred in the old central temple of glorious Sakya Monastery. In the night the spirit let fall a shower of stones, and to some monks he displayed various miraculous apparitions. He appeared in a dream to the Sakya hierarch in which he stood at the entrance to the Tsechen protector chapel in the Phuntsok Ling College of Sakya Monastery in the form of a monk with many eyes.

"Who are you?" asked the hierarch.

"I am that Ganden malevolent spirit," he replied.

Then, blocking out all other form, a huge red hand repeatedly reached through the window into the room outstretched as though begging.

"This one time, what do you want?" asked the Sakya hierarch.

"The previous venerable master pledged to rely on me as one in the ranks of a doctrine protector. Therefore enthrone me as a protector and present me with hand implements."

"In that case," replied the Sakya hierarch, "this is the life essence of all living beings." Taking some leftover dough, he rolled it into a ball and placed it in the hand of the Dharma protector. Immediately it transformed into an actual human heart. Dakchen Vajradhara composed a text called *Request to the Gyalpo: Destroying the Beguilers*, built a protector spirit shrine at Khau Kyelhé, placing in it various offering substances, and enthroned him as a protector of Sakya doctrine.

The substances placed in the shrine included some of great value, and these were later stolen. That thief vomited blood and died. These and other stories can be found in the writings of Sachen Kunga Lodrö (1729–83), who also composed a five-deity offering ritual called *Whirl of Perfect Wishes Fulfilled* with the discipline holder[92] as the central figure surrounded by the kings of the four tantric activities.

A three-dimensional shrine to Gyalchen containing various symbolic substances was constructed in the Mukchung protector chapel at Sakya. Each year the precious Dakchen would come there to perform annual torma-offering rituals. Moreover, in most Sakya monasteries it was the practice to perform Gyalchen propitiation ceremonies, a custom that has lasted to the present day.

It appears that the name Dorjé Shukden Tsal was given by the great Nechung Dharmarāja. In the *Great Wrathful Torma of Shukden* composed by Sachen Kunga Lodrö it says:

> The way this happened was as follows. The succession of incarnations continued up to the Great Fifth Vajradhara, at which time an incarnation bearing the name Panchen Sönam Drakpa appeared, and he possessed wide eyes of wisdom. Others envied his great deeds, which made him unhappy, and finally he died precipitously. Because of this nefarious transition, groans and other sounds could be heard coming from his silver reliquary for about a month, and so the reliquary and his residence were demolished. The timbers were thrown into the river, and they came to rest at Döl White Springs. Remaining there, he became known as the malevolent spirit Dölgyal.
>
> Therefore many rituals of suppressing, burning, and casting were performed, some of which produced signs. However, whether he recovered consciousness or came back from the dead, he simply returned to his old form. This prompted Nechung Dharmarāja to declare, "No one dares compete with him. He is Dorjé Shukden Tsal."
>
> From his being named in this way, can it not be inferred that Dorjé is similar to the explanation of the term *dorjé* found in the Vajra Vehicle, and is it not the kind of name given by Hayagrīva or Guru Rinpoché to

those who have been bound by oath? I leave this question to practitioner scholars.

As described above, he carried a human heart given to him by the Vajradhara Sakya hierarch. He took this and showed it to Morchen Vajradhara,[93] declaring, "This is the hand implement given to me by the Sakya hierarch when he enthroned me as a powerful doctrine protector."

In response, Morchen and Dreu Lhep[94] composed a comprehensive Gyalpo spirit-propitiation ritual containing complete sections on inviting, satisfying and confession, praising and urging, and so on, beginning with the verse:

Beyond recognition, nature of beginningless purity,
unobstructed and effortless, primordially uncontrived,
from the expanse of the great bliss of equality,
come to this place in the play of a single moon
reflected in many a lake.

This work is still recited these days in Riwo Chöling Monastery in Lhokha, in Trokhang Temple in Lhasa, and elsewhere. The Sakya masters composed this work, praising him as Mañjuśrī enthroned as a doctrine protector.

Moreover, Morchen Vajradhara Kunga Lhundrup composed *The Three Activities: Presentation of the Gyalpo Spirit* and expanded the activities of Gyalchen Shukden. At that time some slandered this practice, and these days also there are some who express various perverted doubts regarding the practice of relying upon this Gyalchen. This senseless talk results from failing to understand the definitive reality.

For example, the main lama of the Great Fifth was the precious treasure revealer of Mindröling, Terdak Lingpa Gyurmé Dorjé Tsal. One of his disciples who served him for a long time was the vajra holder Chechok Düpa, or Losal Gyatso. A section of Losal Gyatso's biography was called *Historical Accounts: Dispelling the Darkness of Torment.* This contains miscellaneous works of the master Losal Gyatso compiled in a very natural style by Lelung Shepa Dorjé (1697–1740). In it can be found:

In later times Morchen Vajradhara Kunga Lhundrup encouraged the practice as much as he could, praising the spirit's unbelievable qualities and saying, "Now is the time for all like-minded to rely upon this Gyalchen."

Nevertheless, some said, "This is not good. Those who encourage the activities of this Gyalpo are doing nothing but wrong." They do not understand. It is said that this Vajradhara was the incarnation of a great master and a great illuminator of the doctrine. At that time there was no harm greater than that caused by this Gyalpo and no one who was swifter. Such was of great benefit to Morchen himself. All this was an expression of taming those by appropriate means, and so you should see them both as ultimately having the same intention.

Position of the "Supplemental Explanation"

In *Supplemental Explanation as a Preliminary to the Gyalchen Life-Entrustment*, composed by the tutor to the Dalai Lama, Kyabjé Trijang Rinpoché, it says (520b4):

Later, Tulku Drakpa Gyaltsen performed extraordinary works for both worldly and religious aims. Others envied his deeds, which made him unhappy, and finally he died precipitously under violent circumstances. Such a transition caused him to realize that now was the time to enact the strict pledge he had revived previously. Therefore he rose deliberately in the form of a king of the warrior deities, a protector of the Geluk doctrine, a ruler over the lives of those of the three realms, endowed with the might to accomplish whatever was wished for, a blazing hundred-pronged vajra of unending power, of deeds fierce and swift, a wrathful being sitting as the crown jewel of all imperious deities in existence.

At that time, groans and other sounds could be heard for about a month coming from his silver reliquary in Drepung Upper Residence. Therefore the reliquary and his residence were demolished. The wooden articles were thrown into the river, and they came to rest at Döl White Springs. That is where he settled, and for a while he became known as Dölgyal.

The Great Omniscient Fifth was responsible for preserving, developing, and propagating all old and new traditions. Therefore, in order to protect and develop the stainless doctrine of Lama Mañjuśrī Tsongkhapa in keeping with his previous prayers, this great Dharma protector showed the great conqueror various terrifying ramifications. The great conqueror tried various methods to halt them, but none were helpful. He told the Sakya Rinpoché that methods to stop him must be found. Therefore several powerful masters from the Sakya tradition performed the rituals of suppressing, burning, and casting out many times, and some rituals produced signs. However, they could not cause the slightest harm to this Dharma protector. At that time the great Dharma protector Nechung declared, "No one dares compete with him. He is Dorjé Shukden Tsal," thereby bestowing on him this title.

The torma cast by the Sakya practitioners was returned, and the harms escalated. Everywhere in Central Tibet and Tsang supernatural incidents frightened the people and could not be controlled.

Finally, when the Sakya hierarch Dakchen Vajradhara Sönam Rinchen was giving precious teachings on the path and its results to an assembly at Sakya Monastery, in the night the spirit let fall a shower of stones, and to some monks he displayed various miraculous apparitions. He appeared in a dream to the Sakya hierarch, in which he stood at the entrance to the Tsechen protector chapel in the Phuntsok Ling College of Sakya Monastery in the form of a monk with many eyes.

"Who are you?" asked the hierarch.

"I am that Ganden malevolent spirit," he replied.

He asked Gongkar Dampa Lodrö[95] about this, who remarked, "These days, even in Central Tibet, there is this Dölgyal that nobody can subdue. The monastery should not get riled up, but the venerable Rinpoché should compose a request and offering ritual, and if you construct some kind of temple at Kyelhé and elsewhere, it will be for the good." Accordingly, the Sakya hierarch composed *Request to the Gyalpo: Destroying the Beguilers* and established the Kyelhé Gyalpo shrine.

Examining the Above Excerpts

Commentary on the Praise of Shukden cites Sachen Kunga Lodrö's *Great Wrathful Torma of Shukden*, which states that Drakgyen died and then, for about a month, groans and other sounds could be heard coming from his silver reliquary, that the reliquary and residence were demolished and the wooden articles put into the river, and so on. The *Supplemental Explanation* has a similar account. Let's take a closer look at these accounts.

On the thirteenth of the fifth Tibetan month, July 4, 1656, Drakgyen passed away. The Dharma protector Nechung advised the Great Fifth, "At the time of the cremation of the tulku, you should not be in the vicinity. Return to the Potala."

Accordingly, on August 12, the Great Fifth retreated to the Potala, as is described previously in his autobiography. Therefore, the cremation of Drakgyen definitely took place around August 13–14. That means a month and ten days passed after his death before he was cremated. Was the silver reliquary completed before the cremation? If not, how can one accept that Drakgyen died and then for about a month groans and other sounds could be heard coming from his silver reliquary? In *Heavenly Raiment* (1:264b4) it says, as cited above:

> The great protector said, "Last year when the Depa was at the Tölung hot springs, I advised, through two monastic proctors, that the shrines of the Upper Residence be moved elsewhere because he had been attacked by a demon. The silver reliquary was dismantled and left, but nothing was moved to another place. It is because of this that the Depa is ill. Now the situation is serious, and so you must move the Upper Residence."
>
> There was much talk about whether it was actually necessary to dismantle the building or whether it would suffice to just banish the spirit. It was said that while the eight shrines remained intact, voices and groaning sounds could be heard coming from inside them. Whether this was true or not, the demon of superstition arose, and so there was no decision. The personal possessions were taken to Tölung, and the timber was taken to East River.

This instruction from Dharma protector Nechung was given in the fifth month of the water-dog year, June 1658. Two years had passed since Drakgyen's death. In that instruction, "last year" refers to the iron-bird year of 1657, one year after Drakgyen passed away. In that year, while Desi Sönam Rabten was visiting the hot springs in Tölung, Nechung first gave the advice that the shrines of the Upper Residence be moved. The silver reliquary was dismantled and left, but nothing was moved elsewhere, and because of that the Depa fell ill. Therefore it was *after* Nechung gave his advice on moving the shrines in 1657 that they were finally dismantled. After that the text actually says that the timber was "taken to East River" and not "thrown in the river." This chronology is completely at odds with the narrative in the *Supplemental Explanation*. Therefore, if you want to know the unvarnished truth of an historical event, you should never shun from giving great importance to contemporaneous works composed by authentic compilers.

Also in *Commentary on the Praise of Shukden* it says that "after he had arisen in the form of an imperious spirit he intended to go before the Panchen Dharma king in order to be made protector of Tashi Lhunpo Monastery." But when did Drakgyen actually arise in the form of an imperious spirit? Previously, the same text describes how, at the time of his cremation, a column of smoke traveled to Sangphu, and there he arose in imperious spirit form. Therefore the text is clearly saying that it was around the time of his cremation that he arose in this form. It also states that the purpose for arising in such as form was in order to protect the Geluk teachings and that initially he intended to become a protector at Tashi Lhunpo Monastery.

Let's examine these claims. Having risen in the form of an imperious spirit, he went straightaway to Tashi Lhunpo. Panchen Losang Chögyen lived for six years after the death of Drakgyen. Therefore, Dölgyal going to Tashi Lhunpo fits in with the dates of Panchen Losang Chögyen, and "the Panchen Dharma king" must be a reference to him. Dölgyal is prevented from being in the presence of the Panchen Dharma king, and we are told that consequently he remembers his birth as the venerable Sakya Paṇḍita. But where is the evidence for this recalling of the imprints of having been born in the past as Sakya Paṇḍita? Is it just believing that he remembered it, or saying, "I know because of my clairvoyance of knowing the minds of others"? There is not a single valid reason for advancing this claim, nothing that comes from any research based on reliable accounts from those times.

After Drakgyen rose in the form of an imperious spirit and was unable to be made protector of Tashi Lhunpo Monastery in the presence of Panchen Losang Chögyen, we are told he immediately went to the Sakya hierarch Sönam Rinchen. However, Tulku Drakgyen died in 1656, Panchen Chögyen died in 1662, but the Sakya hierarch Sönam Rinchen was not born until 1705. Thus when Drakgyen died, Panchen Losang Chögyen was alive, but at that time not only was Sakya hierarch Sönam Rinchen not yet born, his birth would not take place for another fifty years.

The passing of Panchen Losang Chögyen and the time when the Sakya hierarch reached age seventeen are separated by sixty-one years. Therefore the account of Tulku Drakgyen arising in the form of an imperious spirit as the exclusive doctrine protector for the Geluk, going to Panchen Losang Chögyen but having no opportunity to be in his presence, then immediately going to be in the presence of the seventeen-year-old Sakya hierarch Sönam Rinchen and being made a Sakya protector is unreliable and nearly impossible to verify.

Furthermore, if it were true that Drakgyen, through his past resolve alone, arose deliberately in the form of an imperious spirit as the protector of the Riwo Genden tradition exclusively, then just because he did not have the opportunity to become a Tashi Lhunpo protector, why would he just cast aside his previous strict pledge? Wouldn't he have gone on to other great Geluk masters and monasteries to become an exclusive Geluk doctrine protector? It does not make sense that he would immediately cast aside his previous pledge like a handful of grass, just because he was not able to be in the presence of Panchen Losang Chögyen, and go to a place that he was able to enter—the residence of the Sakya hierarch Sönam Rinchen—and from the hierarch's window, stretch out his hand again and again, pleading, "Please enthrone me as a Sakya protector."

We are told that through the force of his repeated resolve to become a protector solely of the doctrine of Mañjunātha Tsongkhapa, the time for such an occurrence arrived and he arose in the form of an exclusive protector of the Geluk teachings. At the same time we are told that when he met the Sakya lama, he expressed to him also that a previous Sakya master had promised to rely upon him as a doctrine protector, that he had accepted that position, and now the time had arrived become a protector of the glorious Sakya doctrine. This makes nonsense of the account telling of his arising in the form of an imperious spirit protecting the Geluk teachings exclusively.

It is clear that his main purpose was to find an opportunity to promote his own gratification.

On this point, the master Tsongkhapa, Dharma king of the three realms, said:

> When, by way of the ten Dharma activities,
> I make efforts in the proper practice,
> may I always be helped by the powerful ones,
> and may vast auspiciousness fill every quarter.

If someone is an authentic and powerful doctrine protector, they should help those who are practicing properly and nurture auspicious events. How can it be right to cause hindrances by showering down stones in the night and to show inauspicious omens to the lamas and monks of a great monastery who are properly practicing the precious Dharma?

Also, if you are an authentic and exclusive protector of the Geluk, when somone asks, "Who are you?" you reply, "I am an exclusive protector of the Geluk, a king of warrior deities, called such and such." However, when the Sakya hierarch Sönam Rinchen asked Dölgyal who he was, he replied, "I am that Ganden malevolent spirit." On the basis of this reason alone, there is clearly no need for any great discussion on whether Dölgyal is an authentic and exclusive protector of the Geluk.

In *Commentary on the Praise of Shukden* it says (58b1):

> It appears that the name Dorjé Shukden Tsal was given by the great Nechung Dharmarāja.

This is followed by a citation from Sachen Kunga Lodrö. This is a reference to the time when the Great Fifth and others performed the rituals of suppressing, burning, and casting out, and Nechung Dharmarāja supposedly named him Dorjé Shukden Tsal, as if he were suggesting that it was not right to perform these rituals.

In the *Supplemental Explanation* it states:

> Several powerful masters from the Sakya tradition performed the rituals of suppressing, burning, and casting out many times, and some rituals produced signs...At that time the great Dharma pro-

tector Nechung declared, "No one dares compete with him. He is Dorjé Shukden Tsal."

Thus here too he is given this name and glorified. At every period Dölgyal practitioners have used these citations to promote various baseless claims by way of excessive inflated praise. In reality, if you research the biographies and documents of those times, you will not find, even if you search for an eon, a single syllable of authentic source material that recounts Nechung Dharmarāja naming and praising Dölgyal in this manner.

In fact, the opposite is true. The Dharma protector Nechung advised the Great Fifth to stay in the Potala, as it would not be good to remain in the vicinity of the cremation of Drakgyen. As we also saw in the Great Fifth's autobiography, about a year after Drakgyen died, Nechung advised that the silver reliquary and the shrines of the Upper Residence be moved elsewhere as Desi Sönam Rabten, a.k.a. Desi Sönam Chöphel, had been attacked by a demon. And two years after the death of Drakgyen, Nechung said, "Now the situation is serious, and so you must move the Upper Residence."

The great Dharma protector, as will be described more fully below, also told the Great Thirteenth Dalai Lama that the master Phabongkha had spread the practice of Dölgyal in Drepung Monastery and that this had hastened the demise of the doctrine. As a result, the master Phabongkha wrote a letter to the Thirteenth expressing remorse and a promise of restraint.

Also, these days, Dharma protector Nechung has told the great conqueror, master of the Buddha's entire doctrine on this earth, peerless guide, refuge and protector for all living beings in this and future lives, the Fourteenth Dalai Lama, "It is not right to rely upon Asé Khyampo."[96]

The great conqueror the Fourteenth Dalai Lama asked, "Is Asé Khyampo Dölgyal?"

"It is," came the reply.

Later Nechung told the Dalai Lama that relying upon Dölgyal brings more harm than good and that if you look carefully at those who rely upon Gyalchen these days, you can clearly understand what kind of condemnation they suffer externally, how much mishap they experience internally, and in the end what kind of misfortunes befall them.

Dharma protector Nechung spoke these things about Dölgyal again and again, and so how is it possible that this great Dharma protector would have ever conferred such a name and such praise on Dölgyal?

In the *Supplemental Explanation* it says, "The great conqueror tried various methods to halt them, but none were helpful. He told the Sakya Rinpoché that methods to stop him must be found." And, "The torma cast by the Sakya practitioners was returned, and the harms escalated." And so on. This too is just exaggerated praise born from wishful thinking. No such account appears anywhere in reputable histories or in Sakya biographies of the time. In particular, the most reliable, the clearest, and the most precise sources for the first appearance of Dölgyal—and for what methods to stop him were used—are those in the Great Fifth's autobiography, *Heavenly Raiment*. Had the Great Fifth told the Sakya lamas that methods to stop Dölgyal were needed, then such an instruction as well as an account of the Sakya masters performing these rituals in keeping with the Great Fifth's request would have certainly appeared in *Heavenly Raiment*. The account of the Nyingma masters performing a wrathful ritual aimed at Dölgyal, in accordance with the Great Fifth's instructions, appears in the *Heavenly Raiment*, and so we should expect the above to appear as well. However, nowhere is there any account of the Great Fifth giving such an instruction to the Sakya masters, of the Sakya masters casting a torma at Dölgyal, or of the torma being thrown back to land on top of powerful Sakya masters.

Commentary on the Praise of Shukden cites Sakya Kunga Lodrö as stating, "The succession of incarnations continued up to the Great Fifth Vajradhara, at which time an incarnation bearing the name Panchen Sönam Drakpa appeared." Even this brief historical reference is an example of baseless nonsense. The dates for Panchen Sönam Drakpa are 1478–1554, while the Great Fifth lived from 1617 to 1682. There is a gap of sixty-three years between the two, and Panchen Sönam Drakpa was not alive during the time of the Great Fifth. The incarnation of Panchen Sönam Drakpa was Tulku Sönam Yeshé Wangpo, whose dates are 1556–92. His incarnation was Tulku Gelek Palsang, whose dates are 1594–1615. His false but successful incarnation was Tulku Drakgyen, whose dates are 1619–56. These dates are clearly recorded in the works of the Great Fifth. His next and unfortunate birth has also been described previously with authentic references.

8. Sakya Masters Who Relied on Dölgyal

BOTH *COMMENTARY ON THE PRAISE OF SHUKDEN* and the *Supplemental Explanation* state that the earliest practitioner of Dölgyal was the Sakya hierarch Sönam Rinchen, and *Commentary on the Praise of Shukden* states that he was seventeen at that time. However, before that, when Sakya Sönam Rinchen was only fourteen, the Sakya lama Morchen Kunga Lhundrup (1654–1728) was already relying on Dölgyal. In *Mirror for the Beautiful Woman of Intelligence: A Biography of Morchen Kunga Lhundrup* (288a4), it says, "As Dorjé Shukden Tsal was superior when invoked and in casting curses, he was happily accepted as a protector."

From the words "accepted as a protector," it seems as if Morchen were the first in the Sakya tradition to employ Dölgyal as a protector. This occurred in the earth-dog year of 1718. At that time Morchen was sixty-five, and according to Tibetan reckoning, Sakya hierarch Sönam Rinchen was only fourteen.

Also, in an autobiographical extract within the same biography (298b5), it says, "To the monk proctors and the Gyalchen oracle I offered the extensive Amitāyus and Hayagrīva a hundred times."

It also says (299a2), "I went to perform the consecration of the Gyalchen chapel of Trengpo Ganden Ling." This occurred in the iron-ox year, 1721. Morchen was sixty-eight, and the Sakya hierarch Sönam Rinchen was seventeen.

Further (305a6), "I went to the mantra consecration and so forth of the statue of Gyalchen in Gosur chapel at Trengpo. Gyalchen showed possession of the oracle."

These and other instances demonstrate the relationship between Dölgyal and Morchen from the Sakya tradition.

Also in *Offerings Made to the Jetsok*[97] *Dharma Protector*, Sachen Kunga Lodrö, whose life is detailed further below, states that the practice was with a venerable master of the Sakya and then handed down to his disciple

Morchen. That venerable master of the Sakya was not the Sakya hierarch Sönam Rinchen, because as stated above, Morchen was of an older generation and nowhere in his biography does Morchen speak of taking Sönam Rinchen as his lama. Therefore the venerable master of the Sakya of that time does not fit with Sakya hierarch Sönam Rinchen. So who was this venerable Sakya master? In *Mirror for the Beautiful Woman of Intelligence* (233a1), Morchen says:

> Now I must make sure my life of opportunity and leisure is not wasted. For that, there can be no other than the Vajradhara Khyenrab Jampa Ngawang Lhundrup Tenpai Gyaltsen in glorious Nalendra. I have no other thought in my mind than to go quickly to him.

Therefore Vajradhara Khyenrab Jampa Ngawang Lhundrup Tenpai Gyaltsen, or Lhatsun Khyenrab Jampa Ngawang Lhundrup (1633–1703), was Morchen's primary root lama. Among the Sakya masters of the doctrine of his time, he was unrivaled in his learning, ethics, and goodness, as well as in his wisdom, compassion, power, and so on. He stood high among his peers, like the very peak of a victory banner. He was also included among the inner disciples of the Great Fifth Dalai Lama, guide of men and gods, refuge and protector, as an object of special affection and limitless compassion. When the Great Fifth passed away, Desi Sangyé Gyatso, out of necessity, kept it a strict secret. However, this master had many dreams indicating that the Great Fifth had passed away, and each time these occurred, he had many experiences, in reality or as visions. These were all completely authentic and reliable, as is recounted in his autobiography.

This master lived for a long time after the passing of the Great Fifth, and to see whether he had any relationship with Dölgyal during that time, we have surveyed his early biography, *A Crystal Garland: The Spiritual Achievements of the Chetsun Master of Speech*, and his later biography, *Ambrosia for the Ears of the Fortunate*, as well as the biographies of other lamas of Morchen. We could not find a single word detailing a relationship between these lamas and Dölgyal, or of handing down the practice from this master to Morchen, and so on. Also, while Morchen gives accounts of his own practice of Dölgyal, nowhere does he write of receiving the practice from another lama.

Similarly, in the colophon of *Whirl of Perfect Wishes Fulfilled* composed by Sachen Kunga Lodrö, it says:

This five-deity offering to the Dharma king,
great Dharma protector, protector of great power,
enthroned as doctrine protector by great master Morchen,
glorious one of the Sakya, regent to the Buddha
and preserver of the sun-like teachings of the Buddha,
was spoken by the all-knowing Ngawang Kunga Lodrö,
Sakya guide of the beings of the three realms,
as a whirl of perfect wishes, spontaneously fulfilled,
and a jewel that grants all desires.

The prayer continues and in closing states that it was written by someone called Ānantu. We see that this too states that the first person to enthrone Dölgyal as a protector was Morchen.

The account of a venerable Sakya master handing the practice to Morchen is thus just a case of later Dölgyal practitioners putting their trust in the deceitful words of Dölgyal. Research on the story of the practice being handed down by a venerable Sakya master who existed before the Sakya hierarch Sönam Rinchen and Morchen Kunga Lhundrup reveals it to be nothing but empty words.

However, in Sachen Kunga Lodrö's *Great Wrathful Torma of Shukden* (8a2), also found in the *Shukden Compendium* compiled by a Losang Thupten Trinlé Yarphel (279), it says:

Everywhere in Central Tibet and Tsang supernatural incidents frightened the people and could not be controlled. Finally, in an autumn month of the iron-ox year, the seventeen-year-old Sakya hierarch Dakchen Vajradhara Sönam Rinchen was giving precious teachings on path and its results to an assembly of over three hundred in the old central temple of glorious Sakya Monastery. In the night the spirit let fall a shower of stones, and to some monks he displayed various miraculous apparitions.

Later, in the water-rabbit year, the Dakchen took the immeasurably kind Malak Denyi as consort, and some years after that he had a dream of someone in the form of a monk with many eyes standing at the entrance to the Tsechen protector chapel in the Phuntsok Ling College of Sakya Monastery.

"Who are you?" asked the hierarch.

"I am that Ganden malevolent spirit," he replied.

He asked Gongkar Dampa Lodrö Wangchuk about this, who remarked, "These days, even in Central Tibet, there is this Dölgyal that nobody can subdue. The monastery should not get upset, but the venerable Rinpoché should compose a request and offering ritual, and if you construct some kind of temple at Kyelhé and elsewhere, it will be for the good." Accordingly, the Vajradhara father composed *Request to the Gyalpo: Destroying the Beguilers* and established the Kyelhé Gyalpo shrine, into which substances of great value were placed.

As we saw above, this extract from *Great Wrathful Torma of Shukden* appears in *Commentary on the Praise of Shukden*, and the words and meaning are basically reproduced verbatim. Dölgyal displayed various apparitions such as showering down stones when the Sakya hierarch Sönam Rinchen was seventeen. After that, he took a consort in the wood-rabbit year. This corresponds to the year 1723, when the Sakya hierarch was nineteen. The account then says that it was only some years later that Sakya hierarch Sönam Rinchen began relying upon Dölgyal.

Similarly, it is made clear that the person in whom the Sakya connection with Dölgyal was first made was none other than Sachen Kunga Lodrö's father, the Sakya hierarch Sönam Rinchen. This does not agree with what he stated earlier.[98] Therefore it is not possible to conclusively decide the matter either way. This issue of Dölgyal first appearing in the Sakya tradition through Morchen Kunga Lhundrup and Sakya hierarch Sönam Rinchen requires additional research by impartial scholars.

Reasons the Practice of Dölgyal Appeared in the Sakya Tradition

As cited previously, *Great Wrathful Torma of Shukden* composed by Sachen Kunga Lodrö describes how Dölgyal said, "I am that Ganden malevolent spirit," and displayed various unpleasant apparitions. Fearing the harm that could ensue, Gongkar Dampa Lodrö Wangchuk gave his advice, following which Sönam Rinchen composed *Request to the Gyalpo: Destroying the Beguilers* and built a Gyalpo spirit shrine. The text clearly states that these actions were taken purely out of fear and not out of any newfound trust or faith in Dölgyal. The text clearly states that the composer of *Request to the Gyalpo* was Sachen Kunga Lodrö's father, Sakya hierarch Sönam Rinchen.

However, a few later Dölgyal practitioners have made changes to this text, as will be seen below.

Therefore, out of fear of the harm that Dölgyal might cause, Sakya hierarch Sönam Rinchen composed *Request to the Gyalpo*. Most of the propitiation and invocation texts to Dölgyal up to the present time have been initiated by Dölgyal himself. The reason for the composition of *Propitiation of Dölgyal: Activities That Fulfill All Wishes*, whose section up to the confession was composed by Dreu Lhepa and the remainder by Morchen, is not clear. *Whirl of Perfect Wishes Fulfilled: A Ritual Offering to the Dharma King and Monastic Discipline Holder* and *A Timely Thunderbolt: The Great Wrathful Torma of Dharma Protector Gyalpo Dorjé Shukden Tsal* were both composed by Sachen Kunga Lodrö, the son of Sakya hierarch Sönam Rinchen, and the *Great Wrathful Torma of Shukden* had to be composed because of the urging of Dölgyal. In that text (6) in the *Shukden Compendium* (279), it says:

> In the water-rabbit year, when I was fifty-five, I was very sick, coughing up sputum, for several months. In the fourth month of that year, he appeared in the Mukchung protector chapel at Sakya through a monk-medium from Chökhor Lhunpo Monastery and made a prediction. He said that this was a dangerous time for me, and that it would be good if the repelling torma rituals of Four-Faced Mahākāla and Gyalchen were performed at the end of that month. And so, entreated by Kunga Phuntsok, I at once composed this short ritual and added it to the previously composed *Whirl of Perfect Wishes Fulfilled*.

It also says (9a6, 281):

> On the eighth day of the fourth month of the wood-rabbit year, a monk in whom he had spontaneously appeared said that for the pacification of the disturbances of Sakya Kunga Lodrö, a repelling torma of the Wrathful-Faced One and Gyalchen was necessary. Therefore, because of its necessity from many aspects, as mentioned in the colophon, I wrote this repelling torma to be attached to the previous composition, *Whirl of Perfect Wishes Fulfilled*.

Also in *Amazing Magical Play and Source of the Four Classes of Perfection: The Biography of Sachen Kunga Lodrö*, composed by Sakya Kunga Tashi, it says (348a6):

> The imperious spirit Dorjé Shukden Tsal suddenly appeared within a monk from Chökhor Lhunpo Monastery and declared that it was necessary to cast a repelling torma dedicated to him, and accordingly [Sachen] composed the ritual.

However, it says in the above *Shukden Compendium* (9a3, 281):

> In other later pronouncements Gyalchen stated, "This is how to do it," and so on. That is why this repelling torma ritual lacks the methods found in the authentic works of India and Tibet and follows the general tantric method only roughly.

Therefore this composition of *Great Wrathful Torma of Shukden* was roughly written, following the dictates of Dölgyal, and states clearly that it has no source reference whatsoever in the great texts of India or Tibet.

Nevertheless, in keeping with the dictates of Dölgyal, at the age of fifty-five, Sachen Kunga Lodrö composed *Great Wrathful Torma of Shukden* and performed the repelling torma ritual. This was in May of 1783, when Sachen was fifty-five. However, two months later, on the second day of the later *jyeṣṭha* month, or later fifth month, in the morning at the time of the snake,[99] Sachen Kunga Lodrö passed away.

Author of "Request to the Gyalpo: Destroying the Beguilers"

History texts agree that *Request to the Gyalpo: Destroying the Beguilers* was the first invocation ritual of Dölgyal. Moreover, *Amazing Storehouse of the Sakya Dynasty*, composed by Sachen Kunga Lodrö, says (687, l.7), "*Request to the Gyalpo: Destroying the Beguilers* was spoken by this master," going on to say that this work was composed by Sakya Ngawang Kunga Sönam Rinchen, or Dakchen Sönam Rinchen.

Likewise, Sachen Kunga Lodrö elsewhere speaks of his father, Sakya hierarch Sönam Rinchen, as having composed *Request to the Gyalpo*. For example, in an old Sakya woodblock edition of this invocation, the title page reads, "*Request to the Gyalpo: Destroying the Beguilers*," and in the colophon of the same woodblock edition, it says:

> *Destroying the Beguilers: An Invocation of the Great Gyalpo*[100] was spoken by Sakya Ngawang Kunga. May all be auspicious! Thus the great father, Vajradhara Ngawang Kunga Sönam Rinchen Tashi Drakpa Gyaltsen Palsangpo, composed this brief request to Gyalchen Shukden Tsal. At the time of composition a few similar texts were composed, which had been written down by others with many mistakes. These have been thoroughly corrected by Sakya Ngawang Kunga Lodrö, who dwells in this life, the next life, and the intermediate state purely by the kindness of the great masters.

In *Shukden Compendium* compiled by the Mongolian Losang Tayang, and the later version compiled by a Losang Thupten Trinlé Yarphel, the title page of this work reads, *Invocation of the Great Gyalpo Shukden Tsal: Destroying the Beguilers*. And its colophon reads, "This *Invocation of the Great Gyalpo Shukden Tsal: Destroying the Beguilers* was spoken by Sakya Ngawang Kunga Lodrö. May all be auspicious." These compilers of works on Dölgyal have added "Shukden Tsal" to the title, which does not agree with the old Sakya woodblock edition. Also, they have not even understood that the "Sakya Ngawang Kunga" in the colophon of the Sakya woodblock edition refers to Sakya hierarch Sönam Rinchen, not to Sachen Kunga Lodrö. They thereby attribute *Destroying the Beguilers* to Sachen Kunga Lodrö. Moreover, in the table of contents of the compendium of Losang Thupten Trinlé Yarphel it says, "*Invocation of the Great Gyalpo Shukden Tsal with Black Horse: Destroying the Beguilers*, by Sakya hierarch Ngawang Kunwang Lodrö, four pages in length."

These are huge errors, both in words and meaning.

9. Origin of the Names of Dölgyal

DÖLGYAL IS KNOWN by many names: Dölgyal, Great Gyalpo, Gyalchen, Shukden, Dorjé Shukden, and so on. As the leader of the nonhuman spirits who dwell at White Springs in Döl, in Lhasa Lhokha, he is the Gyalpo of Döl, Döl Gyalpo, Dölgyal, and so on. The great kings in the human realm, the great rulers of the gods, and the leaders of nonhuman spirits are called *gyalpo* ("king"), and as Dölgyal is the ruler of a group of nonhuman spirits, he is the great Gyalpo, or Gyalchen, for short. Because he is endowed with (*den*) the ability or power (*shuk*) to harm others, he is known as Shukden, Dorjé Shukden, and so on.

In *Destroying the Beguilers: Invocation of the Great Gyalpo* it says, "Dharma protector Gyalpo Shukden Tsal with his entourage." And in the invitation, "I invite Dorjé Shukden. Come to this place." And in the wrathful invocation, "*Hūṃ*! Powerful Gyalchen Shukden Tsal, the time has come." Therefore three times he is referred to as "Dharma protector Gyalpo Shukden Tsal," "Dorjé Shukden," and "Gyalchen Shukden." Elsewhere in this work he is mainly referred to as the great Gyalpo. He is referred to as: (1) "Great Gyalpo destroying the beguilers," (2) "Thus, if you wish to perform the torma dedication, invocation, and so on, of the great Gyalpo...," (3) "The great Gyalpo, red in color, with one face and two hands," (4) "Come to this place great Gyalpo with your entourage," (5) "Great Gyalpo and your entourage, accept this vast torma offering," (6) "This cloud of offerings to please the great Gyalpo," (7) "Great Gyalpo and your entourage I invoke your mind," (8) "Dharma protector, great Gyalpo...," (9) "Great Gyalpo, with great anger destroy the enemy hinderers," (10) "Quickly accomplish your terrifying deeds, Gyalchen," and (11) "Great Gyalpo with your entourage."

It is probable that "Gyalpo Shukden," "Dorjé Shukden," and "Gyalchen Shukden" are alterations made to the original invocation text by later Dölgyal practitioners who held him in great esteem, and that Sakya Sönam

Rinchen when he composed *Destroying the Beguilers* had simply written "Gyalchen" instead.

The reason for this is that if the Sakya hierarch Sönam Rinchen had indeed written "Dorjé Shukden" and "Gyalchen Shukden," then instead of "great Gyalpo" elsewhere, he should have written "Dorjé Shukden." Whether from the aesthetics of the composition or the expression of its meaning, we can see that this change would greatly improve the artistry of the composition. However, he did not use these names.

Furthermore, as described in a previous section, someone in the form of a monk with many eyes said to the Sakya hierarch Sönam Rinchen, "I am that Ganden malevolent spirit." The hierarch asked Gongkar Dampa Lodrö Wangchuk about him. In reply Gongkar told him about Dölgyal. At that time he was known only as Dölgyal, and so following Gongkar Dampa's advice when Sakya Sönam Rinchen composed *Destroying the Beguilers*, he referred to him as Gyalchen, which was perfectly commensurate with the preceding events. Before that time he did not know who this being was and had to ask about him. The response was that he was called Dölgyal. Immediately he began to compose the request to Dölgyal, and he would not have used "great Gyalpo Dorjé Shukden Tsal" and so on. Examine this with an impartial mind, and you can understand this to be the case.

Another reason is that *Destroying the Beguilers* had been "written down by others with many mistakes," as described in a previous citation of Kunga Lodrö, the son of Sönam Rinchen. Therefore no one can say that a few later followers did not substitute "great Gyalpo" for "Dorjé Shukden," Gyalchen Shukden," and so on. For example, Sönam Rinchen called the text *Destroying the Beguilers: An Invocation of the Great Gyalpo*, but later even that was changed to *Brief Request to Gyalchen Shukden Tsal*, as cited above.

Even if the names Dorjé Shukden and Gyalchen Shukden, which appear in *Destroying the Beguilers*, had indeed been written by Sakya hierarch Sönam Rinchen, at that time he would have been newly writing a praise specially focused upon Dölgyal, and it can been understood that previous to that time these names were not at all well known, because apart from the single instances of Dorjé Shukden and Gyalchen Shukden, he is mostly referred to as "great Gyalpo" in this text.

Similarly, the accounts of Dharma protector Nechung giving Dölgyal the name Dorjé Shukden Tsal are just exaggerations manufactured by Dölgyal followers.

Also, think carefully about the name Gyalchen Dorjé Shukden as given to Dölgyal by his followers. Dharma protector Nechung, the main warrior deity of the Tibetan government, was known in the past as Gyalpo Pehar, Gyalpo Pekar, Gyalpo Shingja Chen, and so on. At that time Dorjé Drakden was the name of a minister to Gyalpo Pehar, as is clear from old documents. Later, that name of a member of his retinue came to be used for the principal figure himself, and so Dorjé Drakden became the name for Gyalpo Pehar. He is also known as "Dorjé Drakden, the manifested Dharma king," "Dorjé Drakden, the manifested Gyalpo," and "Gyalchen Dorjé Drakden." Therefore it seems reasonable to suggest that a few Dölgyal followers took the name Gyalchen Dorjé Drakden as an example and named Dölgyal as Gyalchen Dorjé Shukden. Nevertheless, it is important for unbiased scholars to research this thoroughly.

10. How the First Sakya Practitioners Praised Dölgyal

IN THE PRAISE section of *Destroying the Beguilers: An Invocation of the Great Gyalpo* it says:

> *Hūṃ.* Gyalchen, whose fearful activities are quickly completed,
> you supernaturally circle the three realms in an instant.
> Whatever activities are entrusted to you
> you accomplish without hindrance.
> Gyalchen and entourage, I offer this praise to you.

Apart from the line about circling the three realms instantaneously, which is just hyperbole, the essential meaning of this verse is: "I praise the great Gyalpo, who with miraculous or supernatural powers quickly completes without hindrance any activity entrusted to him and his entourage."

Thus it is just general praise that makes it easier to use others for one's own purposes. It is not a praise of any unique or special quality. This is acknowledged as being the first praise occurring in the Sakya tradition, as is clear from the previous citation of Sachen Kunga Lodrö.

Furthermore, this text is historically the first invocation of Dölgyal, and when Sakya hierarch Sönam Rinchen first composed this new work, right at the beginning he said, "Thus, if you wish to perform the torma dedication, invocation, and so on, of the great Gyalpo, first arrange the altar. This requires a triangular torma and..." There are also many instances of the terms "torma dedication," "torma offering," and so on. This shows that when Sakya hierarch Sönam Rinchen first composed *Destroying the Beguilers*, Dölgyal was recognized merely as someone to whom a torma can be dedicated.

Propitiation of Dölgyal: Activities That Fulfill All Wishes was composed up to the section on confession by Dreu Lhépa, who did not write any special praises. In the remaining part of the text composed by Morchen, it says:

Kyai! Think of the pledge you took from
the glorious Dīpaṃkara, crown jewel of the five hundred,[101]
Jampal Nyingpo, lord of the doctrine,
and other root and lineage lamas,
and hear my words of compassion.

Thus he is saying that glorious Dīpaṃkara and Jampal Nyingpo[102] and others
placed Dölgyal under oath.

Sachen Kunga Lodrö says in his *Offerings to the Jetsok Dharma Protector*
(1b1):

Kyai!
In keeping with the command of the <u>vajra</u> holder in these
    degenerate times,
you have the name of the one <u>possessed</u> of the <u>skill</u> of <u>powerful</u>
    activities.
In keeping with the binding instructions of mighty Hayagrīva,
the venerable Padmākara, Dīpaṃkara, Jampal Nyingpo,
the venerable Sakya, his disciple Morchen,
and other glorious lamas, holders of tantric knowledge,
do not deviate from your strict pledge
to guard and protect by way of the four kinds of activities
living beings and the doctrine, individually and as a whole.

Up to:

Composed on the third day of the *śrāvana* month
of the *kunden* year, having invited the deity.

On the third day of the *śrāvana* month, which is the seventh month, of the
kunden, or iron-bird year, corresponding to August 1, 1780, this text was
composed. At that time Sachen Kunga Lodrö was fifty-two.

In this invocation the author speaks of glorious Hayagrīva, Padmākara
(or Padmasambhava), Dīpaṃkara (Jowo Atiśa), and Jampal Nyingpo all
binding Dölgyal to an oath. Alongside this, however we have the accounts
of Dölgyal producing various unseemly supernatural activities, such as
showering down a cascade of stones on practitioners of the sacred Dharma,
and appearing and saying, "I am that Ganden malevolent spirit," because of

which, and simply out of fear, a Gyalpo request was composed and a Gyalpo chapel constructed. In the court of the unbiased expounders of reasoning, this cannot but be seen as a serious internal contradiction.

In particular, to say that Hayagrīva, Padmākara, Dīpaṃkara, and Jampal Nyingpo placed Dölgyal under oath is just laughable. Previously the Great Fifth had used his skill to try to placate Dölgyal, but no matter how he tried, the unpleasant supernatural activities and harms grew. At that time Ācarya Padmākara appeared directly before the Great Fifth and said, "In the ruins of Drepung Upper Residence perform the fire offering ritual. Bind the horse of good fortune for the happiness of Tibet." This can be found in *Secret Teachings Sealed by a Pot Marked by Hayagrīva and a Lotus* by the Great Fifth himself.

By this line of reasoning, any accounts of Dölgyal being an oath-carrying deity bound by Padmākara and so on, on the basis of the actual history, are simply inventions. A shred of evidence for it would not be found even if you searched until the end of samsara.

Furthermore, Sachen Kunga Lodrö wrote various praises specifically of Dölgyal, such as those found in *Whirl of Perfect Wishes Fulfilled* and the *Great Wrathful Torma of Shukden*, for example. In the former it says (1b1):

> Generally speaking it can be said that Dharma protector Gyalpo Dorjé Shukden Tsal took birth in the form of an imperious Tibetan geshé. However, in reality, by the force of his prayer and resolve, he was cared for by many buddhas, bodhisattvas, and vajra holders and is someone who has been initiated, oath-bound, and enthroned as a powerful doctrine protector. Although my Vajradhara lama did not actually say these things, the reality was that he established him in the ranks of Sakya protectors. The Dharma king Morchen, who brings benefit to all who meet him, also cast the flowers of enthronement as a doctrine protector more than once. The great Dharma protector Nechung, who sees unhindered all things past, present, and future, was the first to recognize him. He composed a few prayers and so on to him and explained how he was superior to other imperious spirits.

Thus, Sachen Kunga Lodrö tells of (1) how Dölgyal was inducted into the ranks of Sakya protectors, (2) how Morchen enthroned him as a doctrine protector, and (3) how the great Dharma protector Nechung spoke highly of him. The first two accounts contain poor reasons for praise, and the third account contains no reason for praise, as it is devoid of any valid source.

The Tantra of the Seven Precious Gems

In particular, in *Amazing Magical Play*, Sakya Kunga Tashi says (169b3):

> Jetsok great protector, Dorjé Shukden Tsal, declared that he was an incarnation of the great Ācārya Jetari.[103] This is addressed in two parts: (1) in order to generate trust and to prove its sound reference, showing how the great protector delivered this declaration, and (2) the life story of Ācarya Jetari.

For the first, *Tantra of the Seven Precious Gems* from the Nyingma tradition states:

> The one known as the great Gyalpo,
> going by the name of Dölgyal,
> his path is not a perverse path,
> as his nature is Avalokiteśvara.

> However, at the time of kings and ministers,[104]
> he was the minister Thangnak
> and a Bön teacher called Lenmi:
> two living beings at one time.

> Together with Margyen Sa makes three,
> a single mental continuum bringing about harm.
> After that, at times, the three became one;
> at times, each was of a distinct form.

> One such was a disciple from Trewo
> by the name of Dorjé Sengé,
> who accomplished much for the doctrine.

> Finally, he became a disciple of Karmapa
> in the form of a breaker of precepts,
> a powerful tantrika, born in the region of Yartö.

One part held the name of Prajñā
at the time of the Chinese emperor.

Though of different aspects at that time,
they were of one miraculous power, causing harm to all.
Together, finally, they brought about good,
miraculous displays revealing his greatness.
Do not criticize them, therefore.

Thus the declaration was given by one who was of the nature of Avalokiteśvara, and so they are truly incontrovertible words.

Thus limitless praise is heaped upon Dölgyal, stating by way of scripture that his nature of was Avalokiteśvara and that the declaration itself is unmistaken and definitive.

However, the author of this biography is Sakya Kunga Tashi and not Kunga Lodrö, and in *Great Wrathful Torma of Shukden* composed by Sachen Kunga Lodrö it says (7b2, 278):

This Gyalpo in the form of a Tibetan demon does not have the authority of the tantras and Indian scriptures. There is also no life-entrustment, no rites for the four activities, and so on found in the textual, hidden-treasure, or pure-vision traditions. Therefore how can there be a tantric presentation?

Thus Dölgyal has no reference or source in the tantras, Indian scriptures, and the textual or hidden-treasure traditions, and therefore it would not be correct for there to be life-entrustment rituals, rites for the four activities, and so on.

A mere glance at this *Tantra of the Seven Precious Gems* exposes it as the foolish words of some deceitful person of little intelligence, whether innate or cultivated. It has somehow appeared, and yet a thorough research of the three Kangyur volumes of Nyingma Tantras, the Seventeen Dzokchen Tantras along with the *Tantra of Mantra Protectors*, the Nyingma Tantra Collection, and elsewhere has not revealed any *Tantra of the Seven Precious Gems*.

Moreover, *Untarnished Mirror*, the publication compiled by the Amdo

Province Dölgyal Research Committee and published by the Office of the Amdo Central Standing Committee in 2006 (the Tibetan year 2133), transcribes an interview on the above verses with Garjé Khamtrul Rinpoché, alive at the time of writing and a peerless illuminator of the Nyingma doctrine. He says (198.9):

> Generally speaking, in the tradition of the Nyingma school, for example, those tantras, transmissions, and essential instructions that we hold dear are completely validated by scriptural sources. None are the basis for a debate, for example. Up until now I have neither heard of nor seen a *Tantra of the Seven Precious Gems* in the tantras of the Kangyur of the Buddha's teachings, the Nyingma Tantra Collection, the Seventeen Dzokchen Tantras, and so on, and there seems to be no way of knowing how it can possibly exist.

Thinking about these words, it is not difficult to conclude that *Tantra of the Seven Precious Gems* is like one of those "tantras composed by Tibetans" and is not an authentic tantra.

Likewise a few Dölgyal followers continue to insist that Dölgyal is an incarnation of the great Ācārya Jetari, Sakya Paṇḍita Kunga Gyaltsen, Butön Rinchen Drup, Kashmiri Panchen Śākyaśrī, Shalu Lochen Chökyong Sangpo (1441–1527), Dulzin Drakpa Gyaltsen, Panchen Sönam Drakpa, and so on. These too are just assertions, and not a shred of proof from any authentic scripture and reasoning can be found.

A single author, Sakya Kunga Lodrö, sometimes states that of the two Dölgyal practitioners Sakya Morchen and Sakya hierarch Sönam Rinchen, Morchen seems to have been the first, and sometimes he says that Sakya hierarch Sönam Rinchen was the first. He also speaks of how Sönam Rinchen at the age of seventeen came into contact with Dölgyal. On that basis, examination shows that before Sakya hierarch Sönam Rinchen reached the age of seventeen, Morchen was already practicing Dölgyal.

Moreover, he describes how Dölgyal puts on frightening supernatural displays and how, out of fear, Sönam Rinchen composes his *Request to the Gyalpo* and relies upon him out of necessity. At the same time he describes, using poor reasons or reasons without any basis, how Dölgyal is an authentic protector.

Also, Kunga Tashi holds faith with a text claiming to be the words of a Nyingma tantra and strives to prove that Dölgyal is in fact Avalokiteśvara. However, Sachen Kunga Lodrö explains that Dölgyal has no scriptural reference in the tantras, Indian texts, and so on.

These are contradictory statements. It is important for fair-minded scholars to continue to investigate these to a satisfactory conclusion.

11. Sakya Scholars Who Have Restricted Dölgyal

IN *COMMENTARY ON THE PRAISE OF SHUKDEN*, Kyabjé Trijang Vajradhara
says (59a4, 119):

> Moreover, Vajradhara Morchen Kunga Lhundrup composed *The
> Three Activities: A Presentation of the Gyalpo Spirit* and intensi-
> fied the activities of Gyalchen Shukden. At that time some slan-
> dered this practice.

The same text also says (59b2, 122):

> This contains the miscellaneous works of the master Losal
> Gyatso,[105] compiled in a very natural style by Lelung Shepa Dorjé
> (1697–1740). In it can be found the statement:
>
>> In later times Vajradhara Morchen Kunga Lhundrup
>> encouraged the practice greatly, praising his unbeliev-
>> able qualities and saying with special intention, "Now is
>> the time for all like-minded to rely upon this Gyalchen."
>> Nevertheless, some said, "This is not good. Those
>> who encourage the activities of this Gyalpo are doing
>> nothing but wrong."

Thus there were at that time some who restricted this practice.

In particular, in later times, Dzongsar Khyentsé Jamyang Chökyi Lodrö
(1893–1959), second in the dance of the incarnations of Jamyang Khyentsé
Wangpo (1820–92), also known as Pema Ösal Dongak Lingpa, master of the
seven oral transmissions in Tibet and the fifth of the great treasure revealers,
writes in *Dedicating an Effigy Torma to Wealth-Keepers and Oath Breakers*
(359):

Kyai!
Gyalpo Shukden, custodian of wealth and manifested ghost,
chö practitioner Dawa Sengé,
gyalpo demon Bagu and retinue,
Tigyal Lakyap and other mountain ghosts,
demons, ghosts, oath-breaking spirits,
male and female death demons, life demons,
to all of you, this spinal-column effigy torma,
I offer in place of flesh, blood, and life.
Give up forever harming living beings,
such as my attendants, disciples, and sponsors.
Dissolve your violent anger and hostility
and be possessed of the mind of enlightenment.

Thus Dölgyal is referred to as a "keeper of wealth" and a "ghost." Also, the same work says (363):

Uttering the Jvālāmukhi mantra and the four names
and by completing the number of recitations,
I perform the act of the giving of Dharma.
I offer the drops of drink and send these effigy tormas
into the heart of the river.

Kyai! Now you have no place to be.
Gyalchen return to your abode.
You hordes of ghosts, go to the ends of the ocean
and never return. Disobey my word
and you will be ground to dust.

Thus the effigy torma is given, followed by "Now you have no place to be," thereby banishing them to faraway places.

Also, in the biography of Ngawang Yönten Gyatso (1902–59) of Ngor Ewam Monastery composed by Rabten Gelek Phuntsok entitled *A Blessing That Is an Ocean Granting All Desires*, it says (41):

Furthermore, he rode on to the region of Gatö. One day he set up camp and went to a Geluk monastery to pay devotions to the sacred objects there. In the assembly hall he saw a statue of Shukden. He made a threatening gesture at it, saying, "You behave yourself! You are not good!" With that, he slapped the statue with his hand so that dust flew off the clay body.

When it was time to return, it had become dark, and he said to his two monk attendants, "Come off the road. I am going this way." He raced his horse along a rocky road so that sparks flew off the horse's mouth bit.

Some monks at the monastery said, "This lama has done something here," and went inside to look. There they saw his handprint on the clay statue. "We must catch him and beat him," they said.

A wiser monk said, "If he had broken it, there would be something to say. But just doing this on the surface of the clay, it is nothing. Look at the work of this madman. It would be better to just let him get away."

This was spoken by Purong Umik, a high government official.

In Kalsang Monastery [Ngawang Yönten Gyatso] was performing a consecration, and in the room there was a mask of the Gyalpo. When he was doing the ritual of dispelling hindrances, perspiration vapor began to rise and beads of sweat started to drop from the mask.

While he was visiting Denbur Lek Monastery, there was a mural of the Gyalpo on the assembly room wall. Fearing that the lama would erase it, it was covered with a wall hanging. He was asked to perform a consecration of the temple. "The oath-breaker is behind the wall hanging. He does not need consecrating," he replied. He took out his ritual dagger and attacked the mural of the Gyalpo, thereby erasing it.

When visiting Gojo Thangkya Monastery, he said, "You have paintings of Dölgyal." When assured that they had none, with his ability to see what was hidden he saw a mural on an outer porch. He stabbed it with his vajra.

Once he was visiting Silgalen Monastery. The monastery had a painting of the Gyalpo, which they had put in a box and placed it among the sacred objects before requesting consecration. After the lama had left, they took out the painting only to find it was full of holes like a sieve.

There are many extraordinary accounts such as these. Wherever this master went, whether in Kham or Central Tibet, whenever he came across a place where the worship of Dölgyal was being followed, he would assume a wrathful stance and destroy the protector chapel and ensure that the practice was discontinued.

The same book says (48):

At that time a monk had been possessed by Gyalpo Shukden and had thrown a vajra at the abbot. The lama became angry and demanded to know who was practicing Shukden. No one dared to own up. The lama, like a bird flying to its nest, went straight to the offering stand and found behind it a hidden painting of the Gyalpo. He took it and cut it to pieces with a vajra. The monk who was possessed by the evil spirit was cured.

Elsewhere in the same book (61):

Frowning and annoyed, he said, "If the teachings of the root and lineage gurus from the conqueror Vajradhara to one's root guru are not capable of being protected by the Dharma protectors Vajra Guardian of the Tent Mahākāla, Four-Faced Mahākāla, and Chamsing, who are oath-bound and entrusted to guard the teachings, then we certainly don't need this new vicious demon, the oath-breaker Gyalpo Shukden. May it be destroyed!"

The great and overall leader of the glorious Sakya tradition, the Vajradhara throneholder of the Sakya masters, also known as Sakya Trizin Ngawang Kunga Thekchen Palbar Samphel Wangi Gyalpo Rinpoché, who is alive at the time of writing, sent a letter to the Tibetan People's Deputies in 1996, in which he said:

At the recent twelfth Tibetan People's Deputies conference, it seems there was discussion on whether the practice of Dölgyal exists within the Sakya tradition. I would like to say a little on this topic to clarify the reality.

Historically, in the great Tibetan seats of learning, communal recitation of protector liturgies has only included the Dharma protectors eight-deity Guardian of the Tent Mahākāla, Four-Faced Mahākāla, and the Kilaya protectors, and not various protectors such as Gyalpo. Here in our monastic center, our custom is in keeping with these practices of the past. For a while in the Sakya tradition, there were some who privately practiced and relied on Dölgyal as a worldly protector, but it was not widespread.

Moreover, many years ago in Tibet, before the great changes took place, my main root lama, the great guide possessed of the three types of kindness, supreme Vajradhara Ngor Khangsar Khenchen Dampa, as well as Khenchen Ngawang Yönten Gyatso and many other great masters, placed great restrictions on the practice of Dölgyal, and there are well-known accounts of them driving out the practice from various institutions. From that time onward, except for a few, most have forsaken this practice.

Also, following the advice given by the precious Dalai Lama in 1978, there are without doubt no Dölgyal practitioners at all in the main and branch monasteries of our tradition.

I ask that you all please bear this in mind.

The letter continues.

The accounts above show how Dölgyal first arrived in the Sakya tradition, how he was relied on, and finally, up to the present, how great masters presented effigy tormas to him, how the practice was banished from institutions, and how it was banned in this tradition.

PART 3
Twentieth Century:
Phabongkha Rinpoché

12. Restrictions on the Practice of Dölgyal from All Four Traditions

THE FIRST PROPITIATORS of the oath-violator Dölgyal were from the Sakya tradition, as described above. Later, propitiators from within our own Geluk tradition arose, but it is difficult to determine who the first Geluk followers were. Beginning in the eighteenth century, we find restrictions on the practice mentioned in texts by Geluk masters, making it clear that the practice had arisen in some Geluk monasteries in some form by that time. But in these texts of the eighteenth and nineteenth centuries, the status of Dölgyal is that of a vindictive spirit. After a brief survey of these references in this chapter, we will turn in the next chapter to the figure of Phabongkha Rinpoché, who elevated the status of Dölgyal as part of his extensive teaching activities.

In the biography of the Fifty-Fourth Ganden Throneholder Ngawang Chokden (1677–1751) entitled *Biography of the Achitu Nominhan*,[106] completed by his disciple Changkya Rölpa Dorjé (1717–86) on August 18, 1763, it states (66b5):

> Previously, a vicious spirit had entered and possessed a man from the Draksop region. Some interfering, retired monastic officials as well as some of the monastery houses relied on this spirit by professing to make prayers and offerings to it. Also a cairn for the spirit had been built on Jangtsé peak. Observing these wholly inappropriate actions, [Ngawang Chokden] announced in the assembly that since the time of the great master Tsongkhapa and his disciples, there had been no tradition of paying devotions to worldly deities and protectors within the bounds of the monastery. Therefore, from now on, no such practice would be allowed.
>
> The cairn was demolished, and the stones and earth spread among the rocks and soil. The spirit was invoked in the medium

and was ordered not to appear again. It replied, "As this is the order of the precious throneholder, I have no choice but to leave." The spirit left the body and fled to Taktsé Shöl.

The great master went into retreat and then established in the main assembly hall the practice of the Dharmarāja torma-casting ritual composed by the all-knowing Gendun Gyatso. Dharmarāja's punishment was to kill the retired teacher who paid devotions to the spirit, and those monastery houses suffered many a misfortune. Therefore this kind of practice was discontinued, which became very conducive for purifying the monastery.

In *Garland of White Lotuses: The Formation of the Four Great Monasteries and the Upper and Lower Tantric Colleges*, completed by Phurchok Ngawang Jampa (1682–1762) on September 11, 1744, it says (13b1):

> With the exception of the oath-bound Dharma protectors described in the tantras, no shrine to worldly malicious spirits, who become angry at the slightest provocation, was ever built within this monastery while the master Tsongkhapa was alive. Because of this, the teachers lived in harmony, and the studies and practice flourished. Even his birth deity, Machen, was placed outside the perimeter of the monastery. However, these days those who imagine themselves to be his followers don the three robes and mistakenly go for refuge to spirits. Much misfortune will befall them. Therefore, if we ordained monks guard our vows and precepts purely, then those oath-bound protectors who beheld the Buddha in the past will without question fulfill tasks entrusted to them.

Therefore it is clear the practice of the master Tsongkhapa was that, apart from those protectors bound by oath, malicious violators and spirits were never relied on within the confines of Ganden Namgyal Ling Monastery.

The Eighth Dalai Lama Jampal Gyatso (1758–1804) completed his biography of Yongzin Yeshé Gyaltsen (1713–93), *Lotus that Beautifies the Teachings of the Buddha*, on July 24, 1794. It says (187a2):

"Furthermore, I would say to the attendants of the Panchen Rinpoché, in the matter of encouraging the venerable monk in his studies and training, you must all be diligent and very focused. Otherwise, to tell him he is a buddha and does not need to undergo the same rigors as ordinary beings would be to spoil him. Even though he is a buddha, he has taken the form of an ordinary being, and so he must develop and train in the manner of an ordinary being also.

"Scholars who do not learn and practitioners who not meditate only provide a mere semblance, and no more, of the benefits required for the teachings and living beings. Therefore everyone must concentrate on encouraging him in his studies.

"Similarly, this new Tashi Lhunpo protector is bringing ruin to the monastery. Therefore it is important to be content with the protectors relied on by Panchen Losang Chökyi Gyaltsen. If we do not, and we instead start to rely upon harmful spirits, it will become a source of much misfortune. Therefore, all of you, take great care in this."

Like this, he would often give much heartfelt advice.

The speaker quoted here is Yongzin Yeshé Gyaltsen. In the sentence "I would say to the attendants of the Panchen Rinpoché, in the matter of encouraging the venerable monk in his studies and training, you must all be diligent and very focused," the "venerable monk" refers to Panchen Tenpai Nyima (1782–1853).

He also says, "This new Tashi Lhunpo protector is bringing ruin to the monastery," and goes on to say that they should be satisfied with the protectors relied on by Panchen Losang Chökyi Gyaltsen, explaining that if they rely on other harmful spirits instead, it will become a source of great misfortune.

In the biography of Changkya Rölpai Dorjé entitled *An Adornment to the Ganden Teachings*, completed by Thuken Chökyi Nyima (1737–1802) in 1794, it says (221b3):

As he approached the Machen[107] cairn, he said, "The great Tsongkhapa and his disciples never relied on worldly deities and protectors. Therefore even the cairn of Machen, his birth deity, was not placed within the monastery's circumambulation path. In the past, some Ganden throneholders relied on Dölgyal, thereby bringing much misfortune. The Vajradhara throneholder (Ngawang Chokden) demolished his shrine and other objects and banished him from the monastery."

Changkya Rölpa Dorjé was staying at the great monastic seat of Ganden, and one day he went out to the outer perimeter of the monastery, where he conversed with his disciple Thuken Chökyi Nyima. In this biography, Thuken Chökyi Nyima recorded the words of his master on this occasion. From these words we can reasonably infer that the "vicious spirit" mentioned above in Changkya Rölpai Dorjé's biography of the throneholder Ngawang Chokden, in the sentence, "Previously, a vicious spirit had entered and possessed a man from the Draksop region," and the spirit mentioned above by Phurchok Ngawang Jampa in the sentence, "However, these days those who imagine themselves to be his followers put on the three robes and mistakenly go for refuge to spirits," is none other than Dölgyal.

In *Ornament of the Yellow Hat Doctrine*, a biography of Ngulchu Dharmabhadra (1772–1851) composed by his nephew Yangchen Drupai Dorjé (1801–87) in 1855, it says (34a4):

> At that time, some formless creature was sporadically hurling rocks and stones day and night in the Upper Monastery.[108] The monastery requested Lochen Rinpoché to perform a divination. He reported that it was the harmful work of Dölgyal and that if the assembly instituted the recitation of Tsongkhapa's *Hundred Deities of Tuṣita*, all would be well. Therefore the chant leader, Sherap, found a one-folio version of *Hundred Deities of Tushita*, handwritten by Khedrup Ngawang Dorjé, and said, "You (the young Dharmabhadra) know how to read and write. Copy this."
>
> He immediately wrote it out, and instantly he had memorized it.

In *Treasure Pot of Supreme Blessings*, a biography of Yeshé Drup (1781–1835),[109] the fifth incarnation of the Yongzin of Drukpa Dechen Chökhor Monastery, composed by Chökyi Nyinjé (late nineteenth century), the seventh Chöchok incarnation, it says (8a5):

Once while he was in strict retreat, Gyalchen Dorjé Shukden, a very disruptive and disdainful spirit, repeatedly manifested in various forms before the Gyalwang Drukpa in order to test his attainments and to compete with him. After a while Gyalwang Drukpa pacified the spirit. He accomplished this by way of various practices from the paths of sutra and tantra. Finally, the spirit showed his true form and was given instructions and placed under oath. In response the spirit said, "If your disciples make offerings to me, then because I have a very large entourage of very spiteful spirits, they will cause much harm. Therefore I do not seek offerings, but whatever tasks you have for me to do, I will carry out."

With this pledge he left for his abode. Therefore, although this disdainful spirit was a disruptive creature that brought about much harm to those who practice the Dharma, to those of us included in Gyalwang Drukpa's group of disciples, it caused no harm at all. This is solely down to the kindness of this unparalleled guide and refuge.

Thus Yeshé Drup speaks of "Gyalchen Dorjé Shukden" and denounces him as "a very disruptive and disdainful spirit." Moreover, Dölgyal himself is reported as saying, "If your disciples make offerings to me, then because I have a very large entourage of very spiteful spirits, they will cause much harm. Therefore I do not seek offerings."

In the biography of Jamyang Khyentsé Wangpo (1820–92) entitled *Treasure of All-Pervading Joy without Fear*, Dodrup Jikmé Tenpai Nyima (1865–1929) writes (412):

Once when he was giving teachings on Hevajra at Dergé Lhundrup Teng, Gyalpo Shukden came to listen, saying, "As your explanations are excellent and your teachings are good, I want to listen to them."

The master said that there was no impediment to teaching him, and he was able to explain many difficult points of Madhyamaka and Perfection of Wisdom to him.

Thus, as illustrated by the fact that even hostile spirits aspired to drink the nectar of his teachings, his nonhuman disciples were beyond number.

Therefore Jamyang Khyentsé Wangpo, Dodrup Jikmé Tenpai Nyima, and others recognized him as a "hostile" or unruly, disruptive spirit.

In *Sunlight that Brings to Bloom the Lotus Grove Minds of the Faithful*, the biography of the all-knowing Eighth Panchen Lama Tenpai Wangchuk (1855–82), Yongzin Losang Tenzin Wangyal, writing in 1889, says (223b1):

> On the sixth he said to his younger brother and his personal attendant that recently in the topmost quarters of the Dechen Phodrang there had been some disturbances caused by Dölgyal, and therefore on the ninth the quarters should be closed and dismantled.

Also, in *Strict Directive for the Great Monastic Seat of Tashi Lhunpo*, the all-knowing Eighth Panchen Lama Tenpai Wangchuk, writing in 1876, said (121):

> Recently, there have been isolated cases of hostile spirits being channeled within the confines of the monastery. From now on, except for special cases such as Dharma protector Lhamo, no invocation through mediums will be allowed. Apart from those vajra protectors who possess the eyes of wisdom, when it comes to Dharma protectors, going for refuge to and relying on malicious ghosts who fly through the air—Dölgyal and the like—contradicts going for refuge as the gateway to the teachings of the Buddha.

In June 1938, Kyabjé Phabongkha (1878–1941), at the age of sixty-one, was invited by Kyabjé Trijang Rinpoché to Ganden Monastery in order to teach the four commentaries on *Great Treatise on the Stages of the Path* and so on. At that time the Ninety-third Ganden Throneholder and regent of Tsongkhapa was Vajradhara Minyak Amé Rinpoché,[110] and he remarked, "These days, this spreading of the Dölgyal practice is not good at all."

Thus he was completely against it, and this will be widely known among most of the senior monks alive today.

However, in the biography of Kyabjé Phabongkha,[111] it says (635b3):

> That occasion coincided with the Tri Rinpoché Minyak Amé

coming to the Ganden Monastery summer retreat. Therefore the master sought out an audience with him, bringing considerable offerings. In his presence the throneholder lavished praise upon him with elegant words, requesting the great Kyabjé to plant his lotus feet upon the earth for a long time for the sake of the teachings and living beings and so on. However, it is said that secretly, and out of envy, he reprimanded the tulku sponsor and others.

On that occasion the requestor and main sponsor of the teachings was Trijang Rinpoché. Therefore "the tulku sponsor" refers to Trijang Rinpoché.

This passage from the biography of Kyabjé Phabongkha states that the Ganden throneholder was envious. Dölgyal was being heavily propagated at that time, and the reality is that the throneholder was likely displeased about that. Kyabjé Phabongkha was spreading the practice of Dölgyal together with his teachings, after which there was a sudden occurrence of much misfortune, such as the death of many monks at Ganden. This and other accounts are detailed below in chapter 21, "Unfortunate Events Connected with Dölgyal."

It also says in the biography (532a4):

> At that time, the former Ganden Throneholder Tri Rinpoché Jampa Chödrak[112] lived close by in the town of Simmin. He was the most senior of the regents of the master Tsongkhapa and highly regarded by all traditions. The master (Phabongkha) specially set out to meet him. At the audience Tri Rinpoché happily accepted the offerings and said again and again, as an aside during the conversation, "Ah, you have such great merit."
>
> Later the master said, "Tri Rinpoché said this to me repeatedly. Previously, when he took teachings from me, it was not from some ulterior motive or in order to please me but without doubt from a sincere pursuit of the Dharma. So now I cannot understand why he sees me as someone of great merit and not as a lama."

The former Ganden Throneholder Tri Rinpoché Jampa Chödrak was the ninetieth throneholder and was someone held in great affection by the great Thirteenth Dalai Lama. When Tri Rinpoché and Kyabjé Phabongkha met, it was on the third of fourth month of the wood-dog year, corresponding to May 16, 1934, when Kyabjé Phabongkha was fifty-seven. When Kyabjé Phabongkha said that the former Ganden Throneholder did not see him as a lama, it was definitely because Tri Rinpoché was displeased with the amount of Dölgyal practice promoted by Kyabjé Phabongkha.

Likewise, great practitioners from the Sakya tradition, and the present head of the glorious Sakya tradition, Kyabjé Sakya Trizin Rinpoché, in particular, have banned the practice, as related above.

Furthermore, great practitioners from the Kagyü tradition, exemplified by the Sixteenth Karmapa Rangjung Rikpai Dorjé (1924–81), were fundamentally opposed to Dölgyal, and there were several from within that tradition who banned the practice.

Many great practitioners of the past from the Nyingma tradition have also banned the practice and continue to ban it, as illustrated by the great tantrika Pema Trinlé of Dorjé Drak Monastery, the Minling treasure revealer Terdak Lingpa Gyurmé Dorjé, and others, as was described above. These days in the Tibetan exile community also, most Nyingma leaders and lamas have done the same, as illustrated in particular by the Nyingma hierarch Kyabjé Trulshik Rinpoché (1924–2011) and in Tibet the great Dharma king Khenchen Jikmé Phuntsok Rinpoché (1933–2004), who accomplished so much for the Buddha's teachings.

To summarize, up to the present day, for most great practitioners of the Nyingma Sakya, Geluk, Kagyü, Jonang, and Bön traditions, there is no great dispute that beings such as Dölgyal are objects of displeasure that should be banished.

13. The Early Life of Kyabjé Phabongkha

THE FIRST PERSON within the Geluk tradition to declare Dölgyal "protector of the teachings of Mañjunātha Tsongkhapa" or "exclusive protector of the teachings of Mañjunātha Tsongkhapa,"[113] to compose a Dölgyal life-entrustment rite, an exclusive propitiation rite, and to propagate the practice widely was Kyabjé Phabongkha Dechen Nyingpo (1878–1941). At that time the main person who placed restrictions on Dölgyal practice was the supreme leader of the secular and religious systems of Tibet and its people, the Great Thirteenth Dalai Lama.

Therefore, in order to understand clearly the reality of the situation, we will in turn look at a brief account of activities in the early life of Phabongkha, examine whether the Great Thirteenth regarded Phabongkha with special affection, and review how the Great Thirteenth placed restrictions on Dölgyal practice.

For the first of these, in the biography of the venerable Phabongkha compiled by Denma Losang Dorjé (1908–75), *Meaningful and Melodious Speech of Brahma*, it says (262b2):

> At one time, he developed an intense interest in the biographical songs of Jetsun Milarepa, and it was as if his mind had merged with their content. Every day without fail, he would study and contemplate the songs, with the result that he developed an unshakeable conviction and faith in their meanings. Previously, from time to time, he would just enjoy himself in play. But from this time onward that ceased completely. Also, from then on he developed the habit of a pursuing a continual study of various texts from the canon, and like a lotus drinking in the sunlight, the great understanding of the scriptures that was born in him grew day by day.
>
> His mind was helplessly captivated by the life story of the

Mañjunātha Dharma king (Tsongkhapa) and several of his well-written commentaries, and as an early composition, he wrote stanzas of prayer to the great Tsongkhapa by way of acrostic verse.[114]

At this time this master was fifteen years old, and the year was 1893. Later the biography says (263b1):

> At this time he started to compose a history of this meditation hermitage, which took up about five large folios and began with seven verses of homage to the great Orgyen[115] and so forth. It was not quite finished, but realizing that this hermitage was an extraordinary place blessed with the power of enlightened speech, I (Denma Losang Dorjé) offered these verses for perusal by great masters, and as they have not been returned, I cannot present them here.

Also (264a3):

> In the sixth month of that year he traveled to Shang Ganden Chökhor Monastery. There, in response to the fervent requests of the monastery officials, he gave a word-by-word commentary and transmission of the *Hundred Deities of Tushita* to the whole assembly consisting of about five hundred monks. Also, to over two thousand lay people, he bestowed in detail the single-deity, single-vase Amitāyus long-life initiation, together with explanation, from the tradition of Machik Drupgyal. All who were gathered there felt their hairs of faith tingle, and the murmur of praise and appreciation could be heard everywhere.
>
> At that time, he was sixteen years of age, and unlike others he was able to do all this without relying on the support of tutors and senior teachers. This is undeniably an incomparable mark of a superior being.

It continues (264b3):

> In his own words: "From such a young age I thought only of purely following a single-pointed practice. Like the movement of waves in a lake, I continually thought, even by the slightest of

circumstances, that I must become a great yogi who has gained control over the four elements. And even up to the present, I have always thought to spend my whole life in pure practice. But the reality is that I only spend my life pretending to teach the Dharma and doing rituals for householders. This does not seem to be the result of good karma from previous lives."

And (265b6):

In his own words the master said, "When listening to the Dharma, if you fall under the spell of postponing the practice of what you have heard until later, then the time for practice will never come. If what you have heard is ascertained in your mind and immediately integrated into your being by way of contemplation and meditation to ensure that a pure practice arises, then not only will you be able to become a yogi with control over the four elements, but also here in the Mañjunātha Tsongkhapa tradition of sutra and tantra combined, you will definitely be able to attain the Vajradhara state of union in this short life. For if you have accumulated fully and unmistakably the good karma that creates the causes for being able to practice the Dharma, then it is a natural consequence that the appropriate fruit of such a practice will ripen fully and unmistakably."

And (266b6):

In his own words, "At that time, I had immense faith in the Great Ācārya, Padmasambhava, and after my early-morning recitations and during tea, I would recite in full the *Prayer in Seven Chapters*.[116] I also cultivated the yoga of the meditation deity Most Secret Hayagrīva by practicing it in four sessions a day. As a result, I dreamed one night that while looking at the shadow of my head, I saw a horse's head atop my own."

And (267a4):

He returned to Central Tibet and resumed his studies at the monastery. There, in his study and contemplation of the classic texts, his power of understanding reached an extraordinary level and was quite unlike before. Many of those at the college well trained in the art of reasoning remarked, "Since Phabongkha Tulku has returned from Tsang, he has become excellent in scripture."

And (267b5):

At this time, he worked hard in his studies and each day memorized about five pages of *Overview of the Two Truths*.[117]

And (324a6):

While in Sakya he went to the great pilgrimage place of Khau Drakzong.[118] There he took a life-stone[119] of Four-Faced Mahākāla. He then went to the glorious Sakya Monastery, where he received permission initiations of the Sakya Golden Dharmas[120] tradition from the throneholder Dzamling Chegu Wangdü (1855–1919). In his account of the meeting, he mentions that the throneholder told him that the Sakya throne had to alternate between the two Sakya houses of the Drölma Phodrang and the Phuntsok Phodrang, and he suggested that it would be excellent if he were to take teachings from the head of Drölma Phodrang, Vajradhara Drakshul Trinlé Rinpoche (1871–1936).

He went to see this master many times and wrote an account of these meetings. From this master he received several teachings and initiations from the Sakya Golden Dharmas tradition. He also received the initiation of the exclusive life-sustaining White Mahākāla, which is the seventh manifestation of the seventeen aspects of Four-Faced Mahākāla, and the initiation of the manifestation known as the Nine-Deity Increasing Yellow Mahākāla.

Then he traveled to Makhar, and from Mudrak Shö Khensur Rinpoché, he received the complete teachings on the Six Yogas of Niguma.[121]

At that time, in 1909, Kyabjé Phabongkha was thirty-two.

The above extracts are just a brief account of how in the early part of this master's life, he followed nonpartisan studies, contemplations, and meditations, all for the benefit of living beings and the doctrine. If you wish to know more of this, read his biography.[122]

14. The Thirteenth Dalai Lama's Regard for Venerable Phabongkha

THE GREAT GUIDE and refuge the Thirteenth Dalai Lama (1876–1933) spent his whole life, with great endeavor and not without hardship, assuming the responsibility of preserving and developing, both inwardly and outwardly, the nonpartisan precious doctrine of scripture and insight of the Buddha, and in particular of ensuring that the land of Tibet was continually and firmly sovereign and independent. In terms of the economy, education, health, care of the environment, security of the country, and so on, he ensured systematic progress that blended old and new traditions.

Moreover, he did not follow earlier customs of Tibet in which a son was promoted in his father's footsteps and high-class families were entitled. Instead he looked to those with knowledge, capability, and good conduct, taking care to promote those with merit, such as finance minister Lungshar Dorjé Tsegyal,[123] Chensal Thupten Kunphel,[124] and others.

Included in the scope of those for whom he had particular regard was the master Phabongkha Jampa Tenzin, or Dechen Nyingpo. For example, in Kyabjé Phabongkha's biography, it says (338a3):

> With concerns for the long life of the all-knowing guide and refuge, and for a restorative medicine to regain the health and vigor of the secular and religious administration, previously damaged, and for it to flourish again, as well as for several other reasons, a request came from the great seat of government accompanied by a silver-base mandala of the three representations of enlightened body, speech, and mind, which consisted of very rare and untainted celestial substances for the sake of the greatness of the Dharma. The venerable master happily accepted the request.
>
> On the fifteenth of the sixth month he had an audience with the precious leader. Not long after, on the auspicious second

nanda day (21st) of the waning fortnight of the *aṣāḍha* (6th) month in Meru Phuntsok Norbuling Monastery, close to the Lhasa main temple, to a monastic audience of about three hundred dedicated disciples consisting of lamas, tulkus, geshés, and other masters of myriad scriptures, as well as individual monks, from the glorious monastic seats, the two tantric colleges, other colleges, monasteries, and hermitages, he began the reading. He finished in the following year on the second *bhadrā* day (22nd) of the waning fortnight of the *mṛgaśira* (11th) month with an extensive granting of the bodhicitta vows from the tradition of the bodhisattva Śāntideva, in which the vows of the aspiring bodhicitta and engaged bodhicitta are given simultaneously.

This was the giving of a complete transmission of the precious Kangyur of the Buddha. He began with Narthang Monastery edition. Supplementary material not included in that edition, as well as necessary material from the Dergé edition, were also added. He proceeded in a very calm manner, using the Choné edition for making thorough comparisons of alternative text and for corrections, thereby setting a great example of how to maintain the continuity of the Buddha's teachings.

Throughout the transmission the government provided food, drink, and money for the assembly. The great conqueror, through his representative, offered with great pleasure the three representations, a ceremonial scarf, and so on to the venerable master, who accepted them with exceptional respect by immediately rising from the throne and touching them one by one to his head.

Thus, in accordance with the instructions of the Great Thirteenth, the Ganden Phodrang government had requested the venerable Phabongkha to confer the transmission of the Kangyur of the Buddha for the long life of the all-knowing guide and refuge and for the health of the religious and secular administration. At that time, in 1913, this master was thirty-six years old.

This occurred two years after the Chinese army of Lianyu[125] had forcibly invaded Tibet, and the Great Thirteenth had to seek refuge in India. However, soon the inner and outer situation changed, and in 1912 the Great Thirteenth returned to the land he governed. He appointed Dasang Dramdul[126] commander of the Tibetan military, and by uniting the Tibetan people, lay and monastic, he expelled completely the invading force. It was also the second year after the Great Thirteenth officially declared the complete independence and sovereignty of Tibet.

Therefore the ritual requested by the government at that time, whose purpose is described in the above biography as, "With concerns for the long life of the all-knowing guide and refuge, and for a restorative medicine to regain the health and vigor of the secular and religious administration, previously damaged, and for it to flourish again, as well as for several other reasons," was performed for the benefit of the religious and secular administration of Tibet.

The biography states (340b5):

> As a show of gratitude for completing, as instructed, the transmission of the precious Kangyur of the Buddha the previous year, the precious leader granted him an audience, in which he joyfully engaged the venerable master in pleasant conversation.
>
> While staying in the labrang in the upper monks' quarters at Chusang Hermitage,[127] he became very ill. At one point it seemed he would not recover. Drupkhang Rinpoché and two attendants came to the hermitage, and after taking tea immediately went to the labrang. There, in the presence of the Vajradhara, Drupkhang held aloft a mandala of the three representations and delivered the litany calmly and in detail, together with a request from the precious leader that the Vajradhara soon recover from the illness and plant his lotus feet in this world for a long time to come.
>
> The Vajradhara replied by saying how kind it was for the venerable Rinpoché to visit. He offered the equivalent of a mandala of the three representations and a ceremonial scarf, requesting that the universal jewel that brings benefit to the living beings and teachings in the world, the greatest of conquerors, plant his feet firmly here for a hundred eons as a guide for the teachings and living beings. He offered the same to Drupkhang Rinpoché, asking that he too live long.

Also (342a6):

> In response to the request made previously by the Mongolian Bārin Lama, for a period of ten days in the sixth month, the precious leader gave a discourse on *Great Treatise on the Stages of the*

Path within a large marquee set up on the lawns in the eastern part of Norbuling Park to an audience of about fifteen hundred.

Most well-known lamas and tulkus, great and small, from the three great monastic seats and other monasteries around Lhasa automatically had to attend such teachings. Although the venerable lama was recovering from his illness, he had been very ill and there could be no certainty that he was well enough. Nevertheless, he summoned up courage, sent in his request of attendance, and went to the teachings.

The venerable master held only the lowest title of tulku from the ranks of lamas and tulkus within the monasteries and was therefore placed at the back of the assembly row. This was in a place not covered by the marquee canopy, and the sun and rain were particularly fierce. At that time, the precious leader had good eyesight and remarked, "Phabongkha Tulku has been ill and is not very strong. It would not be good if he became ill again because of the heat and cold."

Therefore, each day he was allowed to move closer and closer to the front, until he was under the canopy and close to the high seats.

That event took place in 1914, when this master was thirty-seven. Further in the same work (384b4) it says:

> In water-pig year when he was forty-six, he led the spring Dharma session held at Meru Monastery until the Lhasa Prayer Assembly, a role usually performed each year by the Ganden Throneholder, but in keeping with the instructions of the precious leader, this year was to be performed by the venerable master.

In the water-pig year of 1923, when the venerable Phabongkha was forty-six, he was asked to deputize for the precious Ganden Throneholder, the regent of the great conqueror Mañjunātha Tsongkhapa, at the Meru spring Dharma session. What greater reward and sign of affection could there be for one described above as holding "only the lowest title of tulku from the ranks of lamas and tulkus within the monasteries"?

The Great Thirteenth Dalai Lama, head of the religious and secular administration of Tibet and its people, was someone who again and again, with great love and affection, specially nourished and paid great attention to those people endowed with knowledge, capability, and good conduct, whether in the secular or the religious field. Likewise, with the venerable Phabongkha, if his good deeds had not been compromised by detrimental circumstance, how is it not possible to see the great plans, whether in the religious or secular field, for that time or for the future, that the Great Thirteenth would have had for him?

15. Kyabjé Phabongkha's Connection with Dölgyal

IN THE BIOGRAPHY of the venerable Phabongkha Dechen Nyingpo it says (249b4):

> Once a spirit suddenly entered and possessed an aunt of the young boy [Phabongkha]. Surrounded by the family, it was causing a great disturbance.
>
> "Who are you?" his mother asked the spirit.
>
> "I don't know you," came the reply, and the spirit slapped the mother's head many times.
>
> The young boy was small and could not squeeze between the grown men and so climbed up on the back of one of them. The spirit pulled the boy off the man's back and began touching head to head and making other expressions of joy.
>
> Years later, on reflection, he concluded that this spirit was Gyalchen Shukden. After that incident, there were many occasions of the spirit possessing people in the neighborhood. From that time until he was around twenty, this spirit possessed various people, giving many predictions.

Therefore, Dölgyal began deceiving this master from a very young age. Accordingly, this master went on to inaccurately praise Dölgyal as the exclusive protector of the Mañjunātha lama, Tsongkhapa. As will be described below, however, in the presence of the Great Thirteenth Dalai Lama, Kyabjé Phabongkha stated that Dölgyal was his mother's birth deity. But here we read that when his mother asked Dölgyal who he was, he answered, "I don't know you," not "I am your birth deity." How is all this to be explained?

The biography says (343b3):

In the beginning, the Vajradhara listened to many teachings from many scholars of the Sakya, Nyingma, and Kagyü traditions. He also had some exposure to elements of the Nyingma school from Drakri Gongma and Lama Riku.[128] Therefore he practiced extensively the various teaching traditions in a nonpartisan manner.

However, from an early age, Dorjé Shukden Tsal, the exclusive protector of Mañjunātha Tsongkhapa's teachings, had kept constant watch over him through direct manifestation and through oracles, and had remarked again and again that if the master took hold of a pure philosophy and practice that was unmixed with others, then whatever activities were deemed necessary, he would carry them out exactly in accordance with the master's wishes. This message was also urged upon him through various signs. Accordingly, the master accepted.

In particular, Dakpo Lama Rinpoché[129] told the master that it would be good if he actually relied on Gyalchen, and that although he, Dakpo Lama Rinpoché, did not actually do the practice, Gyalchen was a guard[130] who would carry out his tasks.

Moreover, this great master [Phabongkha] had previously listened to and practiced without partisanship countless teachings of the classic literature and oral traditions of the old and new schools, and as a result he had mastered, without confusing one with another, their views, meditations, conduct, and respective results. Now, by employing with his fine and thorough intelligence a thousand reasons found only in the stainless tradition of the conqueror Tsongkhapa—superior to all others from many aspects, unerring in all the sutra and tantra teachings of the Buddha, and hoisted aloft like the victory standard—a firm and unshakeable conviction had been born within him.

With respect to that, the potential of Gyalchen's past vow had now matured, and having gradually understood the reasons for it, he embarked on single-pointedly nourishing the development of the pure Geluk doctrine. His becoming a wrathful protector of the teachings, effortlessly carrying out, in whatever way possible, all the wishes of the master [Phabongkha], came about this way.

From this we can all understand the following: Dakpo Lama Rinpoché, the person who urged the venerable Phabongkha to actually practice Dölgyal, only used Dölgyal as a guardian; before that time no one had appointed him exclusive doctrine protector of the teachings of the Mañjunātha conqueror, Tsongkhapa. In his early years, Kyabjé Phabongkha engaged in extensive studies without any partisanship, single-pointedly putting into practice all that he had heard. Because of this he possessed all the conducive conditions to become a great master and a matchless upholder of the teachings. Becoming aware of this, this demon of Döl, speaking of the general good while keeping his own desires hidden, made a great show of excessive allegiance to the pure tradition of the master Tsongkhapa and his disciples.

Pretending to be an authentic doctrine protector for Tsongkhapa, he put great effort into deceiving the venerable Phabongkha again and again. He was in reality trying to gain the title "Dorjé Shukden Tsal, exclusive protector of the doctrine of Mañjunātha Tsongkhapa," and as will be shown below, he succeeded.

The biography also says (379b6):

> On the tenth day of the tenth month he [Phabongkha] specially visited Döl White Springs, where the body of the precious Tulku Drakpa Gyaltsen lay. These days only his [Drakpa Gyaltsen] right arm remained, and there in the presence of this precious relic, the master composed a feast-offering ritual for the purposes of making extensive offerings to the manifested and fierce doctrine protector Dorjé Shukden Tsal.

In the colophon of the venerable Phabongkha's *Extensive Libation Offerings* it says (13b2):

> Thus this work, *A Festival Glorious in Every Direction, Being a Feast-Offering Ritual to Please the Manifested Great Deity, Gyalchen Dorjé Shukden*, was composed by the one bearing the name Phabongkha at the age of forty-two in the iron-monkey year on the auspicious tenth day of the tenth month at Döl White Springs, a place I had specially journeyed to, and where lies the sacred shrine in which rests the stainless wisdom of Tulku Drakpa Gyaltsen. In later times parts had been taken away as blessed relics, and so the body was no longer complete. Nevertheless, his right arm remained, and in its presence the actual words of the offering were composed on that day, together with a feast

offering. The overall structure of the ritual from beginning to end was not compiled on that day and was set aside for later. Accordingly, when I was fifty-eight, on the tenth day of the *aṣaḍha* (sixth) month of the wood-pig year, I again worked on it with great joy in Palbar Labrang of Phuntsok Yargyé Ling.

Therefore, at the age of forty-two, according to Tibetan reckoning, on November 21, 1920, he performed a propitiation and made extensive offerings as well as composing a feast offering ritual to Dölgyal.

The death of Drakpa Gyaltsen in 1656 and his subsequent cremation are well documented in *Heavenly Raiment*, the autobiography of the Great Fifth. However, there is not a single word on the construction of a shrine containing the body. Any talk in 1920, 264 years after this event, of the right arm of this body remaining is simply an error of not establishing which historical accounts are reliable and doing the proper research. See chapter 5, "Cremation and Other Postmortem Matters."

Also, as a supplement to *Pure Gold Propitiation of Protectors* by Panchen Losang Chögyen, Phabongkha has added an invocation of Dölgyal:

Protector of the teachings, you are unmatched even by ten
    million
of those endowed with the mighty power of the vajra.
Now, from the palaces of Tuṣita and others where you reside,
come to this place in order to protect the essence
of the conqueror Losang's teachings.

Also, as a supplement to *Enthronement of Dharma Protectors*, by the Seventh Dalai Lama, the conqueror Kalsang Gyatso, he has added:

From the Dharma palace of the Dharma Land of Joy,
great holder of discipline, Dorjé Shukden Tsal,
enthroned as the main protector of the Geluk tradition,
engage in activities to spread pure view and conduct.

From the supreme vajra palace where you reside,
vividly appearing as a powerful layman with entourage,
enthroned as the warrior deity of the Yellow Hat doctrine,
engage in activities to increase the desired wealth of Dharma.

These verses are found in the 1973 Delhi publication of the venerable Phabongkha's collected works (7:477 and 478). In the same edition (7:655):

> These words of Dakpo Kalsang Khedrup Rinpoché carry great significance: "The person offering the torma cannot just be anyone but, in accordance with the thinking of the venerable lama, should be a genuine monastic follower of the Geluk tradition, one with a pure view and conduct and a wide understanding of the paths of sutra and tantra. And they should have a pure perception built on reasons toward this exclusive doctrine protector who guards the teachings of the master Tsongkhapa."
>
> Also, "It is important to do this activity secretly, without it being apparent to others, not mentioning a word of it even to friends. It should also be done swiftly and so on."

For someone who previously was commonly known as the "Ganden oath-breaking spirit" and a "disdainful spirit" to be abruptly promoted to "this exclusive doctrine protector who guards the teachings of the master Tsongkhapa" is an overblown declaration.

Moreover, in the colophon of the same work it says (656):

> Concerning this work, the *Melodious Drum of the Conqueror, Glorious in All Directions, an Extensive Exclusive Propitiation Rite of the Wrathful Five-Family Gyalchen Dorjé Shukden*, mighty warrior deity guarding the Geluk teachings, holder of the lives of the beings of the three realms, oath-bound and manifested deity who cares for others as they would their only child, this monk, Phabongkha Jampa Tenzin Trinlé Gyatso—who from an early age has been lovingly cared for by this doctrine protector, constantly like a shadow—kept in mind the exhortations by this great protector to compose such a work.
>
> Though there are many powerful propitiation rites composed by great masters of the past, none apply the complete appellation of "exclusive protector of the Geluk." Therefore I was lifted up with the joy of composing it. The work was begun on an auspicious day in the waxing half of the *caitra* month of the wood-ox year of the fifteenth cycle. It was taken up again in an encampment on the Naksok road. There, as I reached the invitation

section in the work, the auspicious coincidence arose of me having to go to the opening of a new chapel dedicated to this protector at Sokshö Ganden Phelgyé Ling.

On that day, signs of being welcomed by the protector near the monastery clearly occurred. Also, until the time that the statue had been completed, wild animals that usually hibernate in winter were seen out and about near the monastery chasing people and animals. These and many other alarming magical displays were seen. However, from the day of the purification of the statue and the first propitiation, all such apparitions naturally ceased, and many other extraordinary signs arose. With this my joy increased, and I recommenced the work in the Genden Luksang Kunphel Ling Monastery in Nakshö, completing it on the tenth day of the waxing *caitra* month of the fire-tiger year. The scribe was Shagap Chözé[131] Thupten Wangyal, who held high the banner of renunciation.

Thus it is clear that the composition of this exclusive propitiation to Shukden was initiated by Dölgyal himself, who urged repeatedly, "Compose a propitiation to me." Also, at that time, Dölgyal seduced this master with inappropriate magical displays. Because of this the master began the composition at the age of forty-seven in the third month of the wood-ox year of 1925 and completed it one year later, on April 22, 1926.

The colophon of this extensive exclusive propitiation mentions wonderful signs occurring on the day the propitiation was initiated. However, when an exclusive propitiation rite was initiated in Sok Tsenden Monastery and the practice of relying upon Dölgyal was followed, many inauspicious events, such as trouble within the monastery, killings, and attacks, followed one after another. Finally, the practice had to be stopped. This is recounted below in chapter 21, "Unfortunate Events Connected with Dölgyal."

Moreover, Dölgyal also repeatedly insisted that a life-entrustment rite be composed for him. As a result, this master, at the age of forty-three, in the iron-bird year, or 1921, composed the first Dölgyal life-entrustment rite.

Also, at the age of fifty-eight, finishing on December 22, 1935, he again compiled a life-entrustment rite, from homage to colophon, having received teachings from Takphu Vajradhara.

The composition of both life-entrustment rites was a result of the persistent requests by Dölgyal that such rites be composed for him. This is described in more detail below in chapter 20, "Takphu Vajradhara and the Life-Entrustment Practice."

In the above extract from the colophon of *Melodious Drum of the Conqueror*, it says:

> This monk, Phabongkha Jampa Tenzin Trinlé Gyatso—who from an early age has been lovingly cared for by this doctrine protector, constantly like a shadow—kept in mind the exhortations by this great protector to compose such a work.
>
> Though there are many powerful propitiation rites composed by great masters of the past, none apply the complete appellation of "exclusive protector of the Geluk." Therefore I was lifted up with the joy of composing it.

This indicates that Dölgyal, while keeping his own intentions hidden, set out to deceive the venerable Phabongkha from an early age with his trickery. Not seeing it as deception, this master regarded such activity as being cared for with pure affection. Realizing that up to that point there had been no acknowledgement of this protector as the exclusive doctrine protector of Mañjunātha Tsongkhapa, in 1925, he composed the propitiation ritual with great joy in keeping with the supplications of Dölgyal. This is described in the biography of the venerable Phabongkha (409a3):

> In response to the repeated requests from doctrine protector Dorjé Shukden himself, in the third month he began work on composing an extensive propitiation rite of Gyalchen Dorjé Shukden Tsal called *Melodious Drum of the Conqueror, Glorious in All Directions*.
>
> This is just a brief introduction to the origins of how this master and Dölgyal came into contact with each other.

16. Venerable Phabongkha's Pledge and Remorse

AS DESCRIBED ABOVE, Kyabjé Phabongkha, in the early part of his life, applied himself with great diligence and effort to the disciplines of listening, contemplation, and meditation. This he did purely, never pursuing any of these three disciplines in isolation from the others. As a result, his accomplishment of the three activities of a scholar[133] were glorious in their benefit for the teachings and living beings. When this came to the attention of the peerless leader of the secular and religious administration of the snowy land of Tibet, the Great Thirteenth Dalai Lama, this crown jewel of men and gods, gave him much attention and took care of him with great affection.

There must be a great sense of sadness when the wonderful deeds of a great being destined to be of benefit to others fall under the hindering sway of a malevolent spirit born of perverted prayer. At the age of thirty-seven, in the wood-tiger year of 1914, in the presence of Dakpo Kalsang Khedrup, the venerable Phabongkha was encouraged to rely upon Dölgyal. From then on, by way of a succession of various misleading ploys from this malevolent spirit, and on the basis of his insistent and repeated urgings, the practice of relying upon Dölgyal was spread far and wide, and as much as possible.

When this came to his attention, the Great Thirteenth issued a number of inquiries, to each of which the venerable Phabongkha issued a reply. All these letters, which are replicated in his biography, would take up too much space if reproduced here, and many of them are not relevant. Therefore, in the manner of the saying, "Knowing one thing, liberates all," we produce below the venerable Phabongkha's reply to the last letter of the Great Thirteenth, in which he expresses remorse for his errors and makes a pledge.

In the biography of the venerable Phabongkha, it says (471a2):

Immediately after this came the reply:

"This is offered by your humble subject, the one with the name of Phabongkha. In your instructions that I have received by way of the lord chamberlain, you say:

In your letter of the twenty-second of the twelfth month of last year you state, "By the kindness of the communication of your words, this humble subject sees that he is completely at fault and he has nothing to say in return. Therefore I offer to take your words seriously to the core of my heart, and whatever errors I have made, I beg for forgiveness."

In regard to the three points you mention, there is still much to be debated, but they can be left for the time being.

Previously you said, "I am endeavoring in the practice of refuge." You are someone who propitiates the protector Shukden primarily, and in recent years in Drepung Monastery you have greatly spread the practice of Shukden propitiation among your disciples with your teachings on stages of the path. This is the fundamental reason why Nechung Dharmarāja, who the founder of this monastery, Jamyang Chöjé, appointed and entrusted to be the guardian of Drepung, has complained again and again to the monastery officials that they are hastening the degeneration of the doctrine.

In particular, entrusting an imperious worldly spirit as a companion in this life I see as being counter to the precepts of going refuge. Therefore this seems to contradict your statement, "I have erred because of being obscured by ignorance, but I state sincerely that I have not knowingly entered a wrong path nor have I encouraged others to do so."

How do you explain this?

"In response, I humbly say that my mother informed me that Shukden has been the family deity on the maternal side, and so up to now I have had to propitiate Shukden. However, from now on, with great remorse for my errors and a vow not to repeat them, this humble subject promises from the depths of his heart to never rely on, propitiate, or invoke Shukden again. Whatever errors I have made up to now that have displeased the great Nechung Dharmarāja, and have contradicted the precepts of

going for refuge, I beg for forgiveness from you, with your great
love and compassion, supreme guide who holds the lowest with
the utmost pity."

This was offered with the customary ceremonial offering scarf
and the representative five silver *sang* coins.

This promise was made to the Great Thirteenth in the iron-sheep year of
1931, when the venerable Phabongkha was fifty-four.

At this time, the practice of relying on Dölgyal was being propagated
primarily by the venerable Phabongkha. This had greatly displeased the
Thirteenth, and consequently he placed restrictions on its practice. This
was also the period in which the Thirteenth was restricting the venerable
Phabongkha from giving extensive teachings and from bestowing many
novice and full-ordination vows. Therefore, the statement of the venerable
Phabongkha that "I humbly say that my mother informed me that Shukden
has been the family deity on the maternal side, and so up to now I have had
to propitiate Shukden. However, from now on, with great remorse for my
errors and a vow not to repeat them, this humble subject promises from the
depths of his heart to never rely upon, propitiate, or invoke Shukden again"
coincides with that time.

17. The Passing of the Thirteenth Dalai Lama

The Displays of Dölgyal

The biography of the venerable Phabongkha says (519b1):

> In the seventh month, the Tāsur of Shidé Monastery[134] was in Lhasa. One day before dawn, as he was engaging in spiritual pursuits, there appeared in front of him a monk who seemed to be possessed by Gyalchen Shukden. This monk said twice in a high, clear voice, "After the ninth, it will be on the thirtieth!"[135]
>
> Tāsur immediately thought that he should go at once to the Vajradhara and ask about the meaning of this apparition. Therefore, very early that day he went specially to Tashi Chöling, where he asked for an explanation from the venerable lama, who replied, "Now, it is difficult to say with certainty what it means. We should look at it again later."
>
> The events that had occurred as related by Tāsur, together with the date, were noted down by the venerable lama.

Also (524b4):

> On the thirtieth of that month, the consciousness of the mighty conqueror passed into the dharmadhātu realm.[136] Therefore, concerning the apparition of Dharma protector Shukden speaking to Shidé Tāsur previously, the venerable lama was convinced that the words, "After the ninth, it will be on the thirtieth!" was clearly referring to this time. This is because it was a way of saying that after the ninth month, on the thirtieth day of the tenth month, will be the time when this great being exhibits the act of passing away.

Therefore, more than two months before the Great Thirteenth died, as soon as he realized that the great conqueror would soon pass away, Dölgyal said, "After the ninth, it will be on the thirtieth!" He said this is "in a high, clear voice," meaning that he shouted it out in joy.[137] The reason behind this utterance was likely resentment built on the fact that the Great Thirteenth had previously placed restrictions on Dölgyal. And it is certainly not impossible to infer the nature, aims, and motives of someone, human or a deity, who waits for the death of another and who shouts out in joy when someone like the Thirteenth Dalai Lama, who had been of immeasurable kindness and benefit to the people and the religious and secular administration of Tibet, was about to pass away.

Phabongkha Continues to Propitiate and Propagate Dölgyal

In the letter submitted to the Great Thirteenth, Kyabjé Phabongkha pledged, "From now on, with great remorse for my errors and a vow not to repeat them, this humble subject promises from the depths of his heart to never rely on, propitiate, or invoke Shukden again."

However, after making that promise, there are accounts in his biography of exhortations to those closely connected with the venerable Phabongkha himself to "perform a thousand propitiation ceremonies" of Dölgyal and so on. In particular, as soon as the Great Thirteenth withdrew his physical form into the dharmadhātu realm, the venerable Phabongkha continued extensively propitiating and propagating Dölgyal as he had done previously, before the Thirteenth had placed restrictions on its practice. The way he propagated the Dölgyal life-entrustment rite is one example of this, as will be seen in chapter 20, "Takphu Vajradhara and the Life-Entrustment Practice."

Generally, from the time that the Great Thirteenth had placed restrictions on the practice of Dölgyal, Kyabjé Phabongkha did not have permission from the Great Thirteenth to travel where he liked. However, on December 17, 1933, the mighty conqueror, the Great Thirteenth, passed away, and in 1934 many patrons had made persistent requests to administrator Radreng (1912–47), then the regent of Tibet, for permission to invite Kyabjé Phabongkha. Therefore, in the summer of that year, he gained permission from Radreng Rinpoché to travel as far as Chamdo.

Immediately Kyabjé Phabongkha traveled as far as Chamdo and up to Kyegu Do.[138] There he seized the opportunity to transmit extensively the propitiation and life-entrustment practices of Dölgyal in every place he traveled. Moreover, when he met the all-knowing Ninth Panchen Lama Chökyi Nyima (1883–1937) in Kyegu, he stressed that for the fruitful accomplishment of Panchen Rinpoché's deeds and for the success of his labrang's activities, it was important and necessary to propitiate Dölgyal.

Later Kyabjé Phabongkha traveled to Tashi Lhunpo Monastery. There, using the encouragement given to him by Panchen Rinpoché, he retrieved the image of Dölgyal put away by the Eighth Panchen Lama. He built a statue of Dölgyal in Tashi Lhunpo, recognized an oracle for Dölgyal, and initiated the ritual of propitiating Dölgyal, and so on, in the upper protector chapel of the monastery. These and other deeds, too numerous for the mind to encompass, are clearly related in sources such as Kyabjé Phabongkha's biography *Oral Transmission of the Brave Father-Like Lama*,[139] by Dzemé Rinpoché (1927–96). However, ultimately, they are all without doubt the result of being under the obstructing influence of Dölgyal.

These events will be related in brief in the relevant sections of this book. Those who wish to know of them in greater detail should consult the two works above as well as other sources.

18. The Meeting between the Ninth Panchen Lama and Phabongkha

ON JANUARY 31, 1937, Kyabjé Phabongkha offered Panchen Rinpoché a brief invocation of Dölgyal called *Invocation Speedily Summoning All Fulfillment of Wishes* and encouraged him to recite it every day. However, this practice was no help to Panchen Rinpoché at all in achieving any success for his labrang, as illustrated by Panchen Rinpoché never returning to his monastic seat.[140] Moreover, about ten months later on December 1, 1937, the all-knowing Ninth Panchen Lama died suddenly, as will be described below.[141]

At the beginning of the wood-pig year of 1935, when Kyabjé Phabongkha had left Central Tibet and was traveling in Kham, he received a letter from the all-knowing Ninth Panchen Lama. This letter had been dated by the Panchen Rinpoché April 26, 1934, while he was in the Chashang Palace of Nanjing.[142] In it he tells of how he was making many offerings following the passing of the Great Thirteenth, how he was working to create the favorable conditions that would enable him to return to Central Tibet and Tsang before long, and asking the venerable Phabongkha for information on how they would be able to meet in the near future.

Later, around November of 1935, Kyabjé Phabongkha received a second letter from the all-knowing Panchen, who was staying in Kumbum. In it Panchen Rinpoché writes about his wish to return soon to Central Tibet and Tsang, how important it was to gather as much support as possible for that to happen, and how he was restoring many monastic centers of all traditions in Domé Jangyü that had been reduced to serious state of decline because of the recent troubles, and how it was important to meet before Kyabjé Phabongkha returned to Central Tibet.

In reply, Kyabjé Phabongkha wrote, "For whatever little service I can render, I will definitely come to you at a convenient time and place." And so on.

After that, the all-knowing Panchen Rinpoché wrote a letter from Kyegu

Do, as described in Denma Losang Dorjé's biography of Kyabjé Phabongkha (608a5):

> The all-knowing Panchen sent a letter from Kyegu Do Palace regarding arrangements for a meeting between the venerable lama and himself. It was accompanied by a ceremonial greeting scarf and a map of the terrain from a place a short distance from Chaksam Monastery[143] up to Kyegu Do, and delivered by two bodyguard unit commanders, who were to offer whatever service was needed.
>
> A short time later, having taken a break from the teachings at the monastery, the venerable lama set out for the district of Kyegu Do on the ninth day of the twelfth month, carried aloft on the palanquin of Lama Phakpai Lha, and accompanied by a few important teachers and students. He was escorted by Chaksam government officials and a phalanx of soldiers, and he returned the service and respect paid.
>
> The accommodation on the journey, the people, and the local conditions, as well as the weather, were hostile and rough, and it was also very cold. However, by the compassion and grace of the venerable lama alone, they traveled without discomfort and arrived at Rabshi Lungshö Monastery.[144] There they were greeted by the monastic officials and the monks and escorted by procession into the monastery to a well-prepared reception.
>
> On the day he arrived in Kyegu Do, the highest ranks of the inner circle of the all-knowing Panchen welcomed the venerable lama with ceremonial offering scarves at a place about two miles from the residence of the Panchen Rinpoché. Arrangements had been made for the venerable lama to stay at the residence of the Xining military chairman in the center of Kyegu Do. As soon as he arrived, the labrang of Panchen Rinpoché offered tea, sweet rice, a mandala of the three representations, and so on. The venerable lama showed his delight as if he were receiving blessings.
>
> On the following day, the venerable lama submitted a request for an audience to the all-knowing Panchen Rinpoché accompa-

nied by a ceremonial offering scarf. In the afternoon he engaged uninterruptedly, as was normal, in his usual meditative practices.

This event corresponds to January 1937. At that time Phabongkha Rinpoché was fifty-nine. The biography continues (609a2):

> The next morning, having received a reply, the venerable lama at once set off for the residence behind Kyegu Do Monastery. There, he presented the Panchen Rinpoché with esteemed offerings of the best quality and made greeting prostrations. Panchen Rinpoché was delighted and asked about his health, remarking how pleased he was that they could finally meet. Like close sons who had known each other for a long time, they conversed, took tea and sweet rice, and so on.
>
> At that time, sponsors from the northern nomad community had requested the all-knowing Panchen to confer a Niguma-tradition long-life initiation. The preparatory rituals for the initiation ritual had just been completed when the venerable lama arrived. Seeing this as an auspicious coincidence, he immediately requested to be allowed to receive the initiation. The Panchen Rinpoché came to the lower reception room, where he met the attendants of the venerable lama, and gave them tea and sweet rice. Then the initiation audience assembled, and the Panchen Rinpoché conferred the long-life initiation of the Niguma tradition by way of extensive teachings on its practice. The venerable lama received all the teachings.
>
> Immediately afterward, lama and disciple went to the upper quarters, where they spent the whole day together, enjoying endless feasts of conversation on the profound and vast Dharma, so that the venerable lama was only able to return to his residence in the evening, after which he engaged in his usual profound meditative practices.
>
> That day the all-knowing Panchen said that as the New Year was approaching, the venerable lama should rest and stay here until New Year and that they should meet often. He replied, "Such an occurrence would truly be joyous and fortunate, but administrator Radreng has insisted that I return soon, and

so even these three or four days have been rushed. Also I have already given many promises to continue teachings at Chaksam Monastery, all of which are causes for further delay. I can stay here for about seven days, and then I must request your leave to set out before the New Year."

In reply, Panchen Rinpoché said that if that was the case, then certain matters could be discussed back and forth by message boards[145] and that they should meet face to face a few times more. Accordingly, from the next day onward Panchen Rinpoché sent about five handwritten messages, to each of which the venerable lama replied in his own hand.

Thus this describes Kyabjé Phabongkha meeting the all-knowing Ninth Panchen Lama, Chökyi Nyima.

Events not directly connected with the topic in hand have not been presented here in detail. Those who need to know more should refer to the biography.

Encouraging the Panchen Lama to Practice Dölgyal

The biography says (611a4):

One day the all-knowing Panchen sent Tingkyé Tulku[146] to say, "Our labrang has been hindered many times in accomplishing its affairs, great or small. Would the venerable Kyabjé perform a divination to discern the reason for this and determine which obstacle-removing rituals would be appropriate."

The venerable lama replied, "I have a suspicion regarding this, but it is as if I cannot speak it."

"Well then," came the reply, "Might this be the work of Gyalchen Shukden?"

"That was my suspicion," the venerable lama replied. "It will be difficult for any particular ritual to be of help. I think it is essential that the precious Panchen himself practice Gyalchen Shukden a little."

That evening the venerable lama received a message by way of a secretary saying that they should meet early the following day. Accordingly, the next day the venerable lama went to meet

Panchen Rinpoché. They spent most of the day together, informally discussing a wide range of Dharma topics. On that day too the food and drink provided was especially considerable.

At one point Panchen Rinpoché said, "Concerning the matter raised with you yesterday by way of Tingkyé, you say that lack of success in the activities of Tashi Lhunpo Labrang, which is my business, is the work of Gyalchen Shukden. That seems to be so. When I was young, I once saw a monk with a glowing complexion and wearing Sangphu tiger-boots, walking back and forth by the steps near my rooms at Tashi Lhunpo Labrang. Others saw him too. When I asked the precious tutor about this, he said it was Gyalchen Shukden. He also told me that the previous Panchen Rinpoché, Tenpai Wangchuk, followed practices from the Nyingma tradition. This displeased the gyalpo greatly. Therefore, the tutor insisted, it would be gravely mistaken now for the precious Panchen to muddle his philosophical views, and that he should uphold only pure Geluk view and practice.

"As a consequence, I have never taken up any practice from the Nyingma tradition. However, my predecessor did extensive practices from that tradition. One day as he was preparing for a fire offering, someone had a painting of Shukden commissioned and offered it for consecration. "This is a happy coincidence," he remarked, and he poured molten butter on the scroll and burned it. The covering of the scroll and other peripheral parts were burned, but the central part of the painting was untouched by the fire and was discolored and blackened by grease.

"This act aroused Shukden's hostility. As a way of pacifying that hostility, rituals of contrition, confession, and so on should be effectively performed. Therefore Kyabjé Rinpoché should arrange a deity-to-man introduction between Gyalchen Shukden and myself and give me advice and assistance in offering confession rituals, propitiations, invocations, and so on."

The venerable lama replied, "If such confession rituals and so on could be performed, that would be excellent. It would be very difficult for me, a disciple, to arrange a deity-to-man introduction. Nevertheless, the rituals of invocation, propitiation, and confession that need to be offered, I will perform to the best of my ability. However, more beneficial and more powerful than others performing thousands of these rituals would be for you yourself to perform a short torma offering a few times."

The all-knowing Panchen replied that if Rinpoché possessed a short torma-offering ritual that he had composed, he should give it to him. Accordingly, the venerable lama at once sent someone to fetch from his residence an invocation text called *Invocation Speedily Summoning All Fulfillment of Wishes,* and presented it to Panchen Rinpoché, who placed it to his head and then put it by his pillow.

However, Panchen Rinpoché said again and again that Kyabjé Phabongkha should also perform effective propitiations to Shukden, as service to him. All this I heard from the venerable lama himself.

That day the venerable lama arrived back at his residence just before dark.

Continuing (612b3):

A few days later, the all-knowing Panchen sent secretary Dorjé Denpa to the venerable lama. He brought offering ingredients for a propitiation torma, as well as gifts for service, and asked that the great Kyabjé, while he was staying at Chaksam Monastery, perform five days of effective Gyalchen Shukden propitiation, invocation, confession, as well as feast offering. The venerable lama immediately accepted the task.

The above extracts clearly show that Kyabjé Phabongkha encouraged in person the Ninth Panchen Chökyi Nyima to rely on Dölgyal. He presented him with a text on the invocation of Dölgyal, and accordingly, Panchen Rinpoché began practicing. Moreover, Panchen Rinpoché also requested Kyabjé Phabongkha to perform a propitiation and invocation of Dölgyal.

The extracts above contain no dates for the day-to-day activities described. However, as written earlier, these events took place at the beginning of 1937.

The Sudden Passing of the Ninth Panchen Lama

In the biography, it says (614b6):

The journey continued pleasantly, and as they approached Chaksam Monastery, monastic officials, Giu Tulku, officials from Chamdo, and others arrived to form a welcoming party. A military official with a unit of soldiers lined up to form an escort. The venerable lama acknowledged their service and respect, as he did previously, and continued into the monastery.

Beginning from the following day, and in keeping with the request from the all-knowing Panchen, the venerable lama performed for five days an effective propitiation, invocation, and confession, as well as offerings, for the doctrine protector Shukden. At that time, he composed a complete name-component entrustment verse[147] in order to fulfill the wishes of the Panchen Rinpoché and recited this verse many times during the propitiation. When the rituals were over, he sent a message notifying the Panchen Rinpoché of its completion.

This took place in 1937, after the beginning of the fire-ox new year, when Kyabjé Phabongkha was sixty years old. Also (629a1):

As the venerable lama was traveling near Drigung Yangri Gar,[148] a messenger arrived bearing a letter requesting dedication rituals, together with offerings for same, because the all-knowing Ninth Panchen Rinpoché had ceased his intentions for this life and had passed away in Kyegu Do.

There is no mention of the date of the passing of the all-knowing Ninth Panchen. However, on line five of the same page, it says, "On the twenty-fourth of the tenth month he arrived at Tashi Chöling Hermitage."

Therefore, not long after he received the dedication request letter for the Panchen Rinpoché, Kyabjé Phabongkha Rinpoché arrived at his monastic seat, Tashi Chöling, on the twenty-fourth of the tenth month (December 26, 1937). Therefore, Panchen Rinpoché must have passed away before that date.

Examining the Tibetan Date for Panchen Rinpoché's Passing

Something off-topic needs further explanation. Most Western and Tibetan historical accounts agree that the Ninth Panchen, Chökyi Nyima Rinpoché, passed away on December 1, 1937. However, when this date is transposed to the Tibetan calendar, some confusion crops up. For example, the second volume of Tsipön Shakabpa's *Tibet: A Political History* states that the all-knowing Ninth Panchen Chökyi Nyima passed away on the twenty-eighth of the tenth month of the fire-ox year, which could correspond to December 30, 1937. Paljor Jikmé, a revenue official of the Namsé Ling estate, in his *Various Events Connected with My Life*, citing *Tibet: A Political History*, gives the same date for the passing of the all-knowing Panchen Rinpoché.

However, as we just saw, Kyabjé Phabongkha received the dedication request letter for the passing of Panchen Rinpoché sometime before the twenty-fourth of the tenth month, December 26. Therefore, if the date of his passing were truly on December 30, after the reception of the dedication requests, then clearly something does not tally. However, looking into this more closely, the confusion is easy to resolve: there were two Tibetan tenth months that year. Therefore the date of passing was on the twenty-eighth of the first tenth month, and the dedication requests were received in the second tenth month.[149]

However, a bigger difficulty lies in the following. In the Tibetan translation of *Panchen Rinpoché the Great Master* by Jampal Gyatso,[150] it says (8):

> With the Ninth Panchen Chökyi Nyima passing away in Kyegu Monastery on December 1, 1937, and Gönpo Tseten[151] being born in Bido on February 19, 1938, this means that there are only two months and eighteen days between these two dates.

And later (10):

> Panchen Ertiṇi Chökyi Gyaltsen was born on the third day of the *maghā* month of the earth-tiger year of the sixteenth cycle, corresponding to February 19, 1938, to a farming family of Bido, Yarzi district, Qinghai Kokonor province.

Jampal Gyatso says there are only two months and eighteen days between the passing of the Ninth Panchen and the birth of the Tenth Panchen. But he also says the Tenth Panchen was born on the third day of the maghā month of the earth-tiger year of the sixteenth cycle. The maghā month is the first Tibetan month,[152] and the third day of the first month of the earth-tiger year is March 5, 1938, a duration of about three months and five days from the birth on the twenty-eighth day of the first tenth month of the fire-ox year (November 30, 1937). Therefore it is difficult to ratify the statement that there are two months and eighteen days between these two dates.

If the date of the passing of the Ninth Panchen is December 1, 1937, and the date of birth of the Tenth Panchen is February 19, 1938, the Ninth Panchen passing away corresponds to the twenty-ninth of the first tenth month of the fire-ox year, and the date of the birth of the Tenth Panchen corresponds to the twentieth of the twelfth month of the same fire-ox year.

Scholars who have no vested interest should research this more.[153]

19. Kyabjé Phabongkha's Visits to Tsang

THE BIOGRAPHY STATES (635a4):

> Kadrang Töpa Rinchen Jampal Gyatso from Tsang Khar had
> come many times to Tashi Chöling Hermitage and to Lhasa to
> invite the great Kyabjé to come to Tsang. He requested, if possi-
> ble, to please come to Tashi Lhunpo Monastery and, if not possi-
> ble, then to Palkhor Chödé at Gyantsé to give as many extensive
> teachings as appropriate to disciples in Tsang. Once more he
> arrived at the hermitage to request as before, and the venerable
> lama accepted to visit from around spring of the coming year.

This tells of the invitation to Phabongkha Rinpoché to visit the region of
Tsang from within the larger area of Ü-Tsang and of Rinpoché accepting to
visit Tashi Lhunpo in Tsang to teach the Dharma. This was in earth-tiger
year of 1938, when he was sixty-one. Further (640b4):

> As Kadrang Töpa Rinchen was waiting for the venerable mas-
> ter to come to Tsang, he [Phabongkha] continued at a brisk pace
> his various activities, such as replying to the many letters he had
> received from far-off places, and more or less completed them.
> Then as part of his journey to Tsang, he first visited Lhalu Gatsal,
> as invited by Lady Yangtsé of Lhalu.[154]

And (641a4):

> Then the venerable lama journeyed by way of Paldé and other
> places. Near Palkhor Chödé Monastery of Gyangtsé he was
> met and welcomed by Jampa Chösang, the former abbot of that

monastery and senior monk official of Tashi Lhunpo. Further on, he was welcomed by the current abbot and monastic officials.

This occurred in the earth-rabbit year of 1939. The biography continues (645b1):

> While he was giving teachings on stages of the path, the venerable lama sent word to the Dzasak Lama[155] and others telling of the time he met with the all-knowing Panchen in Kyegu Do while traveling in Kham, and that Panchen Rinpoché had given the venerable lama an instruction to find a way to pacify the hostility of Gyalchen Shukden toward Tashi Lhunpo Labrang. Consequently, the Tashi Lhunpo lamas and officials, noblemen, and senior attendants discussed the fact that Panchen Tenpai Wangchuk had practiced teachings from the Nyingma tradition, thereby arousing great hostility within protector Shukden, meaning that the Panchen was unable to complete his life and his works and that Shukden had been ritually banished to a place under some steps.
>
> In unanimity, they requested that the venerable lama, before he returned to Lhasa, construct a new image of Gyalchen Shukden as an object for reliance on by Tashi Lhunpo Labrang, institute a propitiation ritual, and so on. They would do whatever the venerable lama deemed necessary. The venerable lama acceded to the request.

Also (647a3):

> In response to the request of the keeper of the upper protector chapel, the venerable lama gave the monks of the chapel the transmission of the Shukden life-entrustment, the extensive and middling propitiation rituals, and so forth.

This took place in 1939. According to the biography, in that year Kyabjé Phabongkha only had the time to propagate Dölgyal as described above. He had to hurry back to Lhasa on an urgent matter and would have to wait until the following year to visit Tsang again. He suspended the teachings he was giving and quickly returned to Lhasa.

Propagating Dölgyal on His Second Visit to Tsang

The biography says (653b4):

> Concerning his return to Tsang, Kadrang Töpa Rinchen Jampal
> Gyatso, having requested the visit, had been waiting for some
> time. Therefore, in the third month, [Phabongkha Rinpoché]
> departed from Lhalu and journeyed by way of Tsang Rong.

And (655a4):

> Sometimes he gave many short instructions on the ten wrathful
> protector rituals of protection and averting, the Shukden life-
> entrustment rituals, and so on to small audiences of lamas and
> tulkus.

And (655b1):

> In the previous year, for reasons already mentioned, the venera-
> ble lama had been requested to kindly accept the responsibility
> for Tashi Lhunpo Labrang relying upon and propitiating Shuk-
> den. At this time, the teachings had finished, and although the
> third day of the sixth month was the last day, there were a few
> teachings that had not been completed, such as the transmission
> of the extensive Shukden propitiation ritual to the main assem-
> bly and so on requested by his kinsman Shöl Sharwa. Therefore
> the teachings were carried over to the fourth day.
>
> On that day, when the venerable lama had reached the invi-
> tation section in his transmission of the extensive Shukden pro-
> pitiation ritual, Gyalchen suddenly possessed a senior monk in
> the audience called Tenzin Wangyal from the Upper Protector
> Chapel. He spoke a lot, sometimes clear and understandable and
> sometimes not, and displayed wrathful expressions of displea-
> sure toward the Tashi Lhunpo lamas. This happened about three
> times in that session of teaching and also occurred several times
> during the teachings on Gyalchen propitiation.
>
> In response to this, the venerable lama requested Gyalchen
> many times to cease the hostility toward the Tashi Lhunpo

Labrang and entrusted him with properly carrying out activities
so that he could be restored as a protector of the labrang. However, the venerable lama said that there had been no sign that the
hostility of the past grudges would cease completely.

The above citation raises an interesting point. This took place in the iron-
dragon year of 1940. At that time Dölgyal was still expressing unresolvable
animosity due to the grudge he held against Tashi Lhunpo labrang at the
time of the Eighth Panchen. However, in the *Shukden Compendium* by
Losang Thupten Trinlé Yarphel, it says (1:571a5):

The great previous incarnation, Chökyi Nyima, composed
these vajra pledges, which were given to Gyalchen while he had
entered the body of an oracle and are to be held firmly and without the slightest laxity. There has been a little editing, and they
are included here for the purposes of blessing.[156]

This describes the composition of a work comprising vajra pledges given to
Gyalchen while possessing an oracle and which are to be held firmly and
without the slightest laxity.

If this is true, then from January 31, 1937, the Ninth Panchen Lama
Chökyi Nyima, encouraged by Kyabjé Phabongkha, began to rely upon
Dölgyal. He passed away on December 1 that same year. Therefore, during
the time he was relying upon Dölgyal, he composed the "vajra pledges given
to Gyalchen while possessing an oracle, and which are to be held firmly and
without the slightest laxity." At that time, Dölgyal too can only have pledged
to comply, because there is not a single account of Dölgyal expressing any
of the previous hostility to the all-knowing Panchen, nor is there a single
word about Dölgyal not willingly accepting the vajra pledge given by the
all-knowing Panchen.

However, after Dölgyal had promised to carry out the instructions given
to him by the Ninth Panchen in 1937, three years later in 1940, when the
Tashi Lhunpo Labrang of the Panchen Lama pledged to once again rely upon
Dölgyal as a protector of the labrang, why would he still express the same
open hostility toward the Tashi Lhunpo Labrang of the Panchen Lama?

When the Ninth Panchen announced the vajra pledges, Dölgyal
responded by giving a solemn oath in the presence of Panchen Rinpoché
to do exactly as he instructed. Then, three years later, at a convenient time

when the Panchen Lama was no longer alive, Dölgyal expresses the same previous hostility, which cannot now be pacified, toward Tashi Lhunpo Labrang. This goes against the instructions of the Ninth Panchen Rinpoché, and once again Dölgyal becomes an oath violator.

Some valid explanation is needed to resolve doubts over Dölgyal having hidden intentions, and the reasons behind them, but that is the responsibility of those who still hold Dölgyal to be a trustworthy object of refuge.

The biography continues (656b3):

> Furthermore, Gyalchen, who according to the words of senior Tashi Lhunpo attendants and others had been ritually buried under the steps of the residence, was released, and the venerable lama performed propitiation, confession, and extensive offering rituals. Also, the Dzasak Lama had returned from Lhasa and requested the venerable lama for advice on whether the above-mentioned activities should be completed, on whether the new image should be placed as a protector of the residence and propitiation of Gyalchen be newly instituted, whether a new costume for Gyalchen should be made, and whether the senior monk who Gyalchen possessed previously should henceforth be installed as the oracle for the protector. The venerable lama duly gave advice.
>
> One day the venerable lama was invited to the Kyikyi Naga reception hall. Requests were made to Gyalchen, and he possessed the body of Tenzin Wangyal. While doing so, he performed an angry dance and moved among the crowd. At the back was the elderly monk steward of Sikgyap.[157] Gyalchen grabbed the steward by the neck and punched him several times, causing him to stagger and almost fall.
>
> Several elder monks said the former Sikgyap practiced Nyingma teachings, which aroused Shukden's hostility. As the Sikgyap had died before his time and the old monk had been his steward, this was a sign of Shukden's displeasure. Because of that, there was much talk afterward saying that now there could be no doubt that the one who had possessed Tenzin Wangyal was genuinely Shukden.

This describes an attack on a poor old monk. Further (657a6):

Kyabying[158] requested the venerable lama to compose a text setting out the practices and so on that were to be henceforth followed by Tashi Lhunpo Labrang when relying upon Gyalchen. The venerable lama at once fulfilled their request by composing a detailed directive. Beginning by chronicling the events described above, it went on to describe the general practices to be followed for monthly rituals and specifically took into consideration the proscriptions of monastic discipline, down to stating that Chinese tea be used for the libation and not alcohol. It advised carefully guarding the restraints dictated by the three classes of vows and stressed the need to maintain a pure Geluk view and practice and to generate a strong belief, based on understanding the reasons, toward this fierce doctrine protector.

One night the venerable lama had a dream in which he and several of the finest clergy and laymen had come together and said, "There is something to be resolved." A large figure resembling the Chinese monk in an offering-feast procession appeared, and a fierce Dharma protector attacked him twice. These and other new signs were described by the venerable lama.

Also (657b6):

Having carried out several functions, such as being invited to the homes of the Dzasak Lama and other dignitaries, the venerable lama presented auspicious offering scarves, personally and generally, to those who were escorting him and seeing him off, and then he set off for Central Tibet. On the way, he was invited to Gyangtsé Palkhor Chödé Monastery, and there in the assembly hall he gave many teachings. In Shiné College he taught the whole-day practice as expounded by Ngulchu Dharmabhadra and the transmission of the cycle of Shukden propitiation rituals.

As is clear from all the above extracts, Kyabjé Phabongkha traveled to Tsang, where he gave extensive teachings, and in keeping with the instructions given to him by the all-knowing Ninth Panchen, propagated the practice of relying upon Dölgyal at the great monastic seat of Tashi Lhunpo. This took place in 1940.

In the past, Yongzin Yeshé Gyaltsen had said, "This new Tashi Lhunpo protector is bringing ruin to the monastery. Therefore it is important to be content with the protectors relied on by Panchen Losang Chökyi Gyaltsen."

Also, the Eighth Panchen Lama Tenpai Wangchuk states in his *Strict Directive for Tashi Lhunpo Monastery*, "Going for refuge to and relying on malicious ghosts who fly through the air, such as Dölgyal and the like, contradicts going for refuge as the gateway into the teachings of the Buddha."

Thus great beings had previously advised again and again that it was not right for the great monastic seat of Tashi Lhunpo to rely upon Dölgyal, and yet because of the popularity of this oath-breaking spirit, born of perverse prayers, its practice had spread even to Tashi Lhunpo.

20. Takphu Vajradhara and the Life-Entrustment Practice

As described above, there were those within the Sakya tradition who practiced Dölgyal. Among them, Sachen Kunga Lodrö attached great importance to Dölgyal. However, in his *Great Wrathful Torma of Shukden* it says:

> This Gyalpo in the form of a Tibetan demon does not have the authority of the tantras and Indian scriptures. There is also no life-entrustment, no rites for the four activities, and so on found in the textual, hidden-treasure, or pure-vision traditions. Therefore how can there be a tantric presentation?

This clearly states that at that time there was no Dölgyal life-entrustment ritual, rites for the four activities, and so on. However, in later times the master Phabongkha composed a Dölgyal feast offering and a life-entrustment ritual. In his biography it states (381b5):

> From an early age, the doctrine protector Dorjé Shukden accompanied the venerable lama constantly like a shadow following a body, carrying out his every wish without distraction. Sometimes, this fierce doctrine protector would enter the body of a human, urging again and again that a life-entrustment ritual to him needed to be composed. Accordingly, so as to not ignore the requests of a great Dharma protector, the venerable lama composed a life-force ritual as it arose within his mind.

Therefore, at the insistence of Dölgyal himself stating that a life-entrustment ritual must be composed, this master, in 1921, wrote a Dölgyal life-entrustment rite. From then on, using that rite, he gave the life-entrustment initiation to others. However, later, relying instead upon teachings given by Takphu Vajradhara, the former text of the life-entrustment rite was not much used.

In *Strictly Sealed Chariot of the Gems of Faith Carrying the Jewels of Great Blessings: A Life-Entrustment Rite of the One with the Name of Dorjé, Protector of the Teachings of the Mañjunātha Tsongkhapa, Together with Notes on Drawing the Life-Entrustment Diagram*[159] of the master Phabongkha, it states (500.1):

> Previously, the profound words of the life-entrustment rite of the great doctrine protector Dorjé Shukden Tsal was a profound practice based upon the text of Lama Rinchen Wangyal. However, in later times, the transmission of the initiation was no longer present, and even the text on the subsequent rituals, like the brother of a flower in space,[160] is not to be found anywhere.
>
> The great protector himself has told me, on at least two occasions, that a new initiation must be composed. Once or twice I have disseminated a life-entrustment initiation to students on a one-to-one basis, founded on my own experience and understanding, and I have written down a root text. However, like the offspring of a prostitute,[161] I cannot have any confidence in it.

This raises something that needs to be investigated. The "profound words of the life-entrustment rite" of Dölgyal is here referred to as the profound words of an initiation. However, if these "profound words of the life-entrustment rite," which was "a profound practice based upon the text of Lama Rinchen Wangyal," existed, then what is the source for such a claim? And how are the "profound words" and the "profound practices" profound?

In which century did this Lama Rinchen Wangyal live? Was he an acknowledged scholar and master of the Geluk tradition? If so, then what was the reason that the great masters of those times, who maintained the Geluk doctrine and who were renowned as the sun and moon, did not preserve this profound life-entrustment rite and its text, with the result that in later times the transmission of the initiation was no longer present, and even the text on the initiation rituals became like the sibling of a flower in space?

If, in later times, the text of the Dölgyal life-entrustment had become like the space-flower and was no longer used, then how can it be known that the life-entrustment and the text was "profound"? Also, are we to say that the Geluk masters and scholars of those times did not realize that such-and-such life-entrustment of Dölgyal, and its text, was precious and profound and so its continued transmission ceased?

Furthermore, Dölgyal insisted again and again that the master Phabongkha compose a new life-entrustment to him. Accordingly, this master in 1921 composed the text of a new life-entrustment rite, and using that text, he gave the life-entrustment initiation to his disciples for about fourteen years. Finally, in 1935, if he had not newly credited the source of the life-entrustment as being Takphu Rinpoché, what reason would he have had for regarding the so-called life-entrustment initiation given to disciples for fourteen years or so prior to that time, as one in which he could have no confidence, like the child of a prostitute?

Dölgyal had told the venerable Phabongkha repeatedly, "Compose my life-entrustment rite. If you do so, that will suffice." Venerable Phabongkha obliged. However, the venerable Phabongkha in his own words said that this this would not suffice, and that the rite was like the child of a prostitute, in which he could have no confidence. From this I think we can see that although he praised Dölgyal as the exclusive protector of Mañjunātha Tsongkhapa's teachings and as a Dharma protector manifestation of a great deity and chief protector of the Geluk, in the depths of his heart he knew he could have no faith in the words of Dölgyal and that it would not be proper to have such faith.

Dates for Takphu Vajradhara

Concerning the dates for the birth and death of Takphu Vajradhara, *Encyclopedia of Past Tibetan Masters* says (740), "Takphu Padmavajra was born in the male fire-rat year of 1876. The date of his passing is not known."

However, the *Dungkar Great Dictionary* states (1000), "When he reached the age of forty-seven, in the water-dog year of 1922, he passed away."

If that is the case, he died at forty-six by Western calculation. This means that when Kyabjé Phabongkha visited Kham in 1935, Takphu Vajradhara had been dead for about thirteen years, and they could not have possibly met there. However, as described below, they did meet at that time, and Takphu Vajradhara died very soon afterward. The account that states he passed away in 1922 is incorrect. His dates are 1876–1935.

The Meeting at the Takphu Residence for the Life-Entrustment Teachings

It is recorded that Takphu Padmavajra, or Takphu Vajradhara Losang Jampal Tenpai Ngödrup, was someone who would even compose Bön works when requested by Bön practitioners, that he was a kindhearted man who would always fulfill the wishes of those who made requests of him, and was a very gentle person. In particular, Takphu Vajradhara and Kyabjé Phabongkha had great respect and devotion for each other. Therefore, whatever requests the venerable Phabongkha had, it goes without saying that Takphu Vajradhara would fulfill them.

Kyabjé Phabongkha definitely had this in mind. In his biography, it says (558b3):

> Previously, Takphu Vajradhara of Nakshö had requested the government, by way of the venerable lama, to provide a new monastic constitution for the Takphu monastery of Genden Luksang Kunphel Ling. The venerable lama instructed Governor Shenkhawa to do this. This he accomplished, and the venerable lama received it while setting out from Lhasa. In order to deliver it to the Vajradhara in Nakshö personally, and for other reasons, the venerable lama sent a letter requesting an audience with him. Takphu Rinpoché replied that at that particular time the long and winding road from Bengar to Takphu was difficult, that it would be very tiring, and so he should not come at that time but that both Takphu monasteries would invite him on his way back from Chamdo. There were about three messages saying that meeting on the return journey would be better.
>
> The venerable lama said that there was no way that he could not be in the presence of the Vajradhara at this time. Previously, teachings he had been listening to on the *Four Interwoven Annotations on the Stages of the Path*[162] had been left unfinished, and at this time he would request the Vajradhara to kindly teach them. Moreover, he had a desire to receive the profound words of the short-lineage life-entrustment of the fierce protector as well as other teachings. Therefore, together with these many reasons, he

repeatedly sent by messenger a succession of letters requesting teaching. Finally Takphu Vajradhara happily accepted.

Thus sometime previously, Takphu Vajradhara had asked the Tibetan government to provide him with a new constitution for his monastic seat, Genden Luksang Kunphel Ling. This he had done by way of Kyabjé Phabongkha. Accordingly, Kyabjé Phabongkha had given instructions to Governor Shenkhawa, telling him to ask the government for a new constitution document. The governor obliged, and the document drawn up by the Tibetan government was handed to Kyabjé Phabongkha in 1935 as he set out from Lhasa to Kham. In order to present that document to Takphu Vajradhara in person, Kyabjé Phabongkha sent a special message from a place called Bengar asking if could come to Takphu Vajradhara's residence in Nakshö.

Takphu Vajradhara wrote three times. He suggested that Kyabjé Phabongkha go to Chamdo first and then the Takphu monasteries would invite him on the way back, when it would be easier to travel, stressing that right now the road from Bengar to the Takphu residence was not good.

However, Kyabjé Phabongkha sends a succession of replies by messenger saying that it is not possible that he does not meet with Takphu Rinpoché at this particular time, and that there are many teachings, primarily the so-called "profound words of the short-lineage life-entrustment of the fierce protector," that he needs to receive from him.

Finally, after much persistence, Takphu Rinpoché agrees. This is clearly indicated in the extract.

The Response from the Takphu Labrang

In the above there is one thing in particular that researchers should take an interest in. In the letter of request submitted by the master Phabongkha to Takphu Rinpoché, he mentions the "profound words on the short-lineage life-entrustment of the fierce protector." He is saying that if Takphu Vajradhara were to give pure-vision[163] teachings on Dölgyal life-entrustment and so forth, later these teachings could become those "profound words."

Alternatively, it can be understood that "profound words" refers to venerable Phabongkha requesting Takphu Vajradhara for profound advice and guidance on the life-entrustment he himself had composed earlier. Nowhere, initially, in the letters of request was there mention of "profound initiation of the Dölgyal life-entrustment."

In truth, he could say nothing else because Takphu Vajradhara was not someone who practiced Dölgyal. In particular, he possessed no lineage of Dölgyal whatsoever, either short or long. Therefore saying that he must have something that is nonexistent, like the hair on a tortoise, and that it must be given to him would have been an inappropriate request.

Furthermore, in the biography of Kyabjé Phabongkha, it says (500):

> Therefore, to my sole refuge, the great Takphu, who in reality is the all-pervading Vajradhara, I offered the basic text, together with detailed reasons, and made my request.
>
> This great Vajradhara follows a code of conduct that is not at all evident to the perception of ordinary disciples but is in reality a life of inconceivable mysteries, sporting constantly with mandalas of countless conquering buddhas, all of which transcend the boundaries of the ordinary mind. A fraction of this can be gleaned from his secret biography. There he relates how he received this profound life-entrustment initiation of Gyalchen:

> > Constant deception that has been mixed
> > with the innermost deception of imprints;
> > by prayers made at the behest of the lama,
> > I arrived at the Dharma Land of Joy,[164]
> > where in the presence of the fragrant lotus
> > I offered my request and he smiled with delight.

> > Entrusting a heroic one born from his speech,[165]
> > the rāja was brought from amid the five-faced throne.
> > Entrusted to a servant, it was in accord with the words of
> >   the lama,
> > and supplemented with a few points that are unique,
> > the one called Padma[166] wrote it down in a grove of joy.

> > By its virtue, may the deeds and life of the lama be great,
> > may his disciples, in harmonious mind, be made joyous
> > with the wealth of Dharma, and in particular,
> > may the tradition of Mañjunātha flourish.

> The rite comprising the arrangement of the basic text that I had

offered, and the profound pure-vision short lineage as given by Lama Vajradhara, together with supplementary material, presented in an accessible manner, begins:

In a clean and quiet place....

When the master Phabongkha says, "I offered the basic text, together with detailed reasons, and made my request" he means that he offered Takphu Rinpoché the Dölgyal life-entrustment text he had composed about fourteen years earlier and explained that Dölgyal's insistence was the fundamental reason a new life-entrustment needed to be composed. Moreover, looking at the last three lines of the verses above, I think he was suggesting to Takphu Vajradhara that Dölgyal was a genuine and exclusive protector of the Mañjunātha doctrine who is of great benefit to the teachings of the second Buddha, Tsongkhapa, while also asking for assistance in the activities of his own life.

However, the citation says, "made my request." What exactly was the request for? Was he requesting Takphu Rinpoché to compose a new Dölgyal life-entrustment? Was the venerable Phabongkha asking for support for the life-entrustment he had written previously? Looking at the wording, it seems to indicate that he offered Takphu Rinpoché the text he had written earlier and asked him for advice and instructions on anything that needed adding or removing.

However, there is today a senior monk in his seventies, a former abbot of one of the great monastic seats, who says the master Phabongkha offered the text of the Dölgyal life-entrustment to Takphu Rinpoché and asked him whether it was suitable and whether the time was right for propagating the Dölgyal life-entrustment. Takphu Vajradhara followed the code of conduct of a great mahāsiddha, and in response he drank a large amount of beer, went to sleep, and examined his dreams. The lines from "Constant deception that has been mixed with the innermost deception of imprints" up to "the rāja was brought from amid the five-faced throne" are describing his dream.

Because of who said this, I find this credible. However, up to now nothing concerning Takphu Vajradhara drinking a large quantity of beer and immediately examining his dreams can be found anywhere in the Dölgyal life-entrustment ritual, the biography of the master Phabongkha, or elsewhere.

What is accessible to our purview is that with his three verses from the life-entrustment text beginning "Constant deception" up to "May the tradition of Mañjunātha flourish," Takphu Vajradhara was giving his response to the venerable Phabongkha. Also, by the phrase "deception of deception" in the line "Constant deception that has been mixed with the innermost deception of imprints," it is clear that the event occurred within a dream.

The meaning of those verses is as follows. Takphu Vajradhara arrived at the Dharma Land of Joy in Tuṣita, either in his dream or as a result of his prayer made in order to examine his dreams at the behest of the master Phabongkha. In the presence of the fragrant lotus that was the Mañjunātha Lama Tsongkhapa, he made his request concerning the Dölgyal life-entrustment. The master Tsongkhapa smiled with delight and entrusted the task to a heroic being born from his speech. That disciple brought the rāja, or Dölgyal, from amid a five-face, or lion, throne. All this occurred in the dream of Takphu Vajradhara.

"Entrusted to a servant" refers to Takphu himself. His way of thinking "was in accord with the words" of the master Phabongkha, and there are "a few points that are unique" from those that he has composed. These have "supplemented" his own composition.

By the virtue of this work, may the deeds and life of the lama be great, and may his disciples be in harmony with his thinking and made joyous with the wealth of Dharma, and in particular, may the tradition of Mañjunātha Tsongkhapa flourish.

This is clear from the verses. In particular, these lines state that the Dölgyal life-entrustment composed previously by the master Phabongkha and the way of thinking of Takphu Vajradhara differed only in a few minor points. Therefore it is very clear that Takphu Vajradhara did not make any great changes to the text composed by the master Phabongkha but that fundamentally it was left as it was.

This event is also described in the biography of the master Phabongkha (561b2):

> As a result of previously submitting many requests, now, in the presence of Takphu Vajradhara, the venerable lama received teachings on the *Four Interwoven Annotations on the Stages of the Path* up to the end of the second volume, which had been left unfinished from before, as well the account of how that work came into being, its content list, a transmission of a lineage prayer composed by Lhotrul Rinpoché, and the pure-vision

exclusive short-lineage life-entrustment of the fierce protector of the Geluk tradition, Dorjé Shukden Tsal, together with a one-to-one transmission.

At this point we were called into the presence of the two Vajradharas. The venerable lama said, "Now, in the presence of Vajradhara I have received the great kindness of the life-entrustment of the great Dharma protector. After that, a life-entrustment diagram is necessary, so I have requested Vajradhara for it. You will have to create a new text, so remember how to draw it."

This was clearly hugely important, and so I thought it would be best to write down how to draw the life-entrustment diagram in accordance with its description that arose from the discussion of the two lamas, as their oral instructions merged to become one. Therefore I began to take notes as soon as they began giving instructions. These are as found in the later collected works of the venerable lama. It was made into a root text and was propagated throughout Ü-Tsang, Amdo, Kham, and beyond.

However, the above is just the writing of the biographer. The reality is either that Takphu Rinpoché gave the Dölgyal life-entrustment at that time, or that the two lamas had a congenial discussion about the life-entrustment in which Takphu Vajradhara discussed his thoughts and the signs that had appeared to him in dreams. It is difficult to determine. The lines, "together with a one-to-one transmission" and "At this point we were called into the presence of the two Vajradharas" indicate that at that time, the two lamas were alone in the room with no one else present.

Furthermore, the master Phabongkha says, "Now, in the presence of Vajradhara I have received the great kindness of the life-entrustment of the great Dharma protector." If at that time he had actually received the initiation, he would have said "the life-entrustment *initiation* of the great Dharma protector." This raises a big doubt.

If we examine all this closely, we can see the following: Just as Takphu Vajradhara gave instructions and advice about constructing the Dölgyal life-entrustment diagram, he likewise gave instructions and opinions on the life-entrustment text composed previously by the venerable Phabongkha. Also, in response to a few questions from the venerable Phabongkha, Takphu Vajradhara spoke about the signs he had received in dreams, and because of the power of faith, or for some other reason, it was proclaimed that the Dölgyal life-entrustment had arisen from the pure visions of Takphu Vajradhara. There can be no explanation other than this.

If it is said that Takphu Vajradhara bestowed the Dölgyal life-entrustment initiation on the master Phabongkha, which text did he use to do so? If you say it was the text composed previously by the venerable Phabongkha, that cannot be correct because he saw the text as one "in which he could have no confidence, like the child of a prostitute."

If you say it was given using the text that is widely available these days, that is also not correct because Takphu Vajradhara and the master Phabongkha met in May 1935, and the life-entrustment text was composed on August 25, 1935.

Furthermore, in the collected works of venerable Phabongkha, it says (7:511):

> Because of continuing to hold in the depths of my heart the entreaties delivered more than once by the great protector as described earlier; because of the several requests made by devoted disciples; and in particular, because in his protecting of the tradition of the Mañjunātha Tsongkhapa the execution of his four types of deeds is swift and unobstructed and therefore in the future the spread of his activities will be very great, thus for those who rely upon him properly, a life-entrustment initiation is necessary and timely. Accordingly, this *Jeweled Chariot of Faith Carrying the Gems of Great Blessings: The Way to Confer the Profound Life-Entrustment Initiation of Gyalchen Dorjé Shukden Tsal, Manifested Doctrine Protector*, being an essential instruction practice that combines my experience and the special short-lineage pure vision of the Vajradhara Lama, was written from homage to colophon on the day of the third *bhadrā* (the 27th) of the waning half of the *aṣāḍha* month of the wood-pig year in Shodo Dragom Chöling Labrang[167] by Phabongkha Jampa Tenzin Trinlé Gyatso.

Thus, with Takphu Vajradhara as a source and reference, this master, at the age of fifty-eight, again composed from homage to colophon a Dölgyal life-entrustment on August 25, 1935.

Both the biography and the colophon of the life-entrustment itself are alike in stating that the former and the latter life-entrustment rites were each the result of Dölgyal urging, "You must compose a life-entrustment for me."

The biography also says (580b2), "On that day he also composed the text of the life-entrustment initiation of the fierce doctrine protector and so on." Therefore, as stated in the colophon of the life-entrustment reproduced above, it was composed in Shodo Dragom Labrang after his visit to Takphu Monastery in Nakshö. However, a careful perusal of the biography reveals that a different date for the composition—not the *aṣāḍha*, or sixth month, but the *śrāvana*, or seventh month, or September 24. However, as the colophon of the life-entrustment text carries more authority, it is left as it is.

Misfortunes after the Completion of the Life-Entrustment Text

Something should be evident to all by now. Master Phabongkha saw that if he had not used Takphu Vajradhara as the source, the life-entrustment would not have had authority. He relied on Takphu Vajradhara for support, and with him as reference, he completed the life-entrustment text and began transmitting it to others. Immediately after this, you would expect some auspicious signs to occur. However, instead of that, some very inauspicious signs occurred. For example, when only a little under a month had passed after the life-entrustment rite was completed, on September 21, the consort of Takphu passed away. On the very next day, September 22, Takphu Vajradhara himself passed away.

The biography of Phabongkha states (582b2):

> One day a letter arrived from the Takphu chief attendant, the steward Agyal, and others. It said that recently Takphu Vajradhara and his secret consort had become seriously ill with the fever. No amount of medicine or ritual helped, and the precious consort on the twenty-fourth of the seventh month, and the great Vajradhara on the twenty-fifth, passed away. As soon as he had seen this, the venerable lama seemed sad and upset and did not speak much to those around him.

Also, the Great Fourteenth Dalai Lama, in *Discourses on Dölgyal*, says (2:87):

> According to common knowledge, Takphu Padmavajra received the Dölgyal life-entrustment in a pure vision, and there are those

who say that this pure vision proves that Dölgyal is an authentic protector. Takphu Padmavajra was an unimaginably great master. A compilation of the pure visions that he had was printed on woodblocks, and recently I obtained a copy of this. This text was printed in Tibet. It describes the many pure visions that Takphu Padmavajra received in the early part of his life. It also describes his meeting with the master Phabongkha and mentions various pure visions he received around that time.

If the Shukden life-entrustment really is a pure vision of Takphu, it should definitely be included in this compilation. However, there is no trace of it. That is strange. It certainly raises a doubt. There should be research on whether or not this Shukden life-entrustment is a Takphu pure vision.

The above is extracted from advice specially given by the precious refuge and protector the Fourteenth Dalai Lama during preliminary teachings on January 8–9, 2006, on the occasion of his thirtieth conferment of the great initiation of the glorious Kālacakra at the sacred place of the great Dhānya-kaṭaka shrine.

Also, in the same work (2:31):

If we examine the reason, one year ago I asked Nechung, "This Dölgyal life-entrustment was given by Takphu Vajradhara, and it was pure vision received by him, and so isn't it trustworthy?"

The protector replied, "There are pure visions received by way of divine blessings of the three sources,[168] and there are pure visions received by the power of hindrances. I wonder if this is not a pure vision received by the power of hindrances?"

Ling Rinpoché told me that Phabongkha Rinpoché had told him that there were some Bön teachings included in the collected works of Takphu Vajradhara as requested by his disciples, and that later, he, Phabongkha Rinpoché, took them out in an attempt to keep the collection pure.

The above is taken from the talk given by the precious refuge and protector the Fourteenth Dalai Lama on December 6, 2000, in Dharamsala during the second conference of the Geluk International Foundation, when he attended to preside over the conference.

Conclusions Regarding the Life-Entrustment Rite

To summarize, even those of the Sakya tradition who held Dölgyal in high regard said that he was a Tibetan demon and that it would not be proper for there to be rites of life-entrustment, the four activities, and so on.

Later, a so-called life-entrustment for Dölgyal appeared during the time of Lama Rinchen Wangyal. However, very soon "the transmission of the initiation was no longer present, and even the text on the subsequent rituals was like the sibling of a flower in space."

After that, at the insistence of Dölgyal, the master Phabongkha composed a life-entrustment to Dölgyal, but that too became untrustworthy, "like the child of a prostitute."

Again, using Takphu Vajradhara as source and reference, he composed a life-entrustment rite, hailed as emerging from Takphu pure visions. However, the reality is that when the master Phabongkha went to the Takphu monastery, he only requested for "profound words on the short-lineage life-entrustment of the fierce protector," but there is no clarity whether "profound words" referred to profound words of a life-entrustment initiation or to profound words of advice on life-entrustment.

After that, when the two lamas met in person, the master Phabongkha offered the basic text he had composed earlier, together with detailed reasons, and made his request. Takphu Vajradhara explains his response with three verses, but it is not clarified what the original request was for.

When those verses of response are studied, they emerge as expressions of Takphu Rinpoché's examination of his dreams, but in the life-entrustment text it is not clarified whether these are dreams or not.

In the biography it is written that the master Phabongkha received the pure-vision exclusive short-lineage life-entrustment together with a one-to-one transmission. However, the composer of the biography, Denma Losang Dorjé, was not actually in the company of the two lamas at that time. Therefore, on that day the actual events that went on between the two lamas were not witnessed by the author.

Similarly, the master Phabongkha said, "Now, in the presence of Vajradhara, I have received the great kindness of the life-entrustment of the great Dharma protector." He did not say "I have received the life-entrustment." Nor did he say, "I have received the life-entrustment initiation."

If we think about all the above, we can clearly see that for the purposes of propagating the so-called Dölgyal life-entrustment, it had to be linked to

Takphu Rinpoché. However, to say that the Dölgyal life-entrustment itself came from the Takphu pure visions is simply empty talk. Therefore, short of ignoring all sensible reasoning and simply insisting otherwise, it will never be possible for this so-called Dölgyal life-entrustment to be included in the Takphu cycle of pure visions.

Also, the master Phabongkha uses the three verses purported to have been written by Takphu Vajradhara as a prime source and reference and then completes the text of the life-entrustment himself. Then he says in the colophon, "my experience and the special short-lineage pure vision of the Vajradhara Lama," thereby declaring that the life-entrustment is a short-lineage pure vision, and from then on starts to propagate it in Shodo, Chamdo, and other parts of Kham and Amdo. However, about a month after the life-entrustment text is completed, Takphu Vajradhara and his consort are struck down with a serious illness, for which all medicine and ritual were of no help, and they pass away within a day of each other.

Looking at this, isn't it true what the great Dharma protector Nechung, in the presence of the great Fourteenth Dalai Lama, said concerning the three verses said to have come from Takphu Vajradhara beginning "Constant deception that has been mixed with the innermost deception of imprints" that the pure vision of Takphu Vajradhara was received through the power of hindrance? Beyond that, if we examine all of this carefully, none of it stands up to reason.

Views of Phabongkha because of the Influence of Dölgyal

Because of the hindering and deceptive ways of Dölgyal, there have been many instances of great preservers and propagators of the Buddha's doctrine from all traditions and all places being displeased even with great masters such as Phabongkha Rinpoché who were unrivaled in terms of their learning, ethics, and compassion.

For example, Tseten Shabdrung (1910–85), in his biography of Jikmé Damchö Gyatso (1898–1947), writes (2:315):

> At this time, from Dzongsar Monastery in Dergé Meshö, although they did not know each other, [Jikmé Damchö Gyatso] received a letter, together with customary offering, from the master scholar Chökyi Lodrö (1893–1959), incarnation of Jamyang

Khyentsé (1820–92), incomparable illuminator of the Nyingma tradition. It begins:

> Though the far horizon of knowledge is not apparent,
> that all phenomena, in depth and in number,
> are clearly reflected on the surface of your mirror of
>   wisdom
> is due to the blessing of the venerable Mañjuśrī.
>
> Therefore you are a great heroic being
> who from times past without number
> has engaged in the practices of enlightenment,
> and who, with a glance of compassion toward
> living beings in these times of degeneration,
> appears here now as a spiritual friend.

Thus he continues with several verses of praise of the master's qualities, at the end of which he continues:

> On hearing of your precious life, my mind was filled with joy, which means that we have a connection from previous lives. I would be so happy to meet with you, but by the power of karma I have become very sick and am far away. So there is nothing to be done. However, I continually create in the expanse of my mind the connection of petitions, prayer, and long-life wishes.
>
> Some students of the venerable Phabongkha Rinpoché have been making arguments over the great tenets of the new and old traditions. They have destroyed images of Padmasambhava and other peaceful and wrathful deities. They say that reciting the *vajra guru* mantra is of no use. They have thrown copies of *Lotus Testament*[169] and other works into fires and rivers, and committed many other wrong deeds. Furthermore, they talk a lot about there being no purpose in turning *maṇi* wheels, holding weekly prayers for the deceased, and so on, thereby bringing the people to wrong views.
>
> They hold Gyalpo Shukden as composite of the

Three Jewels and as their supreme refuge. It is said that in the south, Shukden possesses many monks in the smaller monasteries, who then run crazily here and there destroying the three representations of the Buddha, Dharma, and Sangha. In doing so they bring many faults upon themselves and seriously wound the doctrine of the second Buddha, Tsongkhapa.

Therefore, if you could compose a letter that would help the situation, have it printed and distributed throughout Central Tibet, Tsang, and Kham, it would be a great kindness and contribute to the dispelling of this disturbance to the doctrine.

This letter can be seen as a sure sign that [Jikmé Damchö Gyatso] was of unrivaled fame in Kham and Central Tibet in shouldering the responsibility of his own tradition, the holders of the yellow crown,[170] and that the minds of great preservers and propagators of the Buddha's doctrine from all traditions were helplessly swept away by the beautiful white waves of his learning, ethics, and compassion.

21. Unfortunate Events Connected with Dölgyal

THE SECOND VOLUME of *Garland of Pearls*, which is a compilation of the compositions of the Drepung throneholder and former abbot of Gomang College, the master Tenpa Tenzin Rinpoché (1917–2007), contains a piece called "Advice to Kalsang Gyatso[171] in England." There it says (266):

> After the Great Thirteenth had passed away, the master Phabongkha, in a few hermitages in Central Tibet and in many monasteries in Kham, after giving his main teachings, would then encourage the practice of Gyalchen. I heard that just after he returned to Central Tibet, there was much trouble in those monasteries. During assemblies the spirit possessed several monks, causing schism and problems between the old and the new protectors. Images of the old protectors were thrown outside and so on.
>
> In southern Kham too, some prejudiced fools requested images of Lopön Rinpoché[172] to "return to their own abodes." In propitiations they changed the last two words of the phrase, "The most powerful among the masters of tantric knowledge, Padmasambhava," to "Losang Drakpa" (Tsongkhapa). They amended the phrase "In the past, in the presence of the Great Ācārya" to "In the past, in the presence of Losang Drakpa" and so on, thereby erasing the name of Precious Ācārya wherever it appeared. They rewrote the *Pure Dharmakāya Incense Purification Rites*[173] and carried out other acts without the slightest shame or embarrassment, thereby bringing great disgrace to the Geluk tradition.
>
> Because of these events, Phabongkha, whose nature is like that of refined gold, the slander of how he has manifested as a demon,

tainted the Geluk tradition, and so forth has grown far and wide, and it is still evident today.

That the main source of all these bad deeds is solely the machinations of Dölgyal is clear to all. If you say that such a destructive ghost is a protector of the Geluk tradition, then why not say that chief of the demons himself and every other class of demons are protectors of the doctrine?

In *Miscellaneous Comments on What Has Been Seen, Heard, and Experienced Concerning Dölgyal, or Gyalpo Shukden* by former abbot of Namgyal Monastery and the current vice abbot [now former abbot] of the glorious Gyütö Tantric College Jhado Rinpoché (b. 1954) it says (6):

> The sixth incarnation of Drupkhang Rinpoché, Thupten Khedrup, studied in Sera Monastery. He received many teachings from Phabongkha Dechen Nyingpo, during which it is said he received the Shukden life-entrustment. When he had completed his studies, he returned to Shabten Monastery in his homeland of Nakchu.[174] At that time, the protector Nyakré Gyalchen Karma Trinlé,[175] who was the guardian of the line of Drupkhang incarnations, entered the oracle at Shabten Monastery, and in the presence of Rinpoché was not that responsive and made resentful remarks such as, "Now I, a protector appointed and entrusted by the previous incarnations, have become of no use."
>
> Later, Drupkhang Rinpoché amended his practice and rebuilt his bond with Nyakré Karma Trinlé.
>
> As he neared death, he said, "I, the one at fault, am finished. If from now on you do not renounce the propitiation of Dölgyal, it could be the ruin of this monastery."
>
> He summoned Thokmé Rinpoché,[176] a Sera Monastery lama who had given teachings on *Great Treatise on the Stages of the Path* as well as initiations of Guhyasamāja, Vajrabhairava, and Cakrasaṃvara at Jhado Monastery, and who in 1958 performed my crown-hair offering ritual. By now Drupkhang Rinpoché was not at all well and definitely not long for this life. He told Thokmé Rinpoché that after death, in order to suppress and oppose Dölgyal, he would arise as a "blazing doctrine protector." He described the colors, hand implements, entourage, and so on.

He instructed Thokmé Rinpoché to compose a propitiation rite conforming with that description and to recite it to him as he passed away.

Accordingly, Rinpoché composed the rite, and as he was reciting it in the ear of Drupkhang Rinpoché, the lama passed away. As he did so his eyes became very round, blood came from his mouth, and so on. Even his attendants dared not go near him. Therefore, not only the creation of a ritual of generation, but also the corpse itself taking on the form of a protector, is truly remarkable.

Similarly, not only in other parts of Tibet but even in the nomadic regions near my birthplace, and not just during the present time of the Great Fourteenth but in the past also, the matter of Gyalpo Dölgyal has been regarded as important, and many texts and generation rituals have been composed to oppose it.

In the same work (8):

Furthermore, these days there is much misleading talk about how propitiating Dölgyal brings success, of him being superior to other protectors, being a wealth god, and so on. Such devious and arrogant claims are being documented, but there is not a fraction of truth in them.

For example, in Sok Tsenden Monastery, or Sokshö Ganden Phelgyé Ling Monastery,[177] Phabongkha Dechen Nyingpo built a new Dölgyal protector chapel, composed an extensive propitiation text, and encouraged the monks to rely upon Dölgyal. Afterward, disaster followed disaster in the monastery. There was monastic discord, instances of killing and wounding, and so on. The internal strife became a legal action, and the case was brought before the Nakchu governor. In the governor's binding judgment, it was decided that Dölgyal should no longer be propitiated. From that time on, up to the present, there has been no Dölgyal practice in the monastery. That is a remarkable event and is just one story from the times before Tibet was lost.

If Dölgyal were really a deity of good fortune, then especially in the very place where the extensive propitiation was initiated there should have been an unprecedented level of success, and the Shukden protector chapel should have been a place of extraordinary prosperity. However, the very opposite happened.

Such stories have occurred, and continue to occur, not only in my birthplace but all around in neighboring areas also. Nevertheless, since reliance upon Gyalpo Dölgyal was stopped, there continues to be peace and tranquility in that monastery.

In a foreword written by Lama Zopa Rinpoché beginning, "For the people of the world and especially for the people of Tibet,"[178] he says:

Many who rely heavily upon Dölgyal have met death in perilous circumstances. For example, Geshé Yeshé Wangchuk, a learned scholar from Sera Mé College who brought the incarnation of Phabongkha Rinpoché to Tibet and encouraged him to receive the Dölgyal life-entrustment and Cakrasaṃvara body-mandala initiation from Gönpasa Rinpoché,[179] was one day traveling on a bus when it reached a high pass and was involved in an accident.[180] Although there were many people on the bus, he alone fell through a window into a deep ravine and died.

The trader Dorjé Gyaltsen relied heavily on Dölgyal in secret. One day he became very sick. He told his wife to go to the place where he performed his daily Dölgyal requests and offerings and to perform them for him. It was not common knowledge that he was someone who relied on Dölgyal, and his wife was very surprised. She went to perform the Dölgyal invocation and so forth, but there was nothing she could do. The trader said, "This Dölgyal has been deceiving me all this time. Now I see his true form. He is malicious and nothing but a ghost. I have been deceived. I have been mistaken all this time. I must confess to the lamas."

As he took his last breaths, he became very frightened. He looked as if he were being strangled, froth came from his mouth, and he died.

His body was taken to the graveyard and given to the vultures, but even the birds flew off without eating his flesh.

Furthermore, my great spiritual mentor, whose unrivaled kindness is greater than all the buddhas of the past, present, and future and whose name is so hard to utter, Thubten Yeshé, was relying upon Dölgyal. Before his breathing ceased, as he was about to pass into the pure realms, he clearly conveyed that Dölgyal was no good. This was my experience as I remained with him at the point of his passing.

Furthermore, in a document received by this editorial committee entitled *Document on the Position Held by Ganden Dönyi Ling Monastery of Lhodrak, as Presented by Yeshé Dönyö*, it says:

> In the past it was not the practice for anyone at Dönyi Ling, whether lama or monk, to propitiate Dölgyal. However, around 1950 Kyabjé Phara Rinpoché from Ganden Monastery was invited to Dönyi Ling to teach on the stages of the path. While at the monastery he talked emphatically about how good it would be to rely upon Dölgyal, saying that Dölgyal propitiation brought swift results, that if propitiation were practiced by the monastery it would bring huge benefits, and he supported these statements with stories. As a result, a few senior monks immediately approved and promised to rely upon Dölgyal. From then on, a statue of Dölgyal about the size of an eight-year-old boy was built and placed to the left of the Palden Lhamo statue in the Dönyi Ling protector chapel, and propitiation was initiated.
>
> After the practice began a series of inauspicious events. A few monks suddenly died, which was not especially usual. One or two others, including the disciplinarian Gyaltsen Namdren, lost their minds. Trouble and arguments broke out between propitiators and non-propitiators and so on.

In the preface to *Brief Account of the Authentic Origins of the Conflict between Palden Lhamo and Dölgyal*, composed by Gen Ngawang Khetsun, the steward of Gyalrong Khentrul Rinpoché of Drepung Loseling Monastery, it states (1):

> In Tsenlha Chöling Monastery in Gyalrong,[181] Kham, the traditional protector was Palden Lhamo. However, in the first part of the twentieth century, a Geshé Sönam Yak from a monastery in Central Tibet urged Dölgyal to come to Domé Gyalrong, and in

response, Dölgyal accepted. The geshé promptly returned to his homeland but suddenly died on the way.

Not long afterward, Dölgyal possessed a monk called Söpa from Tsenlha Chöling Monastery. A monastery in Okshi Gyalrong, called Okshi Talé Monastery, said that there used to be a Dölgyal oracle in its monastery, and so Chöling Monastery should hand over the new oracle to them. Tsenlha Chöling Monastery refused to do this because of the above reasons. As a result, a conflict arose between the two monasteries.

In the beginning, Chöling gained a few victories, but later Okshi Talé mustered a large Chinese military force, and Chöling was defeated. Over thirty of the ringleaders were captured and locked in the assembly hall to be executed the following day. However, that night they managed to escape and were gone. As a result, the Chinese soldiers confiscated and destroyed all the possessions of Chöling Monastery. Everything apart from the assembly hall and a quarter of the monks' rooms was burned to the ground. Furthermore, except for four young monks, all those who remained, which amounted to over a hundred senior and child monks, were killed. Of the four young monks not killed, one was our esteemed Gyalrong Rinpoché, Jampal Samphel, former abbot of Loseling College, and I, Ngawang Khetsun, have heard this story from his lips many times.

The main military commander of Okshi Talé Monastery at that time was someone called Taya Geshé, and he joked, "I have fulfilled the prophecy, 'There will be a time when the geshés become military commanders.'"[182]

Gyalrong Tsenlha Chöling Monastery was a monastery with a great history. For a while it had over five hundred monks, and as is clear from the above story, when the Dölgyal trouble began, it fell into ruin. When I, Ngawang Khetsun, lived at the monastery there were not more than seventy monks.

The Chöling incarnation, or Khewang Tsenlha Ngawang Tsultrim, returned to his monastery in Tibet after eight years of study at Loseling College in order to restore it. However, the Communist Chinese had occupied Tibet, and so to this day no improvement from its previous state has been possible.

Nevertheless, Dölgyal is well known as a huge troublemaker,

and more than that, the great conflict between Tsenlha Chöling Monastery and Okshi Talé Monastery in Domé Gyalrong, as recounted above, arose fundamentally because of Dölgyal.

In response to an invitation by Kyabjé Trijang Rinpoché, Kyabjé Phabongkha Rinpoché, at the age of sixty-one, came to Ganden Monastery in June 1938. There he taught the *Four Interwoven Annotations on the Stages of the Path to Enlightenment* and also gave many teachings about Dölgyal. At that time an unprecedented epidemic suddenly swept through the monastery. Day after day many monks died of the illness, and among the people it was common knowledge that this was a disastrous omen brought on by the conferring of the Dölgyal life-entrustment and so on.

However, in the biography of Kyabjé Phabongkha it says (635a6), "A contagious illness had been brought in from Sangphu, and a fever from some of the tantric colleges had spread greatly. The venerable lama kindly gave out medicine continually, and the disease gradually subsided." Thus it only mentions that a contagious illness broke out while Kyabjé Phabongkha was giving teachings but that he handed out medicine and the epidemic subsided. It says nothing about many monks dying and so on. It also mentions that he was giving teachings on the *Four Interwoven Annotations on the Stages of the Path to Enlightenment*, but nothing is written about teachings on Dölgyal.

PART 4
Today:
Dölgyal in Exile

22. An Invocation of Dölgyal Ascribed to the Fourteenth Dalai Lama

IN THE *SHUKDEN COMPENDIUM* compiled by propitiators of Dölgyal, there is an invocation to Dölgyal under the name of the Great Fourteenth Dalai Lama. The colophon states:

> The composition of this work, *Song of the Unstoppable Vajra: Invoking the Activity of Gyalchen Dorjé Shukden Tsal, Doctrine Protector of the Mañjunātha Conqueror*, was urged by the great manifested Dharma protector himself in his vajra pronouncements and also unanimously, together with an offering of the three representations, by the teachers and staff of this monastery. Accordingly, I, who bear the title Holder of the White Lotus, and who is called Ngawang Losang Tenzin Gyatso, unparalleled master with command over the three realms, composed it in Tashi Lhundrup Monastery of Dromo Dung. By its virtue, may there be perfection!

Thus it was composed in 1951 in Dromo, when the Great Fourteenth had to seek refuge from the Chinese Communist danger. He was sixteen years old at the time. If the matter of how the invocation was composed, and so on, and the circumstances at that time, were not cleared up now, then those who seek to take advantage could create confusion in the future by pulling people this way and that.

Therefore, on October 1, 2012, we submitted a letter by way of the Private Office of the Great Fourteenth, requesting him to clear up the doubts concerning this invocation. We received a reply promptly, which is reproduced below.

To the executives of the committee compiling a work on the

true history of Dölgyal, representatives of the Geluk tradition exemplified by the three unrivaled monastic seats. The letter that we received recently on October 1, 2012, addressed to the Great Fourteenth, was presented to him. In response to the request for a clear explanation of the circumstances at that time, we present the following:

In 1951, immediately after assuming political leadership as unanimously requested by the people of Tibet, intolerable changes were taking place, and so the Great Fourteenth had to escape the danger and remain for a while in Dromo on the Indian border. At first he stayed in the Dromo governor's house but soon was requested to move into more suitable rooms at Dromo Dungkar Monastery. At that time, not only was Dölgyal being propitiated in that monastery, there were oracles for the peaceful and wrathful forms of Dölgyal. The oracles for the protectors Nechung and Gadong did not travel to Dromo, and to resolve one or two urgent matters, monastic officials from the council of ministers and so forth had to petition the peaceful and wrathful forms of Dölgyal by way of oracles. In this way the connection was made.

At that time, the Great Fourteenth had not turned his attention to or seriously investigated the oath-violator Dölgyal. Moreover, among the people, the tales of the terror and danger of Dölgyal were beyond living memory, and apart from stories of Nechung becoming resentful if anyone from Drepung Monastery should propitiate Dölgyal, it was a time when the true facts were not widely known.

Therefore, in response to petitions from Dulzin[183] by way of oracle, and from the Dungkar Monastery masters and officials, there was no way that the invocation known as Song of the Unstoppable Vajra *by the Great Fourteenth could not be composed.*

At that time, the Great Fourteenth was very young. Moreover, it was the custom followed with all the Dalai Lamas of the past that with compositions required of them, reference notes for illustration would be drafted by their teachers and others who personally served them. Accordingly, for the composition of this invocation, reference notes were compiled by the Darhan[184] teacher of the Dalai Lama, Kyabjé Trijang Rinpoché, who had accompanied him to Dromo.

In summary, this invocation was written at the behest of others under special circumstances, time, and place and with a particular intention and purpose. It can never be interpreted as a source validating Dölgyal when seen in the context of the profound and clear pronouncements, which leave no room for interpretation, made at later times after the Great Fourteenth had, in the eyes of ordinary people, completed his investigations.

Generally, it is well known that if earlier and later pronouncements are contradictory, it is the later that is held to be valid. Also, to illustrate this point with examples evident to all, the reasoning that the Buddha taught a sutra in which he declared that there was a self does not establish that there is a self and that such a teaching was the final thinking of the Buddha, or that the earlier and later teachings of the Buddha are contradictory. Please keep this in mind.

Ganden Phodrang Office
November 20, 2012

Signed as approved by the Dalai Lama

From June 13, 1978, to July 10, 2010, the Fourteenth Dalai Lama gave a series of wide-ranging and profound, eye-opening speeches and teachings on the rights and wrongs surrounding Dölgyal. These were compiled in 2010 by Namgyal Monastery Educational Association and published as *Discourses on Dölgyal* in two separate volumes. We extract some of the essential points made in those books below.

23. Dölgyal and the Tenth Panchen Lama

A DÖLGYAL PROPITIATION reputedly composed by the Tenth Panchen Rinpoché has been inserted in the *Shukden Compendium* by the Shukden group. Also, in the second volume of the collected works of the Tenth Panchen Rinpoché, this propitiation is found on pages 238–64, and on pages 265–67 there is an invocation to both Dharma protector Chamsing and Dölgyal together. Here we will primarily examine the propitiation.

In the empowering section it says:

> *Hūṃ jaḥ*. From the realm of great bliss and non-fabrication
> and to the minds of disciples, manifested by way of
> the pose of the dance of the nine wrathful moods,
> Gyalchen Shukden, in the form of the four activities,
> you are empowered as the embodiment of all refuges.

Thus the author is someone who holds Dölgyal as the embodiment of all refuges. In the invitation section it says:

> Just as you, who were oath-bound in the presence of
> the second Buddha, Losang Drakpa, did promise,
> if you are now invited here for the activities of pacifying,
> increasing, controlling, and destroying,
> come to this place to carry out your deeds.

However, the dates of the second Buddha, Tsongkhapa Losang Drakpa, are 1357–1419, whereas Dölgyal appeared long after that time, around 1656. Therefore there is a difference of 237 years. As they were not contemporaneous, the statement that Dölgyal vowed to protect the teachings in the presence of the master Tsongkhapa is simply speculation and, like so many similar claims detailed previously, contains not a grain of truth.

Also, in the section called "vajra pledges that are to be held firmly and without the slightest laxity," it says:

> *Hūṃ jaḥ*. Supreme and natural expression of
> every pure and exalted wisdom combined as one,
> arising as the doctrine protector, lord of the arrogant,
> known as Gyalchen, possessed of skill, mighty and powerful,
> you, the butcher of all enemies and obstacles within the three
>   realms...

Here, "Every pure and exalted wisdom combined as one" is saying that Dölgyal is the embodiment of the omniscient wisdom of all the buddhas combined to become one. However, whether this makes any sense has already been examined previously and need not be repeated.

The colophon of this propitiation states:

> This composition, *Song Effortlessly Accomplishing the Four Activities: A Propitiation of the Wrathful Five-Family Gyalchen Dorjé Shukden Tsal, Doctrine Protector of the Conqueror Mañjunātha* was composed at the behest of Chief Secretary Tā Lama Losang Gyaltsen of Nordrang, and Vajra Master Losang Jangchup of the upper protector chapel when they requested a brief invocation and prayer to accompany the creation of a new scroll painting of Five-Family Gyalchen. I too have comprehended through actual and inner experience that the time has come for a powerful protection of the teachings in general, and particularly of the tradition of Jampal Nyingpo. Therefore this request coincided with the aspiration to compose a propitiation ritual as an auspicious token, and so with great joy, I the Śākya monk, Losang Trinlé Lhundrup Chökyi Gyaltsen, otherwise known as Tenzin Trinlé Jikmé Chökyi Wangchuk, composed this work in the Sunlight Great Bliss rooms of the Gyaltsen Thönpo Palace of Tashi Lhunpo Monastery, maintainer of the tradition of the pure way of life of the Kadampa. May goodness increase.

Thus there is mention of "the Śākya monk," referring to Panchen Rinpoché, while he was still ordained, and that it was composed while he was residing in Tashi Lhunpo, as referenced by "Palace of Tashi Lhunpo," but there is no date of composition and so forth.

The Tenth Panchen Rinpoché Incurs the Displeasure of Dölgyal

As reproduced above, the colophon of the propitiation text states "Śākya monk," and "rooms of the Gyaltsen Thönpo Palace of Tashi Lhunpo monastery." On that basis we can examine the authorship of this work.

Coming from his birthplace in Amdo, Panchen Rinpoché first set foot in his Tashi Lhunpo monastery on June 23, 1952. At that time the precious Panchen incarnation was a little over fourteen years old. Therefore it can be safely concluded he did not compose the propitiation before this time.

At the end of 1964 the all-knowing Panchen was forcibly taken to Beijing by the Chinese government. There he suffered the hardships of imprisonment and so on. After that, around 1982, he returned to his monastery, but by then he no longer held the vows of a monk. Therefore, he could not have composed the propitiation at that time. In 1963–64 he had to live in the so-called Panchen Residence as arranged by the Chinese government and not in Tashi Lhunpo.

In 1961–62 he embarked on a wide-ranging tour of lands incorporated into the People's Republic of China, and particularly of the whole of Tibet, in order to investigate and learn of the true situation and living standards of the people. It was a very busy period, during which the hardships he witnessed were written down at once and at all times. This was later presented to high-ranking Chinese officials as a seventy-thousand-word document.[185]

If you examine the biography of Panchen Rinpoché, entitled *Panchen Rinpoché the Great Master*, composed in Chinese by Jampal Gyatso, who had the experience of serving as his translator from 1959–62 and again from 1977–81, you can clearly see many good reasons why Panchen Rinpoché, up to the year 1962, did not write such a propitiation of Dölgyal.

To present each reason in detail would take up too much space. Therefore here, in the manner of "knowing one thing, liberates all," we can say that not only did the Tenth Panchen Rinpoché not compose such a propitiation with its overblown praise of Dölgyal, as reproduced above, but Panchen Rinpoché harbored an intense dislike for Dölgyal. The primary proof of this was that one day in 1988, while the Tenth Panchen Rinpoché was still alive, he presented personally to the lamas and tulkus and others studying at the Chinese-Tibetan Institute of Higher Buddhist Studies[186] copies of *Strict Directive for the Great Monastic Seat of Tashi Lhunpo Monastery*, stating:

> Previously, this *Directive for the Great Monastic Seat of Tashi Lhunpo Monastery* was something to be valued primarily within the monastery and was not to be promulgated outside. However, most of you are lamas and tulkus, and in the future you will be responsible for the preservation, development, and propagation of Tibetan Buddhism in the form of its monasteries, teachings, and so on. Therefore, when you do become the guardians of the teachings and the monasteries, it would be excellent if you were to hold this Tashi Lhunpo directive in great esteem. It is complete and comprehensive. Therefore today I am presenting you all with copies of the Tashi Lhunpo directive.

Thus to each of the students of this Buddhist institute in Beijing he gave a yellow clothbound copy of *Directive for the Great Monastic Seat of Tashi Lhunpo Monastery*, or *Yoke of the Shining Golden Vajra Bringing Back the Life of the Two Laws*. This account was told to this committee by the Tsangwa Tulku, Alak Chökyi Nangwa Rinpoché from Golok Dzamthang in Amdo, former abbot of the main Jonang Takten Phuntsok Ling Monastery near Shimla, capital of Himachal Pradesh, who was studying at the Sino-Tibetan Institute of Buddhist Studies in Beijing at that time.

But how does the fact that the Tenth Panchen Rinpoché distributed copies of the *Strict Directive for the Great Monastic Seat of Tashi Lhunpo* to the students of the Beijing Buddhist institute establish that he disliked Dölgyal? This directive has been mentioned earlier and a citation from it reproduced in a previous chapter. However, out of necessity it can be cited again. It states (121):

> Recently, there have been isolated cases of hostile spirits being channeled within the confines of the monastery. From now on, except for special cases such as Dharma protector Lhamo, no invocation through mediums will be allowed. Apart from those vajra protectors who possess the eyes of wisdom, when it comes to Dharma protectors, going for refuge to and relying on malicious ghosts who fly through the air—Dölgyal and the like—contradicts going for refuge as the gateway to the teachings of the Buddha.

Thus he deliberately distributed copies of the Tashi Lhunpo directive that actually named Dölgyal and contained strongly worded proscriptions of him.

Furthermore, the Publications Committee of the Chinese-Tibetan Institute of Higher Buddhist Studies compiled a list of ten monastic directives in *Opening the Doors to a Hundred Fields of Knowledge in the Land of Snow*, and the Tashi Lhunpo directive is included in this as well.

Moreover, the foreword present in all books of *Opening the Doors of a Hundred Ways in the Land of Snow* was personally written by the Tenth Panchen Rinpoché and is signed, "Written by Panchen Erti Chökyi Gyaltsen on the fifteenth day of the fourth month of the fire-rabbit year of the seventeenth cycle, or June 11, 1987."

On January 28, 1989, Panchen Rinpoché suddenly passed away, and although he was no longer alive, in February, the Publications Committee of the Chinese-Tibetan Institute of Higher Buddhist Studies immediately published a preface to the Tashi Lhunpo monastic directive, and in April the Peoples' Printing Press in Beijing printed the first edition of the directive.

Prior to his passing, Panchen Rinpoché must have instructed the Publications Committee that a stand-alone copy of the *Strict Directive for the Great Monastic Seat of Tashi Lhunpo* should be published soon. For while Panchen Rinpoché was alive, the work of the Publications Committee consisted of following and administrating his instructions.

If, as written in the colophon of the Dölgyal propitiation reproduced previously, the Tenth Panchen Rinpoché "comprehended through actual and inner experience that the time had come for a powerful protection of the teachings in general, and particularly the tradition of Jampal Nyingpo," and if, as written in the propitiation, he saw Dölgyal as the "supreme and natural expression of every pure and exalted wisdom combined as one," and if, as stated, Dölgyal took the pledge to protect the teachings in the presence of the second Buddha, Tsongkhapa, and lastly if he regarded Dölgyal as "the embodiment of all refuges" and meditated on him in that way, then it would simply have been impossible for him, having personally presented to his students a document that says, "going for refuge to and relying on malicious ghosts who fly through the air—Dölgyal and the like—contradicts going for refuge as the gateway to the teachings of the Buddha," to then say that in the future you must preserve and develop the teachings and the monasteries in the manner contained within this document. Similarly, how would it have been possible for thousands of copies of this directive to be continuously published and distributed?

Conclusions on the Propitiation

The author of the Dölgyal propitiation to which the name of the Tenth Panchen Rinpoché has been attached is someone who, as previously cited, holds Dölgyal as "the embodiment of all refuges." As to the manner of its composition, it is called *Song Effortlessly Accomplishing the Four Activities,* thus complementing the title of the Dölgyal invocation ascribed to the Great Fourteenth Dalai Lama, *Song of the Unstoppable Vajra.* Examining thoroughly these and other points, we can conclude that this invocation was merely ascribed to Panchen Rinpoché; it was not composed by the Tenth Panchen himself.

Likewise, right now it may not be possible to come to any conclusion on whether the Tenth Panchen Rinpoché was deceived by others and misled into relying upon Dölgyal when he left his birthplace in Amdo and came to Tsang at a very young age. However, after the Communist Chinese released him from prison, not only did the Panchen Rinpoché not rely upon Dölgyal, he had an intense dislike for him, as the evidence cited above establishes.

However, those who claim that Panchen Rinpoché was a Dölgyal practitioner even after he was released from prison by the Communist Chinese government are either speaking nonsense, having done no research at all, or are simply engaged in deliberate and baseless slander. Therefore, as Sakya Paṇḍita says in his *Jewel Treasury of Wise Sayings* (4.16):

> The wise know to use their own ascertainment,
> while the foolish follow whatever is popular.
> When the old dog howls,
> the others senselessly join in.

Had they been able to contemplate this verse beforehand, they would have been better off.

24. Advice from His Holiness the Dalai Lama 1978–98

June 13, 1978

The first set of extracts comes from a discourse on Dölgyal His Holiness gave to an audience that included the Namgyal Monastery abbot Losang Nyima, Geshé Losang Tenzin, twenty-two Namgyal staff and senior monks, five senior monks from Nechung Monastery, two teachers from the Dialectics School, two representatives from the Dharamsala branches of the Gyütö and Gyümé tantric colleges, as well as Ratö Khyongla Tulku and Nyakré Kalsang Yeshé, who lived in the United States and were given permission to attend.

In *Discourses on Dölgyal*, it says (1:8):

> Then I made a mistake. What was that mistake? The previous Dalai Lamas had their own way of doing things, and I was unable to follow them and stand on my own two feet. When I went to Dromo it was arranged that I stay at Dungkar Monastery. At that monastery there was a tradition of invoking through an oracle the wrathful Gyalchen and the peaceful Dulzin.[187] The oracle himself was not someone possessed of scholarly attributes, but when the spirit was invoked, it seems that the predictions were clear and effective.
>
> At that time, I had to leave Lhasa for Dromo suddenly. The Nechung oracle and the Gadong oracle were not in the retinue. In those days, except for the usual summer and winter invocations of Nechung and Gadong, I had not developed the closeness of inviting them privately in my rooms. Basically, up to that time, I been a child growing up. Never mind thinking for myself about deities, I could not generally think about much at all. Nevertheless, the Nechung and Gadong oracles were not there, and from our perspective it was a time of much trouble, as exemplified by the search for agreement between Tibet and China. Among the

officials present, there was one who suggested returning to Lhasa and some who recommended going on to India, and so on. This made any firm decision very difficult indeed.

At that time, there was a reliable medium for Dulzin close by. On one hand, from my side I had great faith in Jé Phabongkha, a factor which made me partial and close to Dulzin. Kyapjé Trijang Rinpoché also had great affection for Dulzin. That was also a factor. Anyway, several factors combined, and finally in my room at Dromo, Dulzin was invited by way of the medium.

During the invitation the *Hundred Deities of Tuṣita Guru Yoga* was chanted using the secret intonation of Takphu. During the actual possession the oracle wore the yellow monastic robe and a pandit hat. He looked very impressive. Facing me he prostrated like a falling tree. When I put to him the questions to be resolved, the answers were reasonably clear. At one time he said, "I have just come from Tuṣita, having asked for the thoughts of Jé Rinpoché." Thus he seemed very decisive, and he spoke impressively.

As I was about to return to Lhasa from Dromo, my intention to rely upon Gyalchen had grown stronger, and so in the reception room of Dungkar Monastery, I invited the wrathful Shukden and presented him with a new set of costumes that had been specially made.

My first connection with Gyalchen was like that. The first mistake of the Fourteenth Dalai Lama, which was that of not being able to stand on my own two feet and not being able to correctly follow the ways of the previous Dalai Lamas, was made at that time.

It goes on to state (1:12):

After that, using the painting belonging to Kyabjé Trijang Rinpoché as a copy, a new painting of Gyalchen was commissioned. This is also recounted in the autobiography of Kyabjé Trijang Rinpoché.[188]

And (1:13):

In a prediction during the time of the previous Dalai Lama,

Nechung had stated, "The much-needed stupa is left black, while the unneeded stone has been painted white." Likewise, I had not developed a deep and special connection with the five-emana-tion protector, and especially Dorjé Drakden, who have had a relation with the succession of past Dalai Lamas, and even further back, with Dharma King Trisong Detsen, and even further back than that, with King Könchok Bang. Here I was, however, developing a relationship with a new deity who had no responsibility for government affairs and no connection with the past Dalai Lamas.

However, I had began summoning Nechung and Gadong in my rooms just before I left for China, and from then on we have gradually become close and know each well. And, as the saying goes, "Deities and humans have the same behavior," so their predictions have become clearer. Asking the questions also has become easier.

Since then there has been no practical need to maintain a relationship with the Gyalchen of Chökhor Yangtsé Monastery[189] or others.

And (1:14):

In 1956, when I was about to leave for India and there were many objections and delaying tactics from the Chinese, Nechung declared, "There will be no problems. Your wishes will be effort-lessly fulfilled." And as he predicted, all ultimately went well.

Also, at that time, there was a lot of concern over whether I should return to Lhasa from India. Nechung and Gadong were summoned, and Nechung in particular gave a clear and decisive prediction that there was no purpose at all to staying in India and that it would be better to return to Tibet.

Then in 1959, during the uprising, Nechung was summoned several times. Finally, the time and date of escaping from the Nor-bulingka, the route to be followed, and so on, were all decided by Nechung, and everything went well with no mishaps. Gadong and Nechung—especially Nechung—were very trustworthy on important matters, definitely reliable.

Then I arrived in India. First, I stayed in Mussoorie and then

in Dharamsala. After a while I wanted to receive from Kyabjé
Trijang Rinpoché the Gyalchen life-entrustment, and so I made
a request to Trijang Rinpoché. At that time, someone, and I
can't think who it is, came and offered to Trijang Rinpoché a
good-quality copy of an old Ganden Monastery edition of *Great
Treatise on the Stages of the Path*. Trijang Rinpoché said that it
was necessary to have a copy of the *Great Treatise* during the
life-entrustment ceremony and that he would use this one. Thus
he set it aside.

One day, sometime after I had moved from Swarg Ashram
to Thekchen Chöling,[190] I summoned Nechung and Gadong.
During the possession Nechung said, "It is not right to rely upon
Asé Khyampo."

I wondered if he were speaking about Gyalchen Shukden,
because during the time of the Thirteenth Dalai Lama there was
talk of Shukden being referred to as Asé Khyampo. I put this
to Nechung, who replied that it did indeed refer to him. I said,
"These days there were many who rely upon Gyalchen, and if the
Nechung Dharma protector declares that it is wrong to rely upon
Gyalchen, the spiritual bond in the minds of many will become
defiled. Therefore, it would be best to keep quiet about this."

He agreed, and for about seven or eight years, until the publication of [Dzemé Rinpoché's] *Oral Transmission of the Brave
Father-Like Lama*, or *Yellow Book*, Nechung said not a word
about it.

And (1:16):

> From that time onward Nechung uttered not a single word about
> that matter. However, I had come to the realization that it would
> not be good to receive the Gyalchen life-entrustment.
>
> If I look at those days, I had a liking for Gyalchen. Also,
> because of the lineage of Kyabjé Phabongkha, I had loyalty. If you
> ask who is it under the heavens that is the one most acquainted
> with Nechung, forget about those with clairvoyance, generally
> among humans the one who has the greatest acquaintance with
> Nechung is me. Also, Nechung is probably the one who knows
> most about me. It is commonly said that Nechung encouraged

Gyalchen, and so therefore it is not possible for there to be any discord between the two. Trijang Rinpoché also said this in his *Commentary on the Praise of Shukden*. Such things are said. But whatever is right to say or not to say, the fact is that there is discord between Nechung and Gyalchen.

From my side if I had to choose between this old deity Nechung and this new deity Gyalchen, I would choose Nechung and never Gyalchen. Therefore, I thought not to seek the Gyalchen life-entrustment, and consequently I did not.

However, making decisions immediately is not a good thing to do, and so Serkong Rinpoché and I discussed the matter. I told him everything that had occurred around that time. This was the time when I was receiving a transmission of Atiśa's *Lamp for the Path to Enlightenment* from Serkong Rinpoché. We were taking tea between the teachings. During the discussions there was a loud thud on the roof, like a stone being thrown. Later I sought the advice of Yongzin Ling Rinpoché, telling him that such and such had happened and asking him what was best to do. Yongzin Rinpoché replied that this was a very important issue and that it was good not to seek the life-entrustment.

Because I had previously made a formal request for the life-entrustment, I explained in person to Trijang Rinpoché all that had occurred and informed him that now I would not be seeking the life-entrustment. At that time, although I had inwardly made the decision on receiving the life-entrustment, I made no change at all to the annual propitiation and the regular invocation, leaving them as they were.

And (1:27):

I thought to myself that up to now I had told Nechung, to put it bluntly, to be quiet. But now to continue with that would not be right. So one day in my rooms I summoned Nechung through the oracle and asked him clearly: "About eight or nine years ago, Nechung said that it was not right to rely upon Asé Khyampo. At that time, I told you sincerely that it would be best to say nothing about this. The Dharma protector on his part has maintained a respectful silence, and I thank you for that. However, now the other side are waving their hands and legs about and saying whatever they like. If I on this side were to keep Nechung from saying anything, that would not be right. Even in law if the opponent can say what they like and the other side is not allowed to say anything, that would not be just. So now Nechung from your side, say what you like. I will back you up."

In a relaxed manner, the Dharma protector went on to recount many stories about Gyalchen Shukden. In essence he was saying that it was more harmful than beneficial to rely upon Gyalchen Shukden, and that if you examine the kind of defamation or personal misfortune experienced by those who these days rely upon Gyalchen, and the unsuccessful outcomes of their endeavors, you find a lot of evidence. If there are Gyalchen practitioners who are yogis that have reached high levels of attainment, and who practice in secret, that is different, but generally, if the present practice is continued, there will be more loss than gain, more harm than good. In particular, relying upon Gyalchen Shukden risks offending and upsetting the mistress of the desire realm (Palden Lhamo).

This is what he said. So like that, I understood the situation regarding Gyalchen.

There had been a lot of talk about whether Nechung and Gyalchen were in accord, but this was the first time I had heard talk of Palden Lhamo being upset. If Lhamo is upset, that is a serious matter and a very important development. Therefore I thought it would be good to be completely sure.

This had all happened in the sixth or seventh month of the rabbit year (1975). I performed the regular invocation as usual. After that, at the end of winter, the dragon year would arrive, and it was the practice to perform the extensive propitiation at New Year. I thought I should seriously investigate whether I should do it. I had recently received the Jinasāgara Avalokiteśvara initiation from Trijang Rinpoché and was in retreat reciting the personal mantra of that deity as well as the six-syllable mantra.[191] At that time, the Namgyal Monastery abbot had gone to Varanasi for dental treatment and was not in Dharamsala. I decided that when he returned we would put on an elaborate offering ceremony for Lhamo and then perform a dough-ball divination rite.

I thought to myself that whatever the result of the divination, I would have to implement it. The focus of my mind would be determined by the divination.

The venerable abbot returned on the 15th or 16th of the twelfth month of the rabbit year (February 1976). On the 18th or 19th, I, the abbot, and about fifteen ritual Namgyal monks performed a propitiation for Lhamo. That day the weather was very stormy, and there was thunder and so on. Just before we rolled the dough balls for divination, we cited the enthronement text, and at the line, "enthroned as the main protector of yogis," there was a power outage and the lights went out. The electricity in Dharamsala was never that reliable, and so I thought maybe it would just be superstition to think it was anything other than that. On the other hand, if it were a sign, then it would be appropriate. Why? Because since the time of Gendun Drup, the First Dalai Lama, Palden Lhamo had been the only protector anyone ever needed and was a composite of every other protector. And yet I was not satisfied with her and was relying upon Gyalchen. Therefore, it was as if "enthroned as the main protector of yogis" were just dry words, while the reality was otherwise. So, if it were a sign, it would be very appropriate, I thought.

In the actual divination, three positions were considered. The first was, "Would it be good to continue relying upon Gyalchen?" If that came out, then I decided there would be no need to change the daily invocation of Gyalchen or the annual propitiation ceremonies. The second question was, "Would it be good to rely upon Gyalchen in secret?" If that position emerged from the divination, I thought that there would be no need to perform the propitiation with the monastery but that I would perform it alone, and I would continue the invocation as before. The third position was, "Would it be good to suspend relying upon Gyalchen?" If that were the case, then there would be no need to perform the propitiation or the invocation, and I would suspend them.

We each recited the mantra of the seven *bhyoḥ* syllables[192] a thousand times and chanted the enthronement rite. Recognizing the importance of what we were doing, we made strong heartfelt prayers and cast the three dough balls. The outcome was that it would be good to stop relying upon Gyalchen.

On the same day I offered a few names by way of dough-ball divination to see who should be appointed the new abbot of Namgyal, and the name of the venerable abbot came out.

After the divinations, from my point of view, it was decided what had to be done, and I felt happy. Likewise, all that Dharma protector Nechung had said had been proven completely correct. Therefore I gained a deep conviction and was astonished at the turn of events.

And (1:33):

Apart from that, in this matter, on one side was the imperious Gyalchen, and in particular my lama Trijang Rinpoché, and on the other side was Nechung and Lhamo. I was in the middle, not knowing how to act. It was very difficult.

And (1:34):

Personally, I felt as if my eyes had been opened on what was to be done regarding the practice of Gyalchen. I would now have to make evident changes to the annual propitiation ceremony performed with the monks from the monastery, and in doing so it would be wrong not to give some explanation. But I felt somewhat as if I could not do it and wondered how best to proceed. From my side, I was completely sure about what was to be done, but I was not sure if I should explain it to others. Therefore I performed a dice divination. I asked, "Is it better not to tell people the results of the dough-ball divination concerning the practice of Gyalchen, and so conceal it and say nothing, or would it be better to tell it to others?"

The reply was that it would be good to tell others.

And (1:39):

I think it was on the twelfth of the first month (March 11, 1976) that the precious tutor (Yongzin Ling Rinpoché) returned from Bodhgaya. I met him and told him everything that had happened. On the thirteenth Trijang Rinpoché returned from Mysore and

I met with him. I explained to him clearly and carefully all that had occurred.

Trijang Rinpoché said, "If that is what the dough-ball divination and Nechung has indicated, then it is true. There is no room for doubt. Nechung, for example, on critical issues gives completely reliable advice and is very clear on what should be done. Likewise with the dough-ball divinations, they were performed in front of the speaking Palden Lhamo painting. As the Fifth Dalai Lama passed away, Desi Sangyé Gyatso cried out in grief in his presence, wondering how many years he should keep his death secret. Although his breathing had ceased, he again revived and said, 'For unimportant matters you can decide for yourself. For the important issues, decide by dough-ball divination in front of the speaking Palden Lhamo painting that was the sacred object for Gendun Gyatso (Second Dalai Lama). It will not deceive you.'

"This is that very painting. There have never been any instances at all of unreliability in any divination made in its presence. It is definitely trustworthy. There really seems to be a reason for these declarations. However, the present discord between Lhamo and Gyalchen Shukden is probably connected with Tibetan spiritual and political affairs. Generally, though, there is no conflict at all between Lhamo and Shukden."

This is what he said.

And (1:41):

Then Trijang Rinpoché asked me whether it would be good to give the painting to a Gyalchen practitioner. I did not recall having a painting of Gyalchen. I had forgotten about it. I wondered whether it would be correct to give it to someone else immediately. Perhaps it would be better to for it to remain together with the other scroll paintings. If for some reason I could not keep it, I would offer it to Trijang Rinpoché. I told Rinpoché that I would decide by dough-ball divination or I would ask Nechung to see whether I should keep it.

The fourteenth was the day of the annual New Year's summoning of Nechung in my rooms, and so there I put my question to him. I said that the recent pronouncements of the Dharma protector and those of the dough-ball divinations were in complete agreement, and so I was very happy. From my side I would follow this course of action. I said that I owned a painting of Gyalchen. If it were all right to keep it, I would do so. If not, I would offer it to Trijang Rinpoché. I asked him what was best.

He replied wrathfully, "It must be expelled now from the residence of the master who is meaningful to behold!"

Immediately after the ceremony I sent a ritual assistant to offer the painting to Trijang Rinpoché. With that I had made a clean break. That was one chapter of the story.

And (1:42):

In the mid-summer of the Dragon year (1976) I was to give the great Kālacakra initiation in Ladakh. Before that I received a request for divination from Jangtsé College of Ganden Monastery. It said that recently there had been much misfortune in the college, and many students were suffering from adversities. Divinations had indicated that generally these were acts of recrimination from a protector. The college had recently asked for advice from Trijang Rinpoché and consequently had produced new ritual sacraments for Palden Lhamo and performed an elaborate offering ceremony for her to that end. They asked me to now do a divination to see whether Lhamo was displeased.

The source of this request for divination was the college of Serkong Rinpoché, a college dedicated to preserving the teachings and a place of study and training. It is because of the kindness of the studies and learning pursued in Ganden Jangtsé that these days I can call upon the services of many like Serkong Rinpoché and the venerable abbot who are willing to do whatever they are asked. Now if there was to be trouble and deterioration in a college of such learning and study, that would bring harm to the teachings of Jé Tsongkhapa, and that would be an important matter. They had asked me to help with a matter they had not resolved. I thought that if I were to make a hasty dice divination, and the matter was decided that way, that would not be right. Therefore, considering its importance, I performed a dough-ball divination. I asked, "Are the continuing troubles in Jangtsé College the result of Lhamo being displeased or not?"

"They are the result of Lhamo being displeased," came the answer.

I asked again, "Is the cause of Lhamo being displeased some other factor, or is it the widespread reliance on Gyalchen?"

"It is the widespread reliance on Gyalchen," was the reply.

The result had indicated first that Lhamo was displeased, and second that the cause of her displeasure was the widespread reliance on Gyalchen, and so again I had confirmation. However, if I were to write this in the reply to the college, I could not predict how it would be seen and what people would think. If I did not write it, that would not be right either because a critical matter had arisen in the college and they had written to me about it, and I would be telling them other than the truth. It was a difficult decision indeed.

And (1:44):

During the annual progress conference of the dragon year, the Loseling abbot Yeshé Thupten, the Jangtsé abbot Gendun Sangpo, and the Sera Jé abbot Lekden were there, and I gave them a full explanation of the matter. I asked Jangtsé abbot Gendun Sangpo what had happened at Jangtsé. He said that he had made changes in the assembly recitations and so on. After I had given this full explanation to them, it seems that the venerable abbot introduced a few more restrictions in the monastery.

Then, as I was about to leave for South India last year, I received a second request for divination from Jangtsé. It said that all the prayers suggested in the reply to last year's divination had been completed and asked me to perform a divination to see whether Lhamo's displeasure had abated and all had been settled.

I took this very seriously. Usually when I make important journeys, I make thousandfold offerings to Lhamo. Therefore, alongside the elaborate offering ceremony, I performed a dough-ball divination. I asked whether Lhamo's displeasure had been pacified. The reply came back that it had not.

I asked, "In that case, would it be best to offer an assembly confession and propitiation to Lhamo, or would it be better to strengthen the restrictions on Gyalchen practice?"

"The restrictions on relying upon Gyalchen must be tightened," was the reply.

And (1:48):

Whatever the case, from the dough-ball divinations and declarations of Nechung, I gained certainty in the unfolding of these events. Likewise, when I examined the accounts and the events I myself had witnessed, it was clear that something strange was certainly happening.

Essentially, the indication I had gotten from the incidental questions put to Nechung when summoned is that one of the main reasons for Lhamo's displeasure is as follows: The protectors entrusted to guard the Geluk teachings are the three protectors of the three types of practitioners on the graded path to enlightenment.[193] However, not being content with those three, it seems that a new protector has become more popular than all the others. This is one cause of Palden Lhamo's displeasure. Another is that the exclusive protector appointed and trusted by the succession of previous Dalai Lamas is Lhamo, and now there is reliance upon a new imperious spirit who seems to be in competition with her. That is also a basis for Lhamo's displeasure.

And (1:49):

I asked Nechung, "In that case, what about Kyabjé Phabongkha, who is truly a yogi, a genuine lama with realizations. He accepted Gyalchen as a genuine protector. He also possessed the lineage of the life-entrustment that came from Takphu Vajradhara, who met Dulzin Drakpa Gyaltsen in his visions. How is this to be explained?"

The Dharma protector replied decisively. Referring to Kyabjé Phabongkha as "a great holder of secret knowledge," he said, "In the latter part of his life the great holder of secret knowledge made great mistakes, but I, Gyalpo Pehar, bear no grudge. If you examine the misfortunes that occurred in the latter stages of his life, you will understand. His incarnation died in India, and if you examine the bad omens that occurred at that time, you will come to know. Moreover, the deeds performed by his future incarnations will not come to successful completion."

Many people know that not everything turned out well for Kyabjé Phabongkha, and in the minds of many it was due to the Nyingma and other traditions casting spells on him because of his great achievements as the vanguard of the Geluk tradition. Thus they put the blame on the Nyingma. But the reality seems to be other than that. It appears that the red and black protectors [Nechung and Palden Lhamo] were punishing him.

Concerning pure visions, Nechung said, "There are two types. There are those received by way of divine blessings of the three sources,[194] and there are pure visions received by the power of hindrances. I wonder if this is not a pure vision received by the power of hindrances?"

Such was the critical situation, and there are some other matters I cannot discuss.

Some years ago, around the time Nechung made his first declaration, I had a dream in which Kyabjé Phabongkha told me that I should receive the Gyalchen life-entrustment. Ling Rinpoché's attendant appeared and said that would be all right to do so. However, there was a scar on Phabongkha's arm that was bleeding. I felt scared and very uncomfortable. Now when I think about it I feel confident that it was the work of some kind of hindrance. But I digress.

These events I have described were hugely critical in nature, and I was unable to bear the responsibility alone. First, I told everything in great detail to Yongzin Ling Rinpoché. He was not that concerned. Then I told everything to Trijang Rinpoché. Not telling Trijang Rinpoché would have been unthinkable, but when I got there I felt as though I dared not tell him.

However, up to the present, the deeds and life of Trijang Rinpoché have been wonderfully complete. Nevertheless, for as long as the teachings of the Buddha are present in Tibet, his incarnations, by way of his firm bodhicitta pledge, must appear. From our side, we must pray and wish for that. It would not be good if things did not turn out well.

On Trijang Rinpoché's reliance upon Gyalchen, this is not a new practice of this life. He relied on him in his previous life. There is no need at all for him to renounce the practice. However, Lhamo is to be recognized as preeminent, and below her is the five-emanation protector. If we use the example of a family estate, he is to be regarded as the manager in charge of the money and with the main responsibility for the estate. Shukden is like an ordinary caretaker below him. Whatever the case, regarding him like a birth deity or local deity and making offerings and asking for assistance, I don't think that is unacceptable.

Anything other than that, such as making him the main focus, thinking of him as having equal or even greater status than the five-emanation protector, runs the risk of displeasing the five-emanation protector. Kyabjé Phabongkha was an inconceivably great lama, but it seems this is what happened to him. I clearly asked Trijang Rinpoché to consider all this.

And (1:52):

In that way primarily, the two tutors came to know and fully comprehended the situation and events. I told Trijang Rinpoché that this was very important information regarding Gyalchen. Now that I was placing some restriction on Gyalchen, there would be people, some more knowledgeable than others, who would come to him and ask his advice. As he was fully apprised of the whole situation, I requested that he must give them appropriate advice. One word of advice from Trijang Rinpoché would be far more beneficial to a Gyalchen practitioner than a hundred or a thousand explanations from me.

Gyalchen is primarily relied on by Trijang Rinpoché. Therefore, were he to give an explanation, having comprehended the reasons, Gyalchen practitioners would have faith in it. I might give an explanation, but there would be those who believed it and those who didn't. Therefore, I said to Trijang Rinpoché that it would be excellent if he were to give advice. I also asked Tutor Ling Rinpoché to give advice.

And (1:54):

> People may come with all kinds of information. If the occasion arises that you have to give an explanation, then what I have just told you are simply the bare facts. If you explain on the basis of this information, then if they are unbiased and given to reasoning, they may well come to an understanding. Therefore, if the occasion arises for you to give explanations and you do so, that is good.

June 25, 1980

The next extract is from a discourse given at a conference of senior monks that included abbots, lamas, and officials from Ganden and Drepung monasteries as well as those from the Sakya and Nyingma traditions.

In *Discourses on Dölgyal* (1:63):

> On this issue, I have reported all the events, from start to finish, to Kyabjé Trijang Rinpoché. He is aware of them all, and it is certainly not the case that I have spoken about something behind his back without his knowledge.
>
> The root source of all of this is the dough-ball divinations done in the presence of Lhamo and the declarations of Dharma protector Dorjé Drakden (Nechung). Take Nechung, for example. From his own experience Trijang Rinpoché accepts him as authentic. He said, "In matters of great importance he will never let you down. There is definitely a reason he said these things."
>
> Similarly, when I told him the of the outcomes of all the dough-ball divinations, he said, "There is total reliability in dough-ball divinations performed in the presence of Lhamo. There must be some inconceivable reason for these." He did not say something like, "That is strange. I wonder what that can mean."
>
> This put my mind at ease.

July 18, 1980

The next three extracts are from a discourse given at a conference at Sera Monastery to current and former abbots of Sera Jé and Sera Mé colleges, officials, senior monks, and the Bylakuppe Youth Congress Standing Committee.

In *Discourses on Dölgyal*, it says (1:74):

> In this life Trijang Rinpoché's work and activities have been successful. But it is not certain what will happen in future lives, and so I asked him to please consider all this. In this matter I have not been like those who will not say something to your face but go and say it behind your back, or bully when possible and shrink away when it is not. In general, that is how things are.
>
> Whether you are from Sera Jé or Sera Mé colleges, or whatever individual monastic house you are from, you should hold primarily to the protector appointed and entrusted by the founder of that monastic college or house. It is unnecessary to create more and more. If on a personal level, through one's individual karma, there is a reason well established by actual results, that is an exception. Otherwise, if you involve yourselves in these various practices, it will turn out for the worse rather than for the good.
>
> I nearly did this. Even someone with the epithet "all-knowing conqueror" was about to fall under the spell of ignorance. There is also the risk that you will fall under it too. Everyone should take care.
>
> Fundamentally, the history of Gyalchen has been to establish Gyalchen as an authentic protector by using Nechung as its root source. There are accounts that he was invoked by Nechung at the outset, that he later petitioned Panchen Sönam Drakpa, and that finally Nechung orchestrated the circumstances of Tulku Drakpa Gyaltsen's fate. If we are going to use Nechung for support, then right now there is no one under the sky who knows Nechung better than I do, and as far as I can see, having thought about it and examined, I can find no support from Nechung at all.

And (1:75):

> I am not clairvoyant, but I have thoroughly examined this matter from all sides. Maybe I am stubborn. Even with something said by a lama, I ask myself, "What did Jé Tsongkhapa say?" And I will

compare it and analyze it. Similarly, I do not immediately accept as fact what one Dharma protector says. I think about it and even cast a divination. I make sure, and I do not do things hastily. That is my nature.

And (1:78):

The practice of the Kadam tradition[195] is the best. They had four deities. As is said, "The Bhagavan Buddha because he is the founder of the teachings, Noble Avalokiteśvara because he is the deity of great compassion, Venerable Tara because she is the deity of action, and Acala because he is the deity who removes obstacles." On top of that were the three baskets of scripture or the three types of practitioner. These are the seven deities and dharmas of the Kadampa. There was no elaboration in the form of incense purification ceremonies or golden vessel libation rites for various spirits. Also, we have not achieved realizations like those of the past lamas. We perform all these offerings and ceremonies that past lamas never did, and we gain no divine assistance or special powers.

So that is what I have to say about Gyalchen. There is no real need to tell all this to others.

April 8, 1983

The next extract is from a talk in Bomdila Tenzin Gang to an audience of about fifty, primarily represented by the monks of the Gyütö Tantric College, as well as nuns and lay people, after the conferment of the initiations of Guhyasamāja, Cakrasaṃvara, and Vajrabhairava (1:89):

Generally speaking, from the perspective of the Geluk tradition, Mahākāla and Dharmarāja are preeminent. If any Geluk practitioner is someone whose life goes hand in hand with their practice, there is no need for many different Dharma protectors. With Six-Armed Mahākāla and oath-bound Dharmarāja, nothing is not possible, nothing is missing. For our connection with the common purpose of Tibet, Palden Lhamo and the five-emanation protector are important.

March 3, 1986

The next two extracts are from a discourse in the Dharamsala Thekchen Chöling temple during a teaching on the Guru Puja (1:108).

As it says in the *Extensive Prayer for the Excellent Geluk Tradition*:[196]

> The main protectors of the three scopes of practice,[197]
> swift-acting Mahākāla, Vaiśravaṇa, and Dharmarāja.

Six-Armed Mahākāla, who is Avalokiteśvara in wrathful aspect in the form of a protector, is primarily the protector of practitioners of advanced scope.

Purely guarding one's ethical behavior is the prime cause for pleasing Vaiśravaṇa. Basically, all nonworldly protectors[198] are pleased by ethical behavior, but this characterization applies to Vaiśravaṇa in particular. The practice of the intermediate scope teaches the three higher trainings,[199] and from those three it primarily teaches the training in ethics. Therefore, Vaiśravaṇa is the protector for those of intermediate scope.

In the practices of the lowest scope, casting off bad deeds and taking on the good in accordance with the law of cause and effect is of greatest importance. Oath-bound Dharmarāja decides between good and bad deeds, as it is said, "Adjudicating the good and the bad, taking the lives of oath-violators." Therefore he is the protector for those whose practice is in common with the lowest scope.

Whatever the case, relying upon a protector within the Geluk tradition should be in keeping with the path you follow. In the special case of Jé Tsongkhapa, his protectors were Mahākāla and Dharmarāja.

And (1:110):

> Sometimes as a joke I say, "If one day it is said within the Geluk tradition that Dharmarāja has died, and requests have been

received for his dedication prayers, then the Geluk will have to start looking for a new protector. Until then there is no need for other protectors." There is some point to that.

December 27, 1986

The next advice comes from a discourse during a Guhyasamāja initiation by way of a powder mandala at Ganden Jangtsé in Mundgod, South India, to an audience of over two thousand, mainly monks from Ganden and Drepung monasteries (1:122):

> I think like this. The special characteristics of Jé Tsongkhapa should be known by way of the eighteen volumes of his collected works. This means by way of what he said with regard to the difficult points of sutra and tantra to bring out the profound features of the teachings and to enrich them. To arrogantly argue for the profundity of the Geluk tradition without knowing anything at all about the truly blessed words of Jé Rinpoché is very sad. If you want to show loyalty, know how to be loyal. Loyalty based on reasoning is best.

And (1:124):

> In the Geluk tradition the actual protectors of Jé Tsongkhapa are Six-Armed Mahākāla and oath-bound Dharmarāja. Of these he entrusted himself to the Dharmarāja inner practice. Jé Rinpoché would not place his trust in an incapable protector. He relied on a capable protector. When oath-bound Dharmarāja has passed away, and we receive requests for his dedication prayers, then the Geluk will need a new protector. Otherwise, until oath-bound Dharmarāja dies, the Geluk has no need for other protectors. That is what I say. Do you understand?

March 21, 1996

The next extract comes from a discourse in Dharamsala's Thekchen Chöling temple on the preparatory day of the Secret Hayagrīva initiation and its secret practice (1:160):

Jé Phabongkha's stance on Gyalchen is clear from his collected works. There are some from the Nyingma tradition and elsewhere who say that Kyabjé Phabongkha Rinpoché is probably a manifestation of the demon Rudra. That is completely untrue. Kyabjé Phabongkha was the teaching master of the stages of the path literature. He was truly an authentic lama who had developed bodhicitta in his mind. When you mention his name among Nyingma and Kagyü practitioners, those who condemn him do not understand this.

How did such condemnation come about? Dölgyal brought only ruin to the work of Jé Phabongkha and never any good. Because of that, even toward the excellent works of Jé Rinpoché (Tsongkhapa), people say dismissively, "Oh, they are Gelukpa works," and other strange things.

Kyabjé Trijang Rinpoché is my root lama. I had single-pointed faith in him. Even in my dreams I meet him again and again as my lama and have excellent connection with him. That is very clear. However, Kyabjé Trijang Rinpoché relied strongly on Gyalchen, whereas I criticized it. When Kyabjé Rinpoché was alive, whatever unfolded, whatever I had investigated, I told him all of it in great detail. Kyabjé Rinpoché from his side said, "There is total reliability in dough-ball divinations performed in the presence of Lhamo." Similarly, in connection with Nechung, he clearly said that in matters of importance, Nechung is trustworthy.

In *Great Treatise on the Stages of the Path* it says, "With wholesome deeds, act accordingly. With unwholesome deeds, act contrarily." Likewise, in Aśvaghoṣa's *Fifty Verses on Guru Devotion*, it states:

If within reason, you cannot do it,
excuse yourself verbally
from what you cannot do.

Consequently, while Kyabjé Rinpoché was alive I asked him to please investigate, saying that this practice was of not much benefit, and moreover it should be expunged.

This is what happened. From the beginning, I reported the whole sequence of events to him, and he listened. He was aware of them. It wasn't that I thought of these things and spoke about them when my lama was no longer alive.

Some people say that the Dalai Lama has destroyed his guru devotion. It doesn't matter what they say. I am an ordinary monk of the Buddha. If I guard my precepts well, people can say what they like. There is nothing more than that.

December 1, 1997

His Holiness made the following comments at a large public gathering at Sera Monastery in South India (1:286):

Some of you might say that relying upon Dölgyal brings success and wealth. That is a mistake. To say that something is special just because it brings in a little money is a sign of not understanding the essence of the teachings of the Buddha.

Some say that this restriction opposes the precept that one's faith is one's choice and that I am not giving you that opportunity. In reality, imposing this restriction protects the precept that one's faith is one's choice. The situation and occurrences in mentioned in the letter written by Khyentsé Chökyi Lodrö[200] that I referred to earlier did not only happen in Kham. There were also incidents in Tsang, Lhokha (in Central Tibet), and elsewhere. Since we arrived in India, there have been many similar incidents. Those who know about these incidents are alive today.

Some say that if a Gelukpa relies on such a deity and practices the tenets of other traditions such as Nyingma and Kagyü, Jé Tsongkhapa will become angry. He will not get angry, but these things are said.

If you say that it is not necessary to wet your lips with other traditions because in the eighteen volumes of Jé Tsongkhapa's compositions there is nothing lacking, nothing that is incorrect with regard to the sutras and tantras, this is a good reason. Other than that, to say that if a Gelukpa follows the practices of the Nyingma or the Kagyü, they will be harmed by a demon or by a deity, and that such scare-mongering is pure Geluk doctrine, is nonsense. It is laughable.

I am putting things right here. I thought I would make good

the teachings of the Buddha in general and specifically the teachings of Mañjunātha Tsongkhapa. Some people pretentiously say that the Dalai Lama is damaging the Geluk tradition. I don't see it that way. To my mind, I am actually cleaning up the doctrine of Mañjunātha Tsongkhapa. It would be excellent if this great lama's teachings, which however you look at them come out as pure within and pure without, were to remain with us. No fault can be found within the eighteen excellent volumes of Jé Tsongkhapa's compositions. There weren't any found six hundred years ago, and there aren't any found today. However, when it is said that this Geluk deity is very harmful, then I take a stand.

This deity has no benefit. Think about this, and don't be stupidly stubborn or pitifully small-minded.

And (1:289):

Whatever the case, this advice I have given you is probably not wrong. In ten, twenty, or even a hundred years' time, I think it will be clear that these decisions were right. I don't think anyone will say that because of these decisions, such and such mistake occurred.

August 27, 1998

This extract is from a discourse to the tenth conference of the Tibetan Youth Congress (1:298):

Anyone who is unbiased and learned would praise the teachings of Jé Tsongkhapa. Several Nyingmapas have done that. There are those from the Kagyü and Sakya traditions also. If you think about the qualities of the Geluk teachings, which are the scriptural teachings and the teachings on the realizations as determined by the Mañjunātha Tsongkhapa, they are totally commendable and no one can find any cause for censure in them.

These days those who rely upon Dölgyal say that if you are a Gelukpa and you take up practices from the Nyingma and other traditions, Dölgyal will destroy you. Because of that, antagonism has developed between the traditions. This is very clear.

September 10, 1998

This final extract from volume 1 of His Holiness's *Discourses on Dölgyal* is taken from a discourse he delivered to listeners from the three regions of Tibet attending a Guru Puja (1:310):

> To the past Dalai Lamas and to me, Nechung has been very special. However, he is a worldly spirit, and I rely upon him as an imperious spirit. If we look at Nechung Dorjé Drakden, no one among the Kagyü, Nyingma, Sakya, and Geluk would say that this five-emanation protector is not reliable. However, he is placed in the category of spirit and not in the category of an object of refuge.
>
> As for Dölgyal, there is disagreement over what kind of spirit he is. The Great Fifth Dalai Lama considered him to be an oath-violator born of perverted prayers. Phurchok Ngawang Jampa, Trichen Ngawang Chokden, Yongzin Yeshé Gyaltsen, Thuken Chökyi Nyima, and others considered him to be a "king spirit."[201] Panchen Tenpai Wangchuk makes that very clear. The previous Sakya masters saw him as a "custodian of wealth." Never was he regarded as an object of refuge.
>
> In more recent times, those who belong to the Dölgyal followers in England regard Dölgyal as a meditation deity. They say that the essence of Geluk practice is the worship of Dölgyal. I told them this is not correct. Such a perception is a huge error. When they say they want the freedom to follow the Dharma they choose, this is not what "following the Dharma" means at all.
>
> If these followers of Dölgyal say, "We are not Gelukpas," thereby setting up a new Dharma in the twenty-first century, that is their right. I have nothing to say about that. What I would say is that if you are claiming to be Buddhist, specifically a Gelukpa, then to do these things that go against the general Geluk doctrine is not right.
>
> If they say they are not Gelukpa, or that they are but they are a present-day special Geluk tradition, or that they are different

to and superior to the Geluk tradition, I have nothing to say to that. But to say that they are those who follow the guidelines determined by Mañjunātha Lama Tsongkhapa and his disciples and yet to do such things, this is not in accordance with the presentation of general Geluk teachings and is not right. This is what I say.

25. Advice from His Holiness the Dalai Lama 2000–2010

December 6, 2000

THE SECOND VOLUME of His Holiness's *Discourses on Dölgyal* records a discourse he delivered to the second conference of the Geluk International Foundation in Dharamsala (2:17):

> Now, let us look at Dölgyal. This title, protector of the teachings of Mañjunātha Tsongkhapa, when was it first awarded? Who awarded it? Did an authentic scholar-practitioner lama formally entrust him and appoint him to such a position? We should look at these things. Kyabjé Phabongkha Rinpoché did not appoint him. Instead Dölgyal threatened him, and from fear he stopped listening to *Excellent Wish-Fulfilling Vase*.[202] That is not good.
>
> Rikgya Rinpoché in his previous life relied heavily upon Dölgyal. At that time, I did too. Rinpoché would joke, "This Dharma protector is unlike any other. From the officials in the government and all the lamas and geshés, he takes hold of the most important ones!"
>
> Later the labrang gave up the practice. His attendant told me that the previous Rikgya's practice of Dölgyal was not a practice stemming from a positive source. When Rinpoché was young, Dölgyal had harmed him and made him ill. Fearful of further harm, he took up the practice. That is sad, isn't it?

And (2:22):

> Whatever the case, among the deeds of Kyabjé Phabongkha Rinpoché and Kyabjé Trijang Rinpoché, I think those involving

Dölgyal were a mistake. This minor, and not so beneficial, part of their activities did not accord with the teachings in general. However, there is simply no one who, by pointing to a small error on their part, could possibly criticize them by dismissing their activities of preserving, developing, and spreading the doctrine, such as their vast teachings on mind training, stages of the path teachings, teachings on tantra in general, and specifically those of the mother tantra Cakrasaṃvara, with deity and consort, all of which are completely in accord with the teachings of the Buddha and the thinking of Mañjunātha Tsongkhapa in particular. Do you understand?

In the homage of Haribhadra's *Clarification of the Meaning*, a commentary on the Perfection of Wisdom sutras, it says:

Vasubandhu, a friend working for the welfare of others,
with his own disposition as influence,
relied on all existence being within
and commentated accordingly.

After that it says:

Vimuktisena, within the ranks of the ārya beings,
realized that it was not as Vasubandhu had done
and opened it up with a mind that dwelled in
   Madhyamaka.

Ārya Vimuktisena's guru, Ācārya Vasubandhu, commentated on Maitreya's *Ornament of Realization*, a text that "dwells in Madhyamaka," according to the Cittamātra position. This reflected Vasubandhu's "own inclination." Ārya Vimuktisena realized that this was not the thinking of *Ornament of Realization* and commented on it from a Madhyamaka perspective. Would it be acceptable, on that basis, to say that Ārya Vimuktisena destroyed his guru devotion? Of course not. Did Ārya Vimuktisena show disrespect to Ācārya Vasubandhu? He did not.

Similarly, the glorious Atiśa's root guru, in dependence on whom he developed the mind of enlightenment, was Suvarṇadvīpa. This guru's philosophical view was that of the Cittamātra school. There is a story of how Guru Suvarṇadvīpa told Atiśa that his view was not right, and that when Guru Suvarṇadvīpa said this, the Madhyamaka view Atiśa held in his mind grew stronger.

Ācārya Dignāga, who was wiser in epistemology than his own guru Vasubandhu, had a disciple named Ācārya Īśvarasena, who in turn had Ācārya Dharmakīrti as a disciple. When Dharmakīrti heard Dignāga's *Compendium of Valid Cognition*, he realized that Īśvarasena had not understood Dignāga's thinking. He asked and received permission from Īśvarasena to present some of his teacher's own teachings as the views of an opponent and then set about refuting them.

These masters were putting right texts of the Buddha's doctrine. In this way, even though it was from their own gurus, if it did not accord with the thinking of the teachings of the Buddha, it had to be explained in another way.

Setting straight something that does not accord with the thinking of the scriptures, whether that is because of a disciple or there is some purpose behind it, is the way of the learned. Doing this ensures that the teachings do not perish.

And (2:31):

If we examine the reason, one year I asked Nechung, "This Dölgyal life-entrustment was given by Takphu Vajradhara, and it was pure vision received by him, and so isn't it trustworthy?"

The protector replied, "There are pure visions received by way of divine blessings of the three sources, and there are pure visions received by the power of hindrances. I wonder whether this is a pure vision received by the power of hindrances."

Ling Rinpoché told me that Phabongkha Rinpoché had told him that there were some Bön teachings included in the collected works of Takphu Vajradhara as requested by his disciples and that later, he, Phabongkha Rinpoché, took them out in an attempt to keep the collection pure. This probably proves that these visions were result of hindrances.

August 2, 2001

This extract comes from a discourse in Sera Monastery (2:40):

> You braved many hardships and dangers to come from Tibet to
> the monasteries in India in order to study, not to worship dei-
> ties and nāgas. In recent times three good monks, epitomized
> by the teacher at the Dialectics School,²⁰³ have been killed by
> newcomers from Tibet, who were thoughtless individuals pos-
> ing as monks. These are forever shameful, disgraceful, despica-
> ble acts.
>
> There are some followers of Dölgyal who say that I have no
> respect for Trijang Rinpoché and that my guru devotion has
> been lost. That is pitiable, a claim made from ignorance. I had a
> connection with Kyabjé Rinpoché from when I was six until he
> passed away. He was my lama. He was immeasurably kind to me.
> I had the closest acquaintance with whatever was in his mind.
> Also, whatever I was thinking and whatever position I held,
> Kyabjé Rinpoché had full knowledge of.
>
> Most of those who are finding fault never met Kyabjé Rin-
> poché or heard his teachings. They are being used by others. They
> become deceived and then just crazily jump in and say all these
> various things.

December 2, 2002

This next extract comes from a discourse delivered at the Tibetan Children's
Home in Bylakuppe, South India, to the teachers, staff, and children as well
as to many monastics and laypeople (2:45):

> Fundamentally, I am speaking to you out of concern from my
> own experience. There is no particular profit in all of this for me.
> I know many will not be pleased with what I say. However, I have
> responsibility in both the secular and religious arenas, and so my
> aim is to avert any unwarranted criticism of the teachings of Bud-
> dha in general and the teachings of the Mañjunātha Tsongkhapa
> in particular. So I am speaking to you about these things as a con-
> cerned friend. Whether you listen is up to you. I am not here to

plead. You can do exactly the opposite, and I will say nothing. All right?

How then does it affect our religious and secular affairs? Is there profit or loss? Does it benefit or harm the teachings of the Mañjunātha Lama? And what is the profit or loss for us as individuals? We must ask ourselves these questions.

It has been difficult for recent incarnations of great lamas who practiced Dölgyal to find success in their activities and lives. If you research this, you will understand. If you remain ignorant and yet still insist, well, that is another matter.

December 6, 2002

His Holiness made the following comments to the governing council of Drepung Monastery while commemorating the 360th anniversary of the founding of the Ganden Phodrang government (2:49):

> The conclusions I have arrived at were reached by investigations made on all levels over the years, by thinking about the reasons, and so on. In particular, while the two tutors still graced us with their presence, I reported all events to them in detail. Kyabjé Ling Rinpoché supported me one hundred percent. Kyabjé Trijang Rinpoché was a Dölgyal practitioner, but because I had come to these conclusions, especially because they were conclusions reached by dough-ball divination, he said that there can be no deception in dough-ball divinations and thus there must be a good reason for these pronouncements.

And (2:51):

> Of the six million Tibetans, more than 99 percent of them will, upon reflection, follow the truth. It would be difficult to find those who would follow lies and pretenses. Therefore, if you, in this one short life, can follow the lead set by the six million Tibetans, that would be wise. Otherwise, if you go your own way, the loss will be yours, and you will become like a white crow in this life. Also, in the next life, as I said at Sera, you run the risk of being reborn in the entourage of a demon. Does that make

sense? If you worship a ghost, the result could well be rebirth as a ghost. This is not good at all. It is a disgrace for the followers of the teachings of Mañjunātha Tsongkhapa, and it is hard to see any benefit in it at all.

January 7, 2004

These two extracts are from a discourse in the Orissa Tibetan settlement (2:53):

> If you are excessive in your propitiation of gods and nāgas, not only do you accumulate the fault of contravening the refuge precepts in your mind, there is a danger of your refuge becoming meaningless. Relying upon and propitiating worldly spirits in general, and particularly this controversial Gyalchen Shukden, an oath-violator born from perverse prayers, is to gather karma destructive in this and future lives, and to both self and others.
>
> Teaching without error the points of practice, in the form of what is to be developed and what is to be discarded, is my responsibility. Whether people listen is their choice.
>
> In the case of Dölgyal Shukden, the result of propitiation is discord among the followers of the Buddha.

And (2:59):

> As is evident, many who supplicate Dölgyal have a particularly nasty character. This is very clear. The principal of the Dialectics School was stabbed sixteen times before he died. When the police were looking for the murderers of the venerable teacher, they found evidence that they had burned their clothes on the roof of the building where they had been staying, suggesting that their clothes had been covered with blood. They left Delhi, and via Nepal sought refuge with the Chinese, then fled to Tibet.
>
> Some Dölgyal followers have organized themselves into a group and continue to oppose and protest the government and the people wherever they can. In India there have been many incidents of attacks on people from settlement leaders down to

ordinary people. Recently the Ganden chant leader[204] was sent intimidating letters and photographs. Still these attacks continue.

March 26, 2004

The next three extracts come from a discourse in Dharamsala's Thekchen Chöling temple during an initiation into Cakrasaṃvara Body Mandala in the Ghaṇṭapāda tradition (2:62):

> He [Phabongkha Rinpoché] was a master of the stages of the path, the mind-training teachings, and a master of the Cakrasaṃvara male and female deity teachings. He was a completely qualified lama. He was tainted by way of Dölgyal, but he was a completely qualified lama.
>
> Fundamentally, as everything exists only in dependence upon something else, in some contexts things are established as method and in other contexts they are established as wisdom. Likewise, in terms of their practice of Dölgyal, Kyabjé Phabongkha Rinpoché was mistaken, and Kyabjé Trijang Rinpoché was likewise mistaken. It was not merely a mistake; it also harmed their life and work. But to cast Kyabjé Phabongkha Rinpoché and Kyabjé Trijang Rinpoché into the category of mistaken lamas on the basis of their error is completely wrong. They were inconceivable lamas. To cite their inconceivable qualities as a reason to revere whatever they did as good, however, goes against the teachings in general. This has been a digression, but I thought it necessary to say.

And (2:63):

> The incarnation of Kyabjé Trijang Rinpoché has said that his reliance on Dölgyal was a distinctive practice of the former incarnation. This is not right. If we are to count the distinctive practices of Kyabjé Trijang Rinpoché, they would be the practices of male and female deity Cakrasaṃvara, and the essentials of the stages of the path corpus and the mind-training literature. It is difficult to say that relying upon a controversial worldly spirit constitutes a distinctive practice.

And (2:65):

> Let me tell you a story of when Kyabjé Trijang Rinpoché was
> alive. Kyabjé Trijang Rinpoché and the previous incarnation of
> Karmapa Rinpoché were very close. They would often joke and
> tease each other. Kyabjé Rinpoché and I would meet often. On
> one of these meetings, he said to me, "Yesterday Karmapa Rin-
> poché arrived at my residence unexpectedly, and I had to sud-
> denly rush around."
>
> "What was the rush?" I asked.
>
> He replied, "Yesterday I was performing the monthly propi-
> tiation of the protector. I had all the offerings set up when word
> came that Karmapa Rinpoché had suddenly shown up. Karmapa
> Rinpoché does not like the protector. Therefore I had to gather
> up all the offerings in a hurry."
>
> If it is a protector of the Geluk, and a Nyingma lama arrives, it
> is all right to show it. If a Kagyü lama comes, it is all right to show
> it. If a Sakya lama comes, it is all right to show it. To say that it is
> a Geluk protector, and then a Kagyü lama arrives and you have to
> hide, where is the sense in that?

December 10, 2004

His Holiness made the following comments at the opening of the new
assembly room for Jadral and Hardong houses (2:68):

> Concerning the practice of Dölgyal and the various restrictions
> I have placed on it over time, my thinking was to ensure respect
> for the teachings of the Buddha in general and specifically for the
> tradition of Mañjunātha Tsongkhapa. I investigated carefully,
> thoroughly, and solidly, and when finally I arrived at reliable con-
> clusions, I imposed the restrictions. It was an ongoing and sys-
> tematic process.
>
> Many great masters of the past of all traditions have imposed
> restrictions on this practice. The Great Fifth and the Great Thir-
> teenth shouldered their responsibility and imposed restrictions. I
> am the present holder of the incarnation of the past Dalai Lamas,
> and my responsibility is to continue their work.

August 8, 2005

The following discourse was given at Samyé Ling settlement in Delhi to newcomers from Tibet who had come for an audience (2:72):

> These conclusions I arrived at are because of events 360 years ago. The Great Fifth Dalai Lama states in his autobiography, *Heavenly Raiment*:

> > There are reports that in Döl White Springs a particularly powerful malevolent oath-breaking spirit, born from perverse prayers, has been causing harm to the people and the teachings, both generally and individually. Since the fire-bird year these have increased, and it has succeeded in many of its intrigues. However, because it did not concern them directly, few did anything about it. At the end of the earth-bird year I had a dwelling constructed at Döl White Springs and moved some items there, hoping that it would become a base for the spirit.
> >
> > However, many in the lay and monastic community have recently been struck down by a contagious illness, and one or two monks have died. Therefore the monks of the college unanimously urged that a wrathful ritual be performed. Consequently, Ngakrampa Döndrup Gyatso as the vajra master of the Dorjé Drolö ritual, and Nangjung Ngakchang Losang Khyentsé as vajra master of the Most Secret Karma Drakpo ritual, headed two groups of ritual practitioners. Also, Rikzin Tulku of Dorjé Drak Monastery, Chögyal Terdak Lingpa, Ukja Lungpa, Drigung Tulku Rinpoché, Katsal Surpa Ngari Könchok Lhundrup, and Palri Tulku spent seven days performing the rituals of Wrathful Guru, Yama, Phurba, Loktri, and so on. This was followed by a fire ritual.
> >
> > There were many wonderful signs of the oath-breaking spirit and its entourage having been burned by this fire ritual. Moreover, the smell of a burning corpse experienced by everyone there was convincing. Directly, this

was the practice of granting freedom from fear by saving the lives of many living beings. Indirectly, those spirits were brought to happiness by being freed from accumulating even more bad actions and having to experience the unending suffering of bad states of rebirth.

At that time, I composed a declaration stating that these spirits were without guide and protection.

Thus at the time of the wrathful ritual, he composed a declaration. This can be found in the *da* volume of his collected works. There are three sections to the collected works of the Great Fifth. They are the exoteric, the esoteric, and the sealed secret collections. This declaration is found in the *da* volume of the exoteric collection.

The declaration begins:

> The false incarnation of Tulku Sönam Gelek Palsang, who was successful because of the manipulations of Lak Agyal of Gekhasa, became an oath-breaking spirit born from perverse prayers and brought much harm to living beings. Consequently, seven groups of practitioners were assembled.

Gekhasa refers to Tölung Gekhasa, the birthplace of Tulku Drakpa Gyaltsen. Lak Agyal was Drakpa Gyaltsen's mother. She was very resourceful. Therefore, while he was not yet the incarnation of Tulku Sönam Gelek Palsang, who in turn was the incarnation of Panchen Sönam Drakpa, she managed to establish him as such, and therefore the "false incarnation...was successful." Finally, because of his perverse prayers he became an oath-breaking spirit and caused much harm to living beings.

In the text of the declaration, it says:

> To the deities Six-Armed Mahākāla, Karmarājā, Palden Lhamo,
> to Four-Faced Mahākāla, Chamdral Bektsé,
> and other oath-bound protectors

that we rely on, offer to, and practice,
I offer to you this precious drink.

This unholy Drakpa Gyaltsen, with pretensions of holiness,
is an oath-breaking spirit born from perverse prayers.
As he is harming the teachings and all living beings,
do not help him or protect him but grind him to dust.

The declaration continues and lists the names of many protectors.

The essence of this matter is as found in the well-known biography of the Great Fifth, and from that biography the declaration is found in the *da* volume of his collected works.

If you ask how did the Great Fifth regard Tulku Drakpa Gyaltsen, the answer is found in the line, "an oath-breaking spirit born from perverse prayers." The Great Thirteenth also imposed restrictions. Previously, on visiting the tantric chapel of Drepung Monastery in Tibet, he observed a statue of Dölgyal. Later, after he imposed the restrictions, he asked that the statue be removed. This is a story told by the older monks.

Whatever the case, the Thirteenth Dalai Lama certainly imposed restrictions. In particular, he reprimanded Kyabjé Phabongkha Rinpoché, saying that when it came to Dölgyal, he was not pleased. This is clearly recorded in the two volumes of Kyabjé Phabongkha Rinpoché's biography compiled in Tibet by his scribe and attendant Denma Losang Dorjé.

So that is what happened. Whatever the case, my former reliance on Dölgyal was a mistake. My imposing restrictions on Dölgyal is not a mistake. The Great Fifth saying that Dölgyal is an oath-violator born of perverse prayers, I rely on. The Great Thirteenth saying that Dölgyal propitiation contravenes the precepts of refuge, I rely on.

My relying on Dölgyal was wrong. In the Vinaya confession liturgy, it asks, "Do you see the mistake as a mistake?"

"Yes, I see it as a mistake," is the response.

Similarly, I see it as a mistake, and that is settled. However, I do not just leave it at that. The founder of the religious and secular administration in Tibet, and the Ganden Phodrang government, was the Great Fifth Dalai Lama. Can you say that one who has broken his bond with the Great Fifth and who has no liking for the Ganden Phodrang is a very special protector to rely upon? He does more harm than good to the religious and secular administration of the Ganden Phodrang. I imposed restrictions for those reasons. That is one point.

The second point is this. I have faith and pure perception for all traditions without prejudice. From my side I have faith and practice pure perception of the Sakya, Nyingma, Kagyü, and many other traditions. As for my studies, I have trained myself by relying upon the extraordinary explanations of the great Mañjunātha lama, Tsongkhapa. Also, I have received initiations, core instructions, and so forth from many Nyingma lamas on the works of Kunkhyen Longchen Rabjampa, Kunkhyen Jikmé Lingpa, and so on. They benefit my practice. I do not do it just to be popular.

The Madhyamaka view, shared by both sutra and tantra, of the reality that is dependent origination was excellently explained by the great Mañjunātha lama, Tsongkhapa, and is an explanation that has not been bettered by anyone. It is something truly wonderful.

The clear-light vajra of the mind spoken of in tantra refers to the primordial clear light. Using the language of the *Guhyasamāja Tantra*, it is the all-empty state of clear light, or fourth emptiness.[205] On top of that presentation, the direct introduction to intrinsic awareness by way of distinguishing the clarity and awareness of mind found in the Kagyü mahāmudrā teachings and particularly in the Dzokchen literature brings a special understanding that helps to determine the fourth emptiness, or the all-empty state of clear light.

Therefore I have developed faith from the basis of knowledge, and the essence of the practices of the Sakya, Kagyü, Nyingma, and Geluk comes down to this point.

Not only that, in Tibet in the past there were many great beings across the traditions. There was also much argument against and refutation of others' traditions from those who only knew their own tradition and had no exposure to others'. Refutation and criticism by way of scholarly analysis has a purpose. As is said, "Scholars are beautiful among scholars." But out of blind attachment and ordinary worldly prejudice, some become angry and biased. That is tragic.

January 11, 2007

The teaching below was given in Sera Monastery, South India, to past and present abbots from various traditions, lamas and tulkus, the monastic assembly, the leader of the Tibetan government in exile, the Home Affairs secretary, local leaders and officials, various organizations, and local residents (2:141):

> To preach that an oath-violator born of perverse prayers, who creates harm both in the short and long term, is a doctrine protector of Mañjunātha Tsongkhapa of the Geluk tradition is a great act of deception. It is completely false.
>
> Recently, a group of Dölgyal followers formed a society to defend Shukden. Let's take the example of the killing of the principal of the Institute of Buddhist Dialectics. He supported my position and wrote some articles on this issue. He was murdered by assailants about a kilometer from where I live. The killers were not Chinese. They did not come from some evil group in India. They were people from our monastic institutions. There were some false Lithang monks from Pomra House of Sera Mé Monastery and Dokhang House of Ganden Monastery. There were one or two from Chatreng also.
>
> After they murdered the Dialectics Institute principal, they fled to Tibet. There they stayed in a Chatreng restaurant in Lhasa, where, through connections with the Chinese government, they were given special hospitality. All this information can be verified from the office of the Dharamsala police, who investigated at the time. At what time the murderers left Delhi, how the murderers were photographed with someone called Chimé, the secretary of the Dorjé Shukden Charitable Society[206] in Delhi, can all be verified there. These events are heartbreaking.
>
> Later, someone with connections to the Dölgyal group sent a letter saying that they had sent me three carcasses and if that were not enough they would offer more.

Campaigns of those who defend Dölgyal often involve violent deeds, such as killing and beating. There have been many such incidents. Here in this area one local leader was beaten and almost killed. These are actual incidents.

It is important to not fall under this deception. For those who have a connection with the events tainted by breaking the sacred bond with the Great Fifth, or events tainted by breaking the sacred bond with my former incarnation, it would not be good if they received initiations and vows from me. Therefore, when I am giving teachings, I am not allowing those who follow Dölgyal to sit among the recipients.

I have no malice or harmful intent toward these people. Quite the opposite: I think it is a pity. It is a cause for compassion. If they are under the spell of wrong ideas, and in their next life Dölgyal can pull them out of the bardo, then good. But that will be very difficult.

Maybe it is not good to say, but the Dalai Lama is better than Dölgyal, not worse. Understand?

January 8, 2008

The following two extracts are from a discourse at Drepung Loseling Monastery in South India (2:199):

I too made a mistake. It was committed out of my own naiveté and lack of concern. There is no blame attached to Kyabjé Trijang Rinpoché. He was a follower of Kyabjé Phabongkha Rinpoché, and he was following the practice of his lama.

As for Kyabjé Phabongkha Rinpoché, there are many elements to consider. In particular, the previous Dalai Lama in the latter part of his life had an unfavorable view of Kyabjé Phabongkha Rinpoché and reprimanded him. Kyabjé Phabongkha Rinpoché was cowed and had to live with that. That was one time.

Once the previous Dalai Lama passed away, Dölgyal rejoiced and considered it good news, which he announced in a high gleeful voice. In the eyes of ordinary disciples, it appears that Kyabjé Phabongkha Rinpoché also, because there was no longer any risk, was, if I may be a little disrespectful, a little disdainful. As soon as the previous incarnation passed away, he took the opportunity and propagated Dölgyal extensively. On that basis was Kyabjé Phabongkha Rinpoché bad? What he did was bad. However, he was an inconceivable lama. He really was the master of the stages of the path and the mind-training teachings. For my part, he is a lineage lama, and I have single-pointed faith in him. To say on that basis, however, that whatever he did was good makes no sense. These two need to be separated out.

And (2:202):

The one with the most knowledge of Dölgyal was the Great Fifth. If I may talk about him in an everyday manner, the Great Fifth was not like some ordinary person given to slander, to coarse anger and desire. He was a genuine lama of high realizations, and he continuously received visions of the lamas, meditational deities, and dākinīs. Likewise, he knew dice divination, the *Arising Letter* elemental divination,[207] and so on.

When someone who investigates using these different methods, and who directly receives the predictions of the lamas, meditational deities, and dākinīs, speaks of "an oath-breaking spirit born of perverse prayers," I consider that to be an authentic declaration.

In the beginning, I was not aware of this declaration and had not seen it. Kyabjé Trijang Rinpoché said nothing. He knew nothing about it and had not seen it. It was as if this weighty declaration of the Great Fifth had remained hidden.

Later, these words of the Great Fifth came to light. They were spoken by a genuine lama who was well-acquainted with the facts, who knew everything about Tulku Drakpa Gyaltsen at that time. When Tulku Drakpa Gyaltsen was alive, he and the Great Fifth were very close. He took many teachings from the Great Fifth. I have seen the two volumes of Tulku Drakpa Gyaltsen's collected works. They are very good. When such a person passed away and was later declared to be "an oath-breaking spirit born of perverse prayers," this is the Great Fifth talking about actual events that occurred at that time.

Therefore there is no need for lots of explanation. The story is that he is "an oath-breaking spirit born from perverse prayers. As he is harming the teachings and all living beings, do not help him or protect him but grind him to dust."

If there is time to study these events in greater detail, I requested a document containing extracts from biographies be put together. Later we can look at it.

July 7, 2008

His Holiness made the following comments in the reception room at his Dharamsala residence during a request to re-enroll in Sera Monastery made by Geshé Thuptén Samphel of Pomra House. Supporting the geshé was the president of the Dharamsala Lithang Welfare Association Tashi Tsering, the Bylakuppe Lithang regional deputy Losang Phuntsok, Thupten Dzinpa, resident of Dehra Dun Mindröling Monastery Drukpa Tashi, and the requestor of the reinstatement, Geshé Losang Jikmé (2:262):

> For example, Yongzin Ling Rinpoché once asked Kyabjé Phabongkha Rinpoché, "The lamas and the senior monks at Drepung say that propitiating Shukden displeases Nechung. Is this true or not?"
>
> Kyabjé Phabongkha Rinpoché replied, "The one who urged Tulku Drakpa Gyaltsen to arise in wrathful form was Nechung. Therefore that cannot be possible."
>
> Usually, whenever he asked Kyabjé Phabongkha Rinpoché to resolve a doubt and received an answer, Yongzin Ling Rinpoché would think, "That is definitely so." However, at the answer he received on that day, he could only wonder, and his doubt was not cleared. Yongzin Rinpoché himself said this.

And (2:263):

> The Shukden Society maintain that the Fifth Dalai Lama composed a propitiation to Dölgyal and say that there were no problems between the Fifth Dalai Lama and Dölgyal. As we have the complete works of the Great Fifth here, I conducted an investigation to see whether they include such a propitiation. The

collected works consist of five esoteric volumes, twenty exoteric volumes, and two sealed volumes. Recorded in them are two incidents of problems between Dölgyal and Palden Lhamo. Whatever the case, after reviewing the whole of the collected works, we found a declaration in the collection of propitiations to the Dharma protectors in the *da* volume of the exoteric collection. That the Great Fifth himself composed this declaration is mentioned in his *Heavenly Raiment* autobiography.

The Gyalpo spirit at Döl White Springs had been appeased in a peaceful way in the beginning, but things steadily grew worse, until finally, a wrathful ritual was employed to expel it. The Great Fifth says that the declaration was composed at that time. That is clear.

Our research uncovered no Dölgyal propitiation text by the Great Fifth, and instead we found this declaration. At the beginning of the declaration it says in small script, "The false incarnation of Tulku Sönam Gelek Palsang, who was successful because of the manipulations of Lak Agyal of Gekhasa, became an oath-breaking spirit born from perverse prayers."

Gekhasa was his birthplace. Lak Agyal was his mother. She was very resourceful. At the time when the Fifth Dalai Lama incarnation had not yet been decided, she almost had Tulku Drakpa Gyaltsen recognized as the Dalai Lama incarnation. When Tulku Drakpa Gyaltsen was not installed as the Lower Chamber incarnation, she made sure he became the Upper Chamber incarnation of Sönam Gelek Palsang, and he was recognized as such.

Therefore, in the declaration it says, "The false incarnation of Tulku Sönam Gelek Palsang, who was successful because of the manipulations of Lak Agyal of Gekhasa, became an oath-breaking spirit born from perverse prayers."

In the actual invocation it says:

This unholy Drakpa Gyaltsen, with pretensions of holiness,
is an oath-breaking spirit born from perverse prayers.
As he is harming the teachings and all living beings,
do not help him or protect him but grind him to dust.

Protectors from Six-Armed Mahākāla up to Setrap are mentioned by name, and after each the above invocation is written.[208]

This invocation can be seen in terms of cause, nature, and
function or result. "This unholy Drakpa Gyaltsen, with pretensions of holiness" means that while he was not in fact the incarnation of the holy being Tulku Sönam Gelek Palsang, he pretended
to be and was successful.

From the lines, "This unholy Drakpa Gyaltsen, with pretensions of holiness, is an oath-breaking spirit born from perverse
prayers," it can be seen that he was born from the cause of perverse prayers. "Oath-breaking spirit" shows his nature. Do you
understand? If he were an oath-breaking spirit born from perverse prayers but he harmed no one, then there is no problem. If
he just sat in a corner being an oath-breaking spirit, then that is
fine. It would make no difference at all.

But what was his function? "He is harming the teachings and
all living beings." What does this mean? Is the Great Fifth lying?
From my side I have faith and trust in the Great Fifth. He was
very kind to the land of Tibet. The Ganden Phodrang, which to
this day has stood up to the Chinese government, was begun by
the Great Fifth. He looked after the Dharma traditions of Tibet,
and in particular, in the case of the Geluk tradition, the expan-
sion of the great monastic seats of Sera, Drepung, and Ganden
was made possible by him.

January 9, 2008

The next discourse was given at Drepung Loseling Monastery in South India
(2:205):

I have something to say during this tea break. I was going to say it
in more detail later, but several of the sponsors are present today
and some will probably be leaving tonight and tomorrow. Therefore, while we are all present, I see it would be good to talk about
it now. Chinese and English translations are also necessary.

You have all heard about Gyalpo Shukden. The issue has been
troublesome since the 1970s. More recently the Chinese government has taken an interest in this problem. When our sixth

delegation met with Chinese officials recently, one criticism those officials leveled at me was that the Dalai Lama had placed restrictions on Shukden and that destroys the principle of one's faith being one's own choice. The atheist Communist Chinese, using a position taken by the Dalai Lama, are saying that they have had to take responsibility on the issue of one's religion being one's choice. They have criticized me officially through their government for destroying, by placing restrictions on Dölgyal, the principle of religious freedom.

I don't think the Chinese government cares anything about the history of Dölgyal. They have seen a political opportunity and used it to criticize me. It doesn't bother me in the least that they find fault with me.

And (2:207):

Recently the Dölgyal group petitioned the Indian government, arguing that the Dalai Lama is denying Dölgyal followers the right to practice as they choose and therefore they are at risk. They are asking for protection, and the Foreign Ministry in turn has responded.

So now the situation is becoming serious. Up to now, I have explained the good and bad of this matter. From my own experience I have spoken of the faults I have witnessed. I have also identified various faults using the words of past lamas. This is my responsibility. Whether you listen is your business. I have never once said you are not allowed to practice Dölgyal. From the beginning I have cited the words of Kashmiri Phalu,[209] "These are the heartfelt words of Kashmiri Phalu. Whether you listen or not is up to you."

Therefore, whether you heed my advice is your choice entirely. In the past I have never said you have to listen to what I say, and I don't say it now. However, now the issue has become confused. There is no way things can stay as they are. It must be clarified. In the Vinaya scriptures, there seven elements to the settling of disputes relating to Dharma matters. They include distributing counting sticks, knotted grass, and so on. So, the time has come to distribute counting sticks. If we explain it in keeping with modern democratic ways, in English there is the word *referendum*, which means to let the will of the people decide. The time has come to ask the people.

Therefore, after the Loseling ceremonies are over, you will return to your monasteries. Once there, you should send out a questionnaire to all the monks. The first question should be whether they wish to rely on Dölgyal. Those who wish to rely on Dölgyal should sign that they do. Those who do not wish to rely on Dölgyal should sign accordingly. You understand?

Then those who wish to associate with Dölgyal practitioners communally and religiously should sign that they wish to do so. Those who do not wish to associate with Dölgyal practitioners communally and religiously should sign to that effect. Understand? This is deciding by the will of the people. No one is forcing you. I am not forcing you.

If those who wish to rely on Dölgyal exceeds sixty percent, then from that day on I will not say another word about Dölgyal. You understand? From then on you will have to carry the responsibility. If, however, more than sixty or seventy percent say that they have no wish to rely upon Dölgyal and no wish to associate on a religious or communal level with Dölgyal practitioners, then we will have to consider what to do.

In reality there is no purpose in Dölgyal followers being in India. We came to India because we could not accept the policies of the Chinese government. Now that Dölgyal followers are being looked after by the Chinese government, now that the Chinese are taking special care of Dölgyal practitioners, it is better that such people go to the place where they are being looked after. There is no point in being here. Understand?

So if the majority decides they want to rely on Dölgyal, then I will say "OK." It makes no difference to me. In the past I relied on him. I was mistaken. I apologized for that mistake to the lamas of the past and corrected my practice. Now if the majority says they want to rely on Dölgyal, that is their right. It doesn't matter. OK? Don't feel you have to flatter or appease the Dalai Lama out of fear or embarrassment.

But do not be misinformed. Tomorrow or the day after I will distribute some documents. They will set out what the great lamas of the past, from the Fifth Dalai Lama onward, said about Dölgyal, how they regarded him, whether they placed restrictions on him. Some have been printed already. There are still some additions I want made, and then they will be handed out.

Before you vote, if there are those who practice Dölgyal, you should make them aware of all that has happened, as described by those who have criticized Dölgyal, from the Great Fifth onward. Those who practice Dölgyal should also explain the reasons for relying upon Dölgyal, the benefits of relying upon him. Recently many books describing this have been published.

You may say, "Dölgyal is a wealth god, and so if you rely upon him you will get money." So first you do the wealth-vase practice, then take the life-entrustment ritual, and then perform the monthly propitiation. That seems to be the way. If you rely upon Dölgyal you will become rich, you will be successful, as the late Drakgom Rinpoché described in his book. There are many of these books around. Everyone has seen them and knows about them.

What are the benefits of relying on Dölgyal? Those who rely upon Dölgyal should make them clear. Those who say there are disadvantages in relying upon Dölgyal should make those clear. Then both sides should be weighed up. Those who say it is not right to do so include the Great Fifth, Trichen Ngawang Chokden, Changkya Rölpai Dorjé, Phurbuchok Ngawang Jampa, Yongzin Yeshé Gyaltsen, and so on. Put them on one side and weigh up against the other. I think this is how it should be done. Sponsors, do you understand? Anyway, this is separating the mouth from the moustache, and fish from turnips,[210] as the sayings go. We have arrived at the point of doing just that.

Whatever the outcome, remember that now the Chinese from their side are taking a strong position. Dölgyal followers have killed, beaten, and threatened, but that is not surprising. However, turning toward the Communist Chinese is strange. We are in dispute with the Chinese government. We're not demanding complete separation. If the Chinese government gives us a meaningful autonomy, one that we Tibetans can trust, we will stay within the People's Republic of China. But at the moment, the Chinese government is pulling us this way and that way as they please. This is unacceptable, and so we are in dispute with them. Amid such a dispute, to side with the Chinese government is tragic, especially to do this in the name of being religious people and then to ostentatiously claim that one's religious freedom is being threatened.

It is not a question of religious faith. As I said yesterday, this is reliance on a ghost. When we say "ghost," we are not talking about a protector who protects. The torma offering text to the fifteen direction protectors in the Vajrabhairava self-generation mentions ghosts and zombies:

> In the presence of the Bhagavan Dharmarāja, Mañjuśrī,
> you vowed to tame the māras and protect the teachings;
> guardian hordes of Yama, ogresses, ḍākinīs, ghosts,
>   zombies,
> all you outer and inner oath-bound protectors...

At the end of the verse it says "oath-bound," not "oath-breaking." So if they are oath-bound with pledges, then it is all right if they are ghosts or zombies. But if it is a ghost who has broken pledges, then that is not good. Some might think it is not that bad if it is a ghost, because in the Vajrabhairava self-generation it says,

> All you outer and inner oath-bound protectors,
> I turn and bow to you with an expectant mind.

So some might think that ghosts are not so bad. A ghost is a ghost, but at the end here it says "oath-bound," whereas we are talking about an oath-breaker. I spoke about this yesterday.

And (2:213):

> In religious matters, when there are disagreements over the Vinaya, the monks decide by casting sticks. The scriptures talk of "settling disputes by the seven points." So it would be good if we hold a referendum, as is done in the world these days, wouldn't it?
>
> You Western monks, will you participate in the referendum?

There is no hurry. You return to your places, and let everything settle down. Discuss all the points, make sure everything is known. Give everyone time to think about it. Then vote. Understand? I thought I would explain this while the sponsors are present.

January 14, 2008

The following extract is from a discourse in which several sourced accounts referring to Dölgyal were presented. It was delivered to several thousand monastics and lay devotees from Tibet and elsewhere at Drepung Loseling (2:250):

There are other reports but there is no need to relate them all here.

During the time I first imposed restrictions on Dölgyal, I gave a talk in the temple at Dharamsala to several staff members, monks, and members of the public who had assembled there. That night I had a dream in which Trijang Rinpoché came with an entourage of two, who resembled Rinpoché with his tall frame and slightly bowed head. As soon as they reached my side, Trijang Rinpoché said, "Placing restrictions on Dölgyal today was excellent."

Then two days later I had a dream of the venerable Gen Nyima in which he said, "Restricting Dölgyal in the three monastic seats[211] is excellent."

Dreams are not so reliable, but that was what happened.

Early in my life, I was not aware of the events described in these biographies. And no one had done any research. I knew that there was some problem with Dölgyal at the time of the Great Fifth and that Drepung had placed some restrictions on the practice. Other than that I didn't know anything. Since the formation of the Dölgyal society, many publications have been distributed, and in them there was talk of the Great Fifth having composed an invocation of Dölgyal. Therefore we had to research the exoteric and esoteric collected works of the Great Fifth to see whether such an invocation had been composed.

Instead of finding an invocation saying, "Composed by the

Great Fifth," we found this frightening declaration [by the Great Fifth that Dölgyal is an oath-breaking spirit born from perverse prayers]. That research has now been compiled as these extracts given here. These accounts were composed by inconceivably great beings, masters truly possessed of learning and practice. Many of them were purely Geluk. When they describe these events, we must grant them some authenticity.

The one responsible for the recent enthroning of Dölgyal as exclusive protector of Mañjunātha Tsongkhapa's teachings was probably Kyabjé Phabongkha Rinpoché. Because of his reliance upon Dölgyal, he suffered many difficulties. In one of the many discussions we had on this matter, Nechung referred to Kyabjé Phabongkha Rinpoché as "venerable"[212] and said that in his early life the venerable Phabongkha Rinpoché was excellent but that in the latter part of his life, because of the influence of Gyalpo Shukden, things were not good. Therefore, "I, Gyalpo Pehar, bear him no grudge. However, the incarnations of the venerable Dechen Nyingpo will not be successful in their activities."

Thus Nechung was decisive in what he said. This is like some kind of proof. So I embarked on research, and these accounts are what emerged.

As I said previously, put on one side those lamas who restricted Dölgyal, regarding him as a malicious spirit and an oath-violator born from perverse prayers, and on the other side put primarily Kyabjé Phabongkha Rinpoché, and some Sakya lamas who regarded him as a protector. Then weigh them up. It is very difficult for the other side to outweigh this side.

Whatever the case, if it is necessary to correct and amend the conclusions of the Great Fifth, which have been followed and supported by many Geluk lamas, then it should be done by someone who has the same level of realization as the Great Fifth. Otherwise, it would be very difficult for we ordinary beings to do it.

Those then are the reasons for the restrictions. Those are the sources. I have distributed documents previously, but these new accounts are more detailed. Examine these documents and explain the situation to new monks. And to those practicing Dölgyal, tell them it is like this and that, and that they should think carefully. If after considering all this information, ascertaining it in their minds, they still have faith in Dölgyal, that is their right. If they act rashly and ignorantly, tell them these stories. Tell them how troublesome it is.

In Tibet too, in such places as Chamdo, Drakyab, in the place of Denma Gönsar Chöjé, Dölgyal is very strong. Most of them follow out of ignorance. It is very important for them to know everything. Understand?

January 8, 2010

His Holiness delivered the following comments in the sacred place of Bodhgaya during profound teachings on Nāgārjuna's *Praise of the Transcendent*, Atiśa's *Lamp on the Path to Enlightenment*, Longchenpa's *Mind at Ease*, Tsongkhapa's *Abridged Stages of the Path*, and an initiation of Avalokiteśvara (2:307):

> One important point is this. In Tibet when they came to learn of the succession of restrictions I had placed on Dölgyal, there were those who said, "This is not the true thinking of the Dalai Lama. He has restricted Dölgyal merely to placate the Nyingmapas. This is playing politics."
>
> That is not the reason I restricted Dölgyal. My reasons are as I have explained. My intentions are sincere. If I come to a decision on the basis of sincere intentions, and then others start speaking in a devious manner, if I then do not reply with a clear explanation and tell the truth, that would be completely wrong.
>
> As the circumstances became clearer, they are revealed to be as they have been presented now. Fundamentally, it is up to you whether you practice Dharma. You can rely upon a god, or on a demon, or on an oath-breaker. Whatever you rely upon, it's in your hands. The choice is yours. However, if you practice out of not knowing the facts, then it is my responsibility. I have come to know of a great many facts. Not to explain what I know would be wrong. This is my responsibility. So I tell you these things, and you decide whether you listen. If you choose not to listen, that is your loss. It is not my business. From the beginning I have always said it is up to you.
>
> If you are a Dölgyal practitioner, then because the bond

between lama and disciple is so important, it would not be right for you to take vows or receive an initiation from me.

September 8, 2010

The final extract comes from a discourse to a group of over 350 South Asians, mainly from Singapore, as well as Tibetan monastics and laity (2:324):

> Some from the Sakya tradition relied on Shukden, but he was seen as "custodian of wealth" and not regarded with any great esteem. Later one or two Geluk lamas said that Gyalpo Shukden was an important protector deity of the Geluk teachings. They also said that the protector of Mañjunātha Tsongkhapa's teaching was Dorjé Shukden.
>
> Think about that well. The Thirteenth Dalai Lama, the previous incarnation, placed restrictions on this practice, and as soon as he passed away, it grew even stronger. Therefore, in the beginning I too knew nothing about this, and so I relied on Gyalpo Shukden. Later, as I began to do some research, I came to understand that I was wrong, and I stopped the practice.
>
> I have heard there are Dölgyal practitioners in Singapore. Therefore I am going off the topic to talk to you about it. There is no need at all to rely on Dölgyal. Particularly if you are a Gelukpa, you should study the eighteen volumes of Jé Rinpoché's compositions. Do that, and that will be your protector. That will be the meditation deity who grants you powers. That will be the Dharma guardian who dispels your obstacles. Anything else, you don't need. Understand? Those bared fangs you don't need!
>
> Within those eighteen volumes of Jé Rinpoché's compositions, in terms of sutra, there are five volumes on the Madhyamaka view: *Clarifying the Intention*, the *Great Commentary on Fundamental Wisdom*, the *Essence of Excellent Explanation: Differentiating the Definitive and the Provisional*, and the special insight sections of his larger and shorter *Stages of the Path*. These five are the works in which Jé Rinpoché determines the ultimate thinking of Nāgārjuna. They are essential.
>
> Likewise, for the topic of the Perfection of Wisdom, there is

his *Golden Garland of Excellent Explanation*. In the tantra collection there is his *Great Exposition of Secret Mantra* and four works on the *Guhyasamāja Tantra*. They are all completely essential. They are our teachers, or lamas, and our meditation deities and Dharma protectors. Do you understand? It is vital that you understand these things.

These pieces of profound advice come from a series of discourses on Döl-gyal given with great love and compassion solely to dispel error and increase virtue by the Fourteenth Dalai Lama, our refuge and protector, the great guide to Buddhists in general and to Tibetans inside and outside of Tibet in particular. They were given over a period ranging from June 13, 1978, to September 8, 2010, and are taken from the two volumes of *Discourses on Dölgyal*.

It is not possible reproduce here every discourse in full, and so those possessing the wide eyes of wisdom, who wish to see the discourses in their entirety, please consult these two volumes.

26. Support Given by Kyabjé Trijang Rinpoché and Kyabjé Ling Rinpoché

FROM THE EARLY days of the great masters of the glorious Sakya tradition up to the early years of the Fourteenth Dalai Lama, several great lamas have had their heads turned by the manipulative methods employed by Dölgyal. As a result, in the perception of ordinary appearance, these lamas believed to be true the deceits produced by his manipulative methods, as well as the exaggerated praises Dölgyal has made of himself, which run counter to factual accounts of the past.

In *Music to Delight the Oath-Bound Protectors: A Biographical Account of the Wonderful Three Secrets of Dorjé Shukden Tsal, Great Deity Guarding the Geluk Doctrine and Emanated Great Dharma King*, more commonly known as *Commentary on the Praise of Shukden*; and in *Supplemental Explanation as a Preliminary to the Gyalchen Life-Entrustment*, both composed by Kyabjé Trijang Vajradhara, tutor to the Fourteenth Dalai Lama, there are several instances of exaggeration in the biographical accounts of Dölgyal. However, it is simply not possible that great and holy beings, such as the great Kyabjé tutor Trijang Vajradhara, crown jewel of millions of scholar practitioners who are like the sky covering the earth, could deliberately compile such false accounts.

The reality could be that they have made these compositions by focusing on Dölgyal's self-aggrandizing praises of himself, which have been directly and indirectly disseminated, and on the inflated praise of Dölgyal perpetuated by some of his later followers who have not considered factual accounts of past events.

With regard to the deeds of great beings such as Kyabjé Trijang Vajradhara, it is difficult to evaluate them conclusively, saying they are this or that. However, the Fourteenth Dalai Lama, after a thorough investigation by various methods, conveyed in great detail the disturbing information concerning Dölgyal to the Kyabjé tutor Trijang Vajradhara. In response, Kyabjé

Trijang Vajradhara approved wholeheartedly and praised what the Dalai Lama had said.

Furthermore, on June 13, 1978, the Dalai Lama gave his first public talk concerning the restriction of Dölgyal. That night he had a dream in which Trijang Rinpoché came, accompanied by an entourage of two who resembled Rinpoché in their tall frame and slightly bowed head. As soon as they reached the Dalai Lama's side, Trijang Rinpoché said, "Placing restrictions today on Dölgyal was excellent."

Similarly, Kyabjé Rinpoché in instructions to his disciples has stressed that they should not create an organization under the name of Dölgyal, that Dölgyal practitioners should not perform Dölgyal propitiation rituals and so forth together and in any extensive and elaborate manner, and particularly that it was not proper for the colleges of the monasteries to practice Dölgyal communally. Many of the recipients of these instructions were disciples of Kyabjé Rinpoché who today are senior monks still living in the monasteries.

It is not possible that a master of scripture and reasoning such as Kyabjé Trijang Vajradhara would place any value upon baseless talk. Therefore if you consider that he composed *Commentary on the Praise of Shukden* and other works on the basis of there being much extraneous and irrelevant claims in the community regarding this matter, no one can say with certainty that these compositions were not expressly written to allow future generations to clear up the confusion regarding Dölgyal.

In particular, these days a few people have proclaimed that all that is contained within *Commentary on the Praise of Shukden* and the *Supplemental Explanation* composed by Kyabjé Trijang Vajradhara represents his final thinking. Also, using Kyabjé Rinpoché's name, and in league with Communist China, who are the enemy of the teachings, they have risen up as opponents to the Tibetan administration and its people. They have targeted serious allegations and slander against the Dalai Lama, the Tibetans at home and in exile, and the Tibetan administration, perpetuating actions that advance the intentions of Communist China.

Let us think about this. Both *Commentary on the Praise of Shukden* and the *Supplemental Explanation* contain various praises and claims regarding Dölgyal that contradict historical accounts. For example, *Commentary on the Praise of Shukden* says:

Praise to you, born from the essence of
your father, King of Hindrance, and your mother, Queen of
    Existence
in Wrathful Palace, where the mandala of your body
became in an instant the complete mandala
of deity and entourage of the five families of Shukden.

Thus, from the united essence of his father, Vināyaka, King of Hindrance, and his mother, the Bön protector Queen of Existence, came the so-called thirty-two-deity body mandala of Dölgyal, or Gyalpo Shukden. Taking this to be a sound reference, Dragom Lama[213] has repeatedly proclaimed that this is how Dölgyal and his entourage first arose, thereby trying to deceive faithful members of the public who are unaware of the facts. In response, the hundredth incumbent of the Ganden throne and regent of the master Tsongkhapa, the unparalleled Kyabjé Losang Nyima Rinpoché, deploying extensive scripture and reasoning, rendered his opponent speechless.[214]

Nevertheless, these days followers of Dölgyal continue to use the name of Kyabjé Trijang Vajradhara and come out with exaggerated praise of Dölgyal while twisting the actual historical truth. Not being able to stand the continuation of such a state of affairs, we have analyzed with pure reasoning, in order to dispel and rectify any inaccuracy. The glorious Candrakīrti said:

Attachment to one's own views
and troubling the views of others are concepts that bind.
Therefore by dispelling attachment and resentment,
analysis with reasoning quickly brings liberation.[215]

As it will, without question, become a peerless offering of practice to delight the mind of Kyabjé Trijang Vajradhara as well, we have roughly examined relevant sections of *Commentary on the Praise of Shukden* and the *Supplemental Explanation*.

These days the Dölgyal groups proclaim, "After Kyabjé Trijang Rinpoché passed away, the Dalai Lama took the opportunity to place restrictions on Dölgyal." That is untrue. The first public discourse by the Dalai Lama referring to placing restrictions on Dölgyal was given on June 13, 1978, as he makes clear on the first line of the first page of *Discourses on Dölgyal*. Kyabjé Trijang Vajradhara passed away November 9, 1981. Therefore the Dalai Lama had finalized his deliberations over Dölgyal years before Kyabjé Trijang Rinpoché passed away. Furthermore he had presented the outcome of those complete deliberations to the two tutors for their consideration, and it was only after that that he began his restriction of Dölgyal. Those who know this will not be deceived by these statements of the Dölgyal groups.

Furthermore, the divisive and misleading statements spread by Dölgyal practitioners that Kyabjé Trijang Vajradhara did not support the restrictions placed on Dölgyal by His Holiness the Dalai Lama are intended to deceive those who are unaware. However, they too are seriously warped statements and not true. As we saw above in the excerpt from *Discourses on Dölgyal* (1:39), His Holiness in 1976 explained to Trijang Rinpoché everything that had occurred in great detail. Rinpoché replied that if that was what the dough-ball divination and Nechung has indicated, then it was true, and that there was no room for doubt.

In his introduction to a document for this committee, Yangteng Tulku[216] writes, "I have compiled factual accounts of how the great beings who were connected with His Holiness, such as the tutor and throneholder Ling Rinpoché, regarded Dölgyal. These are reproduced below." The document continues (2), "Once, when Kyabjé Samdhong Rinpoché came to the Ganden Phodrang government offices, I asked him about to Dölgyal written by Kyabjé Yongzin Ling Rinpoché that was printed in the Varanasi institute[217] prayer book. Rinpoché replied":

> At the beginning of 1970, the Geluk Teachers and Staff General Committee at Varanasi said that the Geluk students needed a refined-gold[218] protector propitiation prayer and that propitiation of Mahākāla, Dharmarāja, Vaiśravaṇa, Palden Lhamo, Shukden, and so on should be included. In response, Kyabjé Yongzin Ling Rinpoché did not compose a new prayer but added one verse each for the invitation and praise of Dölgyal to an existing propitiation prayer. Some years later I had become a student at that institute, and Kyabjé Yongzin Ling Rinpoché said to me, "Previously, the Geluk committee made that request and, not wanting to refuse, I inserted one verse each for the invitation and praise of Dölgyal. Now when I think about it, that was not right. Therefore you should take it out."
>
> Before I spoke with the Geluk committee, I reported to

Kyabjé Trijang Rinpoché what Kyabjé Yongzin Ling Rinpoché had asked me to do. He replied that whatever Ling Rinpoché asks, you should carry out immediately. Therefore I collected all the books that had printed the prayer, pasted a piece of paper over the verses, and blacked them out.

Yangteng Tulku continues in the same document (3):

> During the time of the former incarnation of Bangri Rinpoché of Sera Mé, he had as abbot forbidden the monthly ritual of Dölgyal to be held at the same time as the monastery's monthly protector rituals. I had heard about this but was not sure on the details. The attendant of the former Bangri Rinpoché was still alive, and so I approached him and asked him about it. He told me that when the Dalai Lama appointed the Sera Mé master Bangri Rinpoché to be abbot of Sera Mé, Rinpoché sought the traditional audience with Kyabjé Trijang Rinpoché, who told him that previously, in Tibet, it was not the practice for the Sera Mé main assembly to perform the propitiation of Dölgyal. However, it seems that these days it had become part of the assembly recitation in exile. If that is true, Trijang Rinpoché continued, it is not necessary to perform this propitiation, and it would be better for the monastery to follow the traditions initiated by the masters of old.
>
> Therefore Bangri Rinpoché, while he was abbot, asked those who were regularly reciting the Dölgyal invocation and those who had received the Dölgyal life-entrustment, who were reciting the monthly Dölgyal rituals in the main assembly together with the monastery monthly rituals, to desist from this practice. All the monks were aware of this request.

In *Miscellaneous Comments on What Has Been Seen, Heard, and Experienced Concerning Dölgyal, or Shukden,* Kyabjé Jhado Rinpoché says (1):

> These days, there has on the Internet and in other media been a smear campaign and the pursuit of vile activities aimed at the wish-fulfilling jewel that is the Dalai Lama, Avalokiteśvara,

holder of the lotus and general personification of all the buddhas of the three times in the play of a monk holding the three vows, the mighty guide for us snow-mountain dwellers in all our lives. These have been unbearable to hear and impossible to watch. This unthinking nonsense has been far greater than even the perverse claims made about Dölgyal. They boast that none of their activities go beyond the boundaries of the wishes of Kyabjé Yongzin Trijang Vajradhara and are completely in accord with his thinking. They have spread and continue to spread these outrageous claims that deceive and confuse those who do not know the facts.

Therefore, I, bearing the name of Jhado Tulku from Jang Namtso, former abbot of Namgyal Monastery, will write a little of what I have seen in my life and stories I have heard connected with these events.

First of all, to the false claim these activities are completely in accord with the thinking of tutor Kyabjé Trijang Vajradhara, I would like to say this. In 1980 when I was studying at Sera Mé College, the Sera Mé abbot, Bangri Rinpoché, in keeping with the wishes of the wish-fulfilling jewel, the Dalai Lama, issued an order that the monthly recitation of the Gyalpo Shukden propitiation in the Sera Mé protector chapel should cease. This displeased many who were engaged in the wrong path. Toward the end of that year, Kyabjé Yongzin Trijang Vajradhara visited Sera Monastery, and in Sera Mé College he gave the lineage-entrustment initiation of the Sixteen Arhats by way of a powder mandala. At that time, a group of officials headed by the Sera Mé manager Gen Dönyö of Chatreng and Losang Thupten from Chatreng, who was the manager of the Sera governing council, gained an audience with Kyabjé Vajradhara. They said to him, "The precious abbot has stopped the Shukden propitiation," and so on.

Kyabjé Vajradhara replied clearly, "What the Sera Mé abbot has done is good. In the past, in Tibet, there was no tradition of performing the Dölgyal Shukden propitiation during the monthly college propitiations, and there is no special reason for initiating it now when it was not there in the past."

That Kyabjé Trijang Vajradhara could actually utter these words, which are in complete agreement with the wishes of the wish-fulfilling Jewel, the Dalai Lama, I see as truly extraordinary and difficult for ordinary people to comprehend. If Kyabjé Yongzin Trijang Vajradhara were alive today, I believe he would see all of what the Dölgyal groups are doing as wrong, and I have no doubt that there would not be even a corner of his mind that would approve.

These are conclusive, fact-based accounts and give proof that Kyabjé Trijang Vajradhara fully supported the wish-fulfilling jewel, the Dalai Lama, in his restriction of Dölgyal.

Not only in matters relating to Dölgyal but in general, Kyabjé Trijang Rinpoché held His Holiness the Dalai Lama in great esteem. Evidence of this and just how high this esteem was is illustrated by the following examples.

Compendium of Compassionate Advice is a 2010 work that collects advice from His Holiness and from the great scholar Kyabjé Samdhong Rinpoché. There Samdhong Rinpoché says (35):

> In the autumn of 1952 Kyabjé Trijang Rinpoché gave a detailed teaching on the stages of the path in Drepung Gomang Monastery. On the final day he bestowed the bodhicitta vows and performed the dedication prayers, followed by a discourse in which he declared, "If it is made possible by the communal karma of Tibet, you should have no doubt that the deeds and qualities of the great Fourteenth Dalai Lama will be greater than those of the omniscient Gendun Drup, the Great Fifth Ngawang Losang Gyatso, and the Seventh Dalai Lama combined."
>
> Then, jokingly, he remarked, "Don't think that I am flattering just because I am someone who lives off the government! What I say is true. If it can be carried by the communal karma of the Tibetan people, this Dalai Lama incarnation will without doubt be a very special and holy being with qualities of compassion, ethics, and learning not seen before. Everyone needs to make prayers and to accumulate communal karma."

Also, in his autobiography Trijang Rinpoché tells a story about inviting Phabongkha Rinpoché to his house for a feast offering on March 22, 1941 (156):[219]

At one point, [Phabongkha Rinpoché] said, "If he does not fall prey to hindrance or obstacle, His Holiness the present Dalai Lama will without doubt be as great as Kalsang Gyatso, the Seventh Dalai Lama. Should you be called on to serve him, you must do so with skill and pure motivation."

It seems that this was a prophecy in which he foresaw my future, first in serving His Holiness as a mentor and then bearing the title of his tutor, thereby continuing to perform religious service for many years up to the present day.

In the autobiography, Trijang also recounts the following lines he wrote for His Holiness in response to a request that Trijang live long (294):[220]

Possessing the **power** of a myriad buddhas inexpressible by
    speech,
wondrous clouds of interweaving miraculous deeds far beyond
    the **mind**,
maintaining the beautiful pose of enlightened form **revealed**
    clearly to all,
an ocean of benefit and happiness whose **extent** cannot be
    perceived.

The waves moved by the compassion of your mind
and the nectar stream of your well-spoken words
fall upon the head of this stupid old man.

And so on up to:

When adversity and obstruction has arisen all around
and people wield the machinations of cruel deceit,
in such unending times of horrendous misfortune,
you wear the armor of the great power of undaunted
    patience.

And if the buddhas and bodhisattvas from the hidden realms
praise and exalt you as a lion among men,
aside from the stupid and the ignorant animals,
who with intelligence would not revere you?

Kye! Kye! Great protector, treasure of compassion,
held vividly as an image in the center of my heart,
seize with your iron hook of compassion
this old man who makes this resounding plea.

The autobiography also relates these events from November 3, 1971 (371):

After I had given the permission initiation of Three Wrathful
Forms Combined and a longevity initiation from the Niguma
tradition to a large audience of ordained and lay people, I
requested them all to carry out their religious and secular duties
in accord with the wishes of His Holiness the Dalai Lama.

This advice was given by Kyabjé Trijang Rinpoché to a gathering of laypeople and monastics exemplified by the monks of Sera Jé and Sera Mé and
the Gyütö and Gyümé tantric colleges. There is a lot more similar advice
found in the autobiography.

Also, in the longevity prayer for His Holiness composed by both Kyabjé
tutors, it says:

Bless the life of Tenzin Gyatso, guide of Tibet,
for it to remain indestructible for a hundred eons,
and for his wishes to be effortlessly realized.

Also:

May the nectar stream of the blessings of the Holder of the
    Lotus
nourish forever the very essence of our heart,
and by the service of offering him a practice
of acting in accordance with his words,
may we cross the oceans of excellent practice.

These and other lines are from an extensive prayer made for all the great
wishes of His Holiness the Fourteenth Dalai Lama to be quickly realized
without obstruction.

How Kyabjé Ling Rinpoché Regarded Dölgyal

It is well known that Kyabjé Yongzin Ling Rinpoché had no liking for Döl-gyal. Yangteng Tulku has written:

> In November 2012, the Ganden Phodrang secretary Kungo Dre-sang, along with Ratö Khyongla Rinpoché, his Western atten-dant, and I, Yangteng Tulku, were called into the Private Office reception rooms to discuss and receive advice on the compilation of the list of teachings His Holiness had received. At one point His Holiness asked Ratö Khyongla Rinpoché, "Rinpoché, did tutor Kyabjé Ling Rinpoché ever give you any advice regarding Dölgyal?"
>
> Khyongla Rinpoché replied to His Holiness, "Yes. In Tibet once I asked Yongzin Ling Rinpoché how it would be if I relied on Dölgyal. Yongzin Rinpoché replied with a disapproving expression, 'I don't like new friends and new deities.'"
>
> Moving on from that, His Holiness recalled that in 1951 when he and Yongzin Ling Rinpoché were staying in Dromo, there were oracles for wrathful and peaceful forms of Dölgyal. The oracles for the government protectors of Nechung and Gadong had not traveled to Dromo. Therefore some high officials from the government put questions to Dölgyal, and this was the first connection made between Dölgyal and the government. At that time, Losang Lungrik, the Ling Labrang manager, asked Kyabjé Yongzin Rinpoché if it would be good to rely on Dölgyal. "Not necessary," was Rinpoché's reply.
>
> Later, after he had returned to Lhasa, the manager again asked, "Kyabjé Trijang Rinpoché relies upon Dölgyal. There are also increasing numbers of Geluk lamas, tulkus, and so on doing this practice. Therefore wouldn't it be good if the Ling Labrang did the same?"
>
> Yongzin Ling Rinpoché replied, "We are from the glorious Drepung Monastery, and we depend upon the old deities. There is no need to take up new ones. Kyabjé Trijang Rinpoché has a relationship from past lives, and so he is different."
>
> This is what His Holiness told us.
>
> The present manager of Ling Labrang, TT-la, or Thupten

Tsering, also told the Ganden Phodrang secretary Kungo Losang Jinpa that Yongzin Ling Rinpoché had made these comments.

Furthermore, His Holiness, continuing on the same topic, said, "Loseling Gala Rinpoché asked Yongzin Ling Rinpoché if he could practice Dölgyal. 'The old spirits are better than the new gods,' was the reply. Gala Rinpoché told me this himself."

His Holiness also said, "In 1960, at a Tibetan transit school in Khanyara, near Dharamsala, a group of teachers held an extensive propitiation of Dölgyal in the school one day. When Dzemé Rinpoche came to hear of this, he severely reprimanded the teachers and told them not to do it again. Clearly Dzemé Rinpoché did not consider it necessary to propitiate Dölgyal simply because one is a Gelukpa."

27. The Incarnation of Trijang Rinpoché

KYABJÉ TRIJANG VAJRADHARA passed away to the pure realm in 1981. In the following year his incarnation was born. After that the Dalai Lama recognized him as the incarnation and proceeded to care for him with exceptional love and compassion. Not only did His Holiness constantly urge him and advise him on the importance of his studies, but he appointed Lati Rinpoché, the former abbot of Ganden Shartsé, to be the young incarnation's tutor.

Because he was the incarnation of Kyabjé Trijang Vajradhara, the precious incarnation was the object of great hopes by the government and the people. For example, in terms of the Dharma, they hoped that he would be the sole son-like disciple of the wish-fulfilling jewel, His Holiness the Dalai Lama, and become an ornament of the teachings of the Buddha. Also, in terms of political administration, people both inside and outside of Tibet, as well as in the government, prayed that in these difficult and dangerous times he would provide key support for the Dalai Lama and the government, becoming the right hand of the Dalai Lama in whom all Tibetans could place their hope and trust.

Similarly, His Holiness held the strong desire that all the initiations, transmissions, oral instructions, and so on that he had received from Kyabjé Trijang Vajradhara would be returned to the precious Kyabjé Trijang incarnation as the Dharma being returned to the Dharma master, in the manner of one full vase being poured into another without the scent of the blessing being lost.

In 1996, when the precious incarnation was fourteen, followers of Dölgyal began to circulate lies that if he remained in India his life would be in great danger. This deceived the young incarnation. He was encouraged to not remain in the monasteries and to instead be taken abroad. This created nothing but obstacles to his being able to sit in the presence of His Holiness and receive teachings and to pursue his studies in the monastery.

These Dölgyal followers said that they followed the teachings of their root guru, Kyabjé Trijang Vajradhara, and were simply serving their lama, but the reality was that they had fallen into complete contradiction with the thoughts and wishes of Kyabjé Vajradhara. By deliberately pleasing the Communist Chinese, they were simply amassing the bad karma of pleasing their enemies and hurting their friends.

Nonetheless, whenever the opportunity arises, His Holiness the Dalai Lama gives advice and clarification to those connected to Trijang Rinpoché, such as the attendants of Trijang Labrang, saying that it is vitally important for the precious incarnation to return quickly to the monastery and to properly engage in his studies so that he may enact his own great deed of becoming an ornament of the Yellow Hat teachings. Therefore, the labrang, the college, and the monastic houses should consider this well and work hard to do what is right so as to avoid regret later on.

His Holiness has also stated from the beginning that it is not good for anyone to rely upon Dölgyal in general but that Kyabjé Trijang Vajradhara was a qualified lama who had the capacity to employ worldly spirits as servants. Moreover, the precious incarnation was the incarnation of his root lama. Therefore, for him an exception can be made, but not for others.

In this way, His Holiness made an exception for the precious incarnation. However, the Dölgyal followers held that Kyabjé Trijang Vajradhara's own practice and unique quality was his reliance upon Dölgyal and its propagation, and they perversely declared that it was the responsibility of the precious incarnation not only to practice Dölgyal but also to propagate it, that he was capable of doing this, and that Denma Gönsar[221] and others had great hopes for him doing this. They also broadcast statements that are painful to take in, dismaying to listen to, and simply alarming, such as that these days even the main tradition of Jé Tsongkhapa rests upon reliance on Dölgyal, that the Dalai Lama has not granted to them the principle "one's faith is one's own choice," and so on.

Therefore His Holiness the Dalai Lama has reiterated, among other things, that whether it is good for the life and deeds of the precious incarnation of Kyabjé Trijang to rely or not rely upon Dölgyal should be decided by a dough-ball divination and not by the Dalai Lama using his own wisdom.

In short, throughout this period, His Holiness the Dalai Lama has thought about what would benefit the life and work of the precious incarnation, what would bring him back to the monasteries and properly engage him in his studies, and how to give to the incarnation the complete transmission of teachings on sutra and tantra that he himself received from Kyabjé Trijang Rinpoché. At appropriate occasions, he has given much advice publicly and privately to those connected with the incarnation.

Whether the Dölgyal followers have listened to His Holiness's advice, whether they have come between His Holiness the Dalai Lama and the Trijang incarnation as lama and student, whether they have blocked and prevented His Holiness the Dalai Lama from transmitting to the precious Trijang incarnation the complete initiations, transmissions, and core instructions he himself received from Kyabjé Trijang Vajradhara, and whether this has harmed or helped the precious incarnation in working for the benefit of living beings can be clearly understood from seeing how Dölgyal followers obstructed the precious incarnation from taking the initiation of the Sixteen Drops of the Kadampa[222] from His Holiness the Dalai Lama. If you know about this, then, as the saying goes, "Seeing all with just a glance"[223]—you will definitely understand everything.

To show how they obstructed the precious incarnation from taking this initiation, we reproduce an extract from a discourse by His Holiness on October 2, 1997, in the Dharamsala Thekchen Chöling temple to many monastics and lay people (*Discourses on Dölgyal*, 2:249):

> This Sixteen Drops of the Kadampa initiation has been a little troublesome. Several days ago I met with Ganden Shartsé Geshé-la [Tsultim Gyeltsen] in the United States. I told him I would be doing a retreat of the Sixteen Drops of the Kadampa. Geshé-la asked if he could sponsor it, and I accepted. Before that I had thought about the fact that I had first received the Sixteen Drops of the Kadampa initiation from Kyabjé Trijang Rinpoché, and therefore I thought that I could offer this initiation to the precious incarnation. I had great hopes for that. Recently, when I was doing the retreat, I had an excellent dream in which I met Kyabjé Trijang Rinpoché. He was very pleased and presented me with a copy of *Great Treatise on the Stages of the Path*. I was very happy and thought to offer this initiation to the precious incarnation.
>
> In the beginning I held discussions with Lati Rinpoché, and at that time there was talk that the precious incarnation was coming here at the end of September. Shartsé Geshé-la also confirmed this was true. We discussed how good it would be if at the end

of September, during the teaching, I was able to bestow the Sixteen Drops of the Kadampa initiation on the precious incarnation. However, I received a reply from Switzerland (where the incarnation was living) that said that the precious incarnation would not be able to come. They said they had received many phone calls from India stating that if the precious incarnation were to come to Dharamsala, his safety could not be guaranteed. Therefore, unless Rinpoche was accompanied by twenty or thirty bodyguards, it would not be acceptable. Therefore it would not be convenient for him to come.

The office immediately wrote a letter to the precious incarnation. The government ministers also wrote a letter to him saying how good it would be if he could come, and that the Private Office and the council of ministers would take responsibility for his safety. After that the office received a letter in English written by Gönsar Rinpoché,[224] saying that the precious incarnation had finalized plans to visit other places, that it was not convenient for him to come to Dharamsala, and that generally the Dalai Lama had decided not to give initiations to those who practiced Dölgyal.

Last year after I had come to conclusions regarding Dölgyal, I called in the precious incarnation as well as Norbu Chöphel, because he was a senior attendant. Two other attendants also came. I said that whether the precious incarnation should practice Dölgyal in the future I would determine by way of doughball divination, and if for special reasons it was determined by the divination that he should, then the incarnation of Kyabjé Trijang Rinpoché, like the first portion of food put aside for offering up, would be set aside as an exception. Anyone else, for as long as they were practicing Dölgyal, I did not want them present when I was giving initiations. This I had already decided. I explained this to the precious incarnation that he was an exception. The attendants also understood this.

Last year when I went to South India I met with the manager, or attendant, of Trijang Labrang called Chözé as well as the secretary. I explained these points to them and entrusted them with this information. The attendants who had accompanied the precious incarnation were also aware of these points, but none of them told anyone else? It seems so by this letter. Whatever the case, I saw that Gönsar Tulku wanted to make trouble. It doesn't matter. It was a case of the humble trying to help, as they say.

That happened, and the precious incarnation was unable to come. I believe it would have been good had he come. I only had sincere and genuine motives. There was no other reason. According to what some have been saying recently, the incarnation of Trijang Rinpoché not returning here is probably because I was making trouble. That is simply not the case. I do not have to prove that.

Whatever the case, the forces of unconducive circumstances have prevented the precious incarnation from being here. Therefore this time the Sixteen Drops of the Kadampa initiation will be postponed. If Geshé-la came here specially, and even if he has to return empty-handed, it doesn't matter. If you think about it, you will understand. What must be done in the future, we will wait and see.

Some people behave strangely. It doesn't matter to me. If there is time tomorrow or the day after, I will talk about Dölgyal. The reason I am being so thorough about this is the three hundred years of history. I am not just talking about it because I feel like it.

This extract mentions how the Private Office received a letter written by Gönsar Tulku in English. On this one matter alone there are two main speculations held within the Tibetan community. The first is that when Gönsar Tulku—who is Tibetan and who holds the name of tulku—presents a written document to the office of His Holiness the Dalai Lama, leader of the religious and political administration of Tibet, and writes not in the language of the people of Tibet but in English, that this shows a disregard and contempt for the country of Tibet, the leader of Tibet, the Tibetan people, and its language and culture.

The second speculation is that Gönsar Tulku is not sufficiently educated in Tibetan to present to the Private Office a letter written in Tibetan.

Gönsar Tulku was born in 1949 in Shigatsé in Tsang. Around the age of six he was enrolled in Jadral House of Sera Jé Monastery and became a student of Geshé Rabten. However, in 1959 he came into exile and spent about three years studying in the monastery set up at Buxa, West Bengal.[225] Apart from those times, he did not come into contact with an opportunity for any further studies in the monasteries.

In 1962 he moved to Dharamsala and from then on studied English and Hindi languages. In 1969 he became interpreter for Geshé Rabten. In 1974 with Geshé Rabten, he moved permanently to Switzerland. Geshé Rabten passed away in 1976, and Gönsar Tulku took over Geshé-la's Dharma center. In recent times he was at the forefront of those who turned the head of the precious incarnation and is a main obstacle to the continuation of his studies.

28. The Criminal Acts of the Shukden Society

THE DISCOURSES ON the issue of Dölgyal given by Holiness the Dalai Lama over a long period, for the sake of the fundamental well-being of the Tibetan religious and political systems, can be seen to contain sound reasoning. And so, mindful of the kindness of the great Fourteenth Dalai Lama, the main pillar of the Tibetan religious and political systems—who from the age of sixteen up to the present day has worked tirelessly with great hardship, without a moment's relaxation, as if a single day was a whole life, for the sake of increasing our happiness in this life and the next, for the succession of the Dalai Lamas in general, and specifically for the land of Tibet and its people—most of those outside and inside Tibet who previously relied on Dölgyal have awoken from their sleep of ignorance and happily offered to stop the practice for good. These people are greatly praised by Tibetan brothers and sisters both in Tibet and in exile, the same flesh and blood.

However, there are a few who carry the name of Dölgyal in their mouths, and at this critical and dangerous time when the Tibetan religious and secular administrations, its people, and its culture are on the verge of disintegration, they have calculatedly joined forces with the enemy of the Buddha's teachings, the Chinese Communist regime. They claim that the Dalai Lama, by placing restrictions on Dölgyal, has denied them the principle of religious freedom and that Dölgyal is the exclusive protector of the Geluk tradition. They have cast slanderous and totally baseless aspersions on the person of His Holiness the Dalai Lama, the wish-fulfilling jewel and master of the Buddha's entire teachings here on earth.

Still they sow dissension between His Holiness and the Tibetan people inside and outside of Tibet. They sow dissension between the Tibetans in Tibet and those in exile, between the Tibetan religious traditions, between the government and the people, between His Holiness and the religious traditions, between Westerners and His Holiness, between His Holiness and the Chinese people, between the Tibetan people and the Chinese people, and so on.

Moreover, on April 4, 1996, they formed the Society for the Protection of Men and Gods by the Power of Unwavering Faith in Dorjé Shukden, Protector of the Teachings of Mañjunātha Tsongkhapa.[226] Since that time this group has planned and carried out a series of violent and horrifying acts within the Tibetan exile community. In particular, they have shown hostility toward those who willingly obey His Holiness. They have burned, beaten, killed, and carried out all manner of violent and frightening acts toward those who distribute and promote the advice of His Holiness, lama officials from the monasteries who have given friendly advice on the need to follow directly the advice and instructions of His Holiness, those in the service of the government in exile, and even ordinary people.

We will list some of these well-sourced incidents:

1. On May 27, 1996, a group of so-called monks from the Shukden Society, wearing lay clothes, their faces hidden by masks, carrying axes, knives, and petrol, came in the night to the residence of Trehor Thupten Wangchuk Rinpoché, former abbot of Ganden Shartsé in Mundgod, South India. They poured petrol through his window and set it on fire. His room was burned down, and Rinpoché himself suffered serious burns and had to spend a long time in hospital.

2. On January 26, 1997, at 4:00 in the afternoon, a group of men sent by the so-called Shukden Society lay in wait in Manjukatilla in Delhi and attacked Lubüm Geshé Trinlé Tenzin of Ganden Jangtsé Monastery, who was the chairman of the Mundgod Tibetan settlement conference. They severely beat him with stones, bamboo rods, metal wire, and so on. He nearly died and was unconscious for an extended period.

3. On the evening of February 4, 1997, the venerable Losang Gyatso, principal of the Dharamsala Dialectic School,[227] was in his room with two of his students, the monks Ngawang Lodrö and Losang Ngawang, translating Buddhist works from Tibetan into Chinese. Suddenly six men, their faces covered with masks, forcibly entered the room. They were so-called young monks of the Shukden Society, coming from Dokhang House of Ganden Monastery and Pomra House of Sera Mé Monastery. Their origins were

Lithang and Chatreng. They stabbed the venerable Losang Gyatso sixteen times and the two students more than ten times. After they had committed this heartless and unthinkable crime they fled to China. This and other facts have been verified by the Indian police, as His Holiness stated above in the chapters containing his discourses on Dölgyal.

4. On April 12, 1999, at about 6:30 in the evening, Geshé Phurbu Samdrup from Lhasa Phenpo district, and belonging to Tsawa House of Sera Jé Monastery, was in Delhi walking behind Samyé Ling Tantric College when he was set upon by six young men wearing lay clothes but with shaven heads. They carried stones and sticks wound with barbed wire up to the handles. They beat him so severely that Geshé-la had four different wounds on his head alone, while the rest of his body was covered in cuts. He collapsed to the ground, his body soaked in blood. He was taken to the hospital, where he had to receive treatment for a long time.

5. In October of 2000, in Dokhang House of Ganden Monastery in Mundgod, the Shukden Society gathered to hold their national conference. Prior to this the Shukden Society itself had advertised that they planned to hold a meeting to discuss protests against His Holiness and the government. Therefore, the local people knew that the Dölgyal leaders were coming. On the day of the actual meeting, hundreds of monks from Ganden and Drepung, as well as many lay people, spontaneously and of one mind marched in a peaceful demonstration to the conference. The Shukden Society had made preparations, and from the roofs of the buildings they threw stones, bricks, and bottles onto the crowd below. About seventy people were injured and had to be taken to the hospital.

6. On October 19, 2000, Phurbu Sitar, head of the Tibetan settlement at Bylakuppe in South India, and his wife Losang Chödrön were sleeping when, in the middle of the night, ten so-called monks of the Shukden Society arrived with their faces covered and carrying knives, iron bars, and sticks. They climbed up on the roof of the house, tore off the slates, and jumped in. They beat Phurbu Sitar and his wife so severely that their entire bodies were covered with wounds. With his broken ribs and other injuries, Phurbu Sitar fell unconscious and was dragged outside.

7. During the summer retreat of 2003, a letter tied with an offering scarf and looking like a petition for prayer recitation appeared on the table of Geshé Norsang-la, the chant leader for Ganden great assembly.[228] He was from Maldro Gungkar near Lhasa and belonged to Hardong House of Ganden Jangtsé Monastery. The letter read:

> Although it has never been the custom in the Ganden great assembly hall in the past, you have been reciting various prayers such as the long-life prayer of the Dalai Lama, the *Words of Truth* prayer,[229] and verses such as:
>
>> Those beings, whether formless or possessed of form,
>> who by the force of perverse prayers harbor hostility
>> toward the teachings of the Buddha
>> and who engage in acts from wicked thought and deed,
>> by the words of truth of the Three Jewels,
>> may they all be totally destroyed.
>
> Do not recite these kinds of prayers. If you continue to recite these types of prayer, we have no wish to attend assembly. If you do not listen to what we say, there is only one place for you to go. For those who do not like us, we have a place to send you to. Where that is, you must know.

Regardless of this letter, the assembly chant leader continued to recite the long-life prayer of the Dalai Lama and the *Words of Truth* prayer. One night he received a phone call on his residence landline. A voice said, "Recently we sent you a letter. Didn't you see it? If you do not control what you do, then one day we will send you somewhere. Then it will be too late."

The assembly chant leader's phone had caller identification. Therefore he was able to get the number of the person who phoned him. After the security office at the Mundgod settlement had investigated the phone number, they verified that it belonged to the Dölgyal practitioner Gyara Tulku from Yangteng Dapa in Kham of Dokhang House. They issued a warning saying, "Any bad incidents that happen to the assembly chant leader will lead to no one but you, and on that day you will be driven out of India."

8. Focusing solely upon diminishing the splendor of the influential and beneficial activities of His Holiness the Dalai Lama, and of nullifying the just struggle of the Tibetan people for autonomy, the Shukden Society has joined hands with the Chinese Communist regime, the enemy of the Buddhist teachings, and engaged in slander and calumny against His Holiness the Dalai Lama, the refugee community, and the government in exile.

For example, in 2002, the so-called Nga Lama[230] went to China, and on his return on July 19 stated in a Nepalese newspaper, "The Dalai Lama and Bin Laden are the same."

Also, they make claims such as that under the instruction of the Dalai Lama, the Tibetan monasteries in India and Nepal are waging a campaign of violence against China. By doing so they are deliberately causing dissension and schism between the Indian and Chinese governments on one side, and Nepal and the Tibetan exile administration on the other.

Wherever His Holiness goes in the world, amid the many thousands of the faithful who come to see him, the Shukden Society seize the opportunity, and with no trace of shame, raise their fists in the air, wave their various banners, and protest against him.

9. In 2008, on the day commemorating the March 10 uprising,[231] the Tibetans in Tibet staged a peaceful demonstration against the suffering and mistreatment they had endured for so long under the heavy yoke of the Chinese regime's oppression. In response the Chinese government instigated a frightening and blood-stained violent repression in which hundreds of Tibetans were killed and thousands thrown in prison. At this very time, when the Tibetan people, inside and outside Tibet, were plunged into deep grief and mourning, the Shukden Society on May 12 brought a writ petition against His Holiness the Dalai Lama and the head of the government, Kyabjé Samdhong Rinpoché, at the High Court in Delhi, accusing the Dalai Lama and the government of mistreating and harassing Dölgyal followers.

For about two years the High Court investigated the case, and finally on April 5, 2010, Justice S. Muralidhar of the Delhi High Court concluded, "The allegations that the Shukden followers were being systematically harassed and mistreated are found to have no basis." Also, "There is no clear evidence of any attacks being carried out on Shukden practitioners."

Thus the High Court announced that the petition would not be considered.

10. The Ganden Shartsé proctor Geshé Ngawang Tsering and the Shartsé chant leader Geshé Tenzin Namdak both followed the wishes of His Holiness the Dalai Lama. Consequently, they both received phone calls from public telephones from Dölgyal practitioners. One said to Geshé Ngawang Tsering, "When you have finished your term as disciplinarian, we will send you a gift of thanks." Also, knives wrapped in ceremonial scarves were thrown more than once over the wall surrounding his house and in his doorway. In such a way he was threatened repeatedly.

Geshé Tenzin Namdak, similarly, was walking along the main street in Mundgod town one day when a Dölgyal monk took hold of the collar of his upper garment and, with his teeth bared, he threatened, "It would be best if you behave. Otherwise, we will not leave you be." However, the chant leader meditated on patience and did not reply.

Members of the Shukden Society have set fire to private houses, public buildings, private possessions, government and private buses, and even grazing land for livestock. They have smashed the windows of buses that take children to and from school as well as the windows of government and private houses. These incidents, together with evidence and dates, have been recorded in other publications. This is just a summary enumeration of some of the worst incidents. Because of their length, the episodes have not been presented in any detail.

29. A Discourse on Dölgyal by the Hundredth Ganden Throneholder

Venerable Losang Nyima (1928–2008), the Hundredth Ganden Throneholder, gave many discourses on why it is improper to rely on Dölgyal. The one reproduced here was given in 1996 to a large audience from both the monastic and lay communities. It is from a compilation put together by the Domé Dölgyal Research Committee called *Spotless Mirror: An Examination of the Coming of Dölgyal and the Ensuing Controversy.* He says (388):

> Just stating that it was a practice of great lamas of the past and that one's faith is one's own choice is not that helpful. The great lamas of the past were able to unite the peaceful and wrathful meditation deities with their minds, and through that, their perception was totally pure. This is completely different from our devotional practices in which our karma-led perceptions are bound up in a procession of ordinary perceptions and clinging.
>
> Using this as a basis to slander His Holiness the Dalai Lama by saying that there is disharmony between him and the great masters of the past is to hold to the lamas as ordinary beings and is a slanderous wrong view brought on by mental afflictions. Therefore know this to be very heavy karma. You must be very careful.
>
> If a protector is genuine, it should protect the people. A protector that needs to be aided and protected by the people is no protector. Is it right to cause trouble, become angry, saying whatever nonsense comes to your mind, thereby disrupting the peace and harmony of everyone, just to please the Dharma protector? Is this what the great masters of the past wanted? Will it fulfill their wishes? How many of the volumes of teachings, exemplified by

those works on the stages of the path and on mind training, state these things?

Also, further on:

The Mahayana teachings say that we should sacrifice a little for the sake of the many and that it is right to do so. For the cause and benefit of the Tibetan people and for the well-being of His Holiness the Dalai Lama, why can't we, who claim to be Mahayanists, stop relying on these dubious gods and protectors? The monastic codes of the Vinaya say that an issue should be settled by the use of counting sticks, and the minority accepts the will of the majority. If a position is supported by ninety-five percent and five percent refuse to listen, there exists provisions such as the four punishments, the seven removals, and the four convictions.[232] Therefore they really should stop the practice. That is the right thing to do.

If from our own side we respect and adhere to the precepts and the vows, and are able to preserve, develop, and spread the teachings, then because there are genuine Dharma protectors as many as the stars in the sky, there is no point in scratching our heads and wondering about unquestionably genuine protectors.

If the protector is not genuine, then far from carrying out your wishes, reliance on such a protector would be like taking hold of a thunderbolt with your bare hands.[233] Therefore His Holiness has quoted from the biography of Ganden Throneholder Ngawang Chokden composed by Changkya Rölpai Dorjé, which relates how, with his innately pure mind, free from the stains of misconception, he expelled Dölgyal from the bounds of the monastery. Also, in the biography of Jamyang Khyentsé Wangpo (1820–92) by Dodrup Jikmé Tenpai Nyima, it is written that once, when Khyentsé was giving teachings on Hevajra at Dergé Lhundrup Teng, Gyalpo Shukden came to listen, saying, "As your explanations are excellent and your teachings are good, I want to listen to them." The text goes on to say, "Therefore, not only humans but even hostile spirits came to drink the nectar of his teachings."

When great masters across all traditions recognize such creatures as being not fit for them to rely upon, as described above, then without doubt the same is true for us with our karma-created perceptions.

In his *Great Commentary on Kālacakra Tantra*, Khedrup Jé describes how the māra Garab Wangchuk[234] would constantly hinder the venerable Galo[235] with his various apparitions, sometimes pretending to protect him and at other times pretending to encourage him to practice. However, Galo had received the initiation of Red Yamāntaka and was impervious to such attacks. There are many such accounts of false apparitions, of carrying out trivial activities, and so on, none of which engender trust.

At times, even reliance upon authentic deities has had to be stopped. During twenty-one days of the Great Prayer Festival in Lhasa, invocation of and requests to Karmasha[236] through oracles were prohibited.

There was a wicked headman from Chushur called Tenpa Tsering who at death was born as a spirit in the entourage of Samyé Pehar. This malicious spirit put poison in the tea cauldron meant for the monastic assembly at the Great Prayer Festival. But Dharma protector Nechung pierced a hole in the bottom of the cauldron with his ribbon-adorned spear, thereby ensuring that afternoon tea could not be served.

They say, "One's faith is one's own choice," but they have not understood the meaning of these words. A short explanation will loosen the knots of doubt. These expressions—"Having faith or not in a particular Dharma is one's own choice" or "Believing or not believing in any Dharma is one's own choice"—mean that no one is forced to practice or not practice the Dharma. Therefore all that is being said is, "Others can do as they please. We have faith and belief in the Dharma." However, if you say, "There are no restrictions on what doctrine you can or cannot follow, because one's faith is one's choice," or, "There are no restrictions on what deity or protector you follow, because one's faith is one's own choice," and then with no respect for the laws of the country, as in the saying, "the people reject the law, and the horse rejects the saddle," someone who has entered the Buddhist path then goes and practices Hinduism or Islam, how can that be acceptable? If someone who has entered the Buddhist path goes and practices a path with tenets completely incompatible with those of Buddhism, that is a breach of the precepts of refuge, and in that case it is unacceptable to say, "One's faith is one's choice."

If it were unnecessary to have any boundaries to "one's faith is one's choice," then there would have been no monastic rules in the past stating that novice monks seeking entrance to the monasteries had to join the monastic houses corresponding to the area of their birth, and that incarnate lamas had to join the monastic houses of their predecessors, and were not allowed to change monasteries. When these rules were broken they resulted in litigation. There were many such cases, and here too some houses are engaged such disputes. Therefore, by understanding properly the saying, "one's faith is one's choice," we must put an end to these arguments so that these troubles do not arise.

If having undivided faith in a worldly deity is not a downfall in your refuge precepts, then what is it? Furthermore, there is no one here who has not received teachings from His Holiness the Dalai Lama, and from those teachings we have all received tantric initiations, transmissions, and instructions. The fault of having contempt for the vajra master carries a weight that is unbearable even to imagine. Therefore, if someone who believes in the law of cause and effect engages in such wicked act with eyes closed, unconcerned, with no attempt to avoid it, and entices others to do the same and is not even a little bit concerned, that is extraordinary.

If you can contemplate a little about what is taught concerning devoting oneself to a spiritual master in the stages of the path work by the Kyabjé Vajradhara,[237] that would be good. The *Guhyasamāja Root Tantra* says:

> Even though living beings commit heinous acts,
> such as those bringing immediate retribution,
> they will still find attainment in the supreme vehicle,
> the great ocean of Vajrayana.
> But should they from the heart despise the vajra master,
> they may practice, but there will be no attainment.

Also, in the *Vajrapāṇi Empowerment Tantra* and elsewhere, it says that the faults committed in devotion to the spiritual master are beyond explanation. If we who profess to be tantric practitioners do not think about this, then who will?

Not following the advice in the discourses by His Holiness, which are given for developing what is good and reducing what is wrong in the political and religious systems of Tibet, and because some little thing does not fit your views and you are not happy with the advice, you immediately disregard what he has said and instigate a campaign: this is simply a case of having no altruistic thoughts for the cause of Tibet and its people.

When Jé Tsongkhapa founded the new Kadampa school, if he had done so on the basis of devotion or nondevotion to this violent deity, then fine. But Jé Rinpoché did not divide the old and new Kadampa traditions on the basis of deity devotion. Such ideas are extreme, and not to consider that carefully is not good.

If we continue to jump up and down like a child who has received a present from his parents just because we have become a little wealthier, then we don't have to search far for evidence of Jé Tsongkhapa's prophecy, "Later my teachings will be destroyed by the pleasures of the senses."

30. Resolutions and a Referendum

ON JANUARY 1, 1998, at the monastic seat of Sera Thekchen Ling, a plenary conference of the Geluk tradition was held. It was chaired by the Ganden Throneholder and attended by Jangtsé Chöjé Rinpoché, past and present abbots of the three monasteries and their six colleges, of Gyütö and Gyümé tantric colleges, of Namgyal Monastery, Tashi Lhunpo, Ratö Monastery, Mön Tawang Monastery, and others. The conference produced a joint resolution that states:

> Therefore the many past and present abbots of the three monasteries, the lamas and tulkus who from the beginning did not practice Dölgyal, and those who in the past did practice it hold in great esteem the words of His Holiness the Dalai Lama, and together with the Tibetan people of the three regions, we now oppose, directly, indirectly, and in other ways, those who have not renounced the practice.

Also:

> From now on, we sever all connection with those who refuse to renounce the practice of relying upon Dölgyal and with those Dölgyal followers who by differentiating the mouth from the moustache, assign each river to a different country. We place ourselves directly under the guidance of His Holiness the Dalai Lama, whose advice brings benefit now and in the long term.

As can be seen from these extracts, from the past up to now, conferences of the Geluk tradition alone, as well as the leaders of the Sakya, Geluk, Kagyü, Nyingma, and Bön traditions in their plenary meetings and elsewhere, have delivered resolutions calling for restrictions on Dölgyal.

The Geluk Referendum on Dölgyal

Based on the authentic historical accounts transcribed above, and particularly on the message of the advice and guidance given by His Holiness the Dalai Lama, the leaders of the religious traditions in Tibet, the lamas and officials of the monasteries and colleges, those who serve the people, as exemplified by the leaders of our democratic government, those with a sincere sense of responsibility, those of sensible, intelligent thinking—in short, all those with a love for our traditions and our people—have explained to Dölgyal practitioners again and again in great detail, until they could do no more.

However, it was like talking to the stones and the earth. They did not listen or learn. And more than that, the Shukden Society, solely for financial and material gain, joined forces with the Chinese regime and instigated all manner of divisive campaigns within the Tibetan community. Day by day and year by year, this became clearer and clearer. Many students from the monasteries became appalled by the activities of the Shukden Society. They were unhappy at having to go to places where Dölgyal practitioners were gathered, such as at the annual Jangun debate gathering, and for a while even the staging of this annual gathering was met with problems. It was fast coming to the critical point where if this situation continued, the continuity of the Jangun gathering was in serious jeopardy.

At this time on January 9, 2008, at the opening ceremony of the Drepung Loseling assembly hall, His Holiness the Dalai Lama announced that there would be a referendum. In the Vinaya scriptures there were seven ways of settling disputes relating to Dharma matters. They included distributing counting sticks, knotted grass, and so on. This practice would now be initiated to decide whether to rely on Dölgyal, whether we should associate communally or religiously with those who practice Dölgyal. Being able to settle this matter decisively by way of a referendum, in keeping with modern democratic ways, would be very beneficial. This was his announcement.

Consequently, for two days on January 18 and 19, 2008, on the upper story of Drepung Loseling's new assembly hall, a conference was convened to informally discuss the matter. The head of the administration, or Kalön Tripa, the venerable Samdhong Rinpoché, was specially invited. The meeting was attended by the Sharpa Chöjé and Jangtsé Chöjé, representatives from the six colleges of the three monastic seats, Gyütö and Gyümé tantric colleges, Namgyal Monastery, Tashi Lhunpo, Ratö Monastery, Dzongkar Chödé Monastery, Mön Tawang Monastery, and others, comprising all past and present abbots, college disciplinarians, chant leaders, and managers, the chant leaders and managers of the three governing councils of the three monastic seats, a representative of the Tibetan people in the form of the regional people's deputy, representatives of the Mundgod Dögu Ling Tibetan settlement, including the chairman of the people's deputies, the director of the settlement, and the secretary of the director's office.

They discussed whether there were any way besides a referendum to quell the serious ongoing problems within the Tibetan community brought about by Dölgyal practitioners. The meeting unanimously agreed that a referendum was the best means to accomplish this. Consequently, twelve people were appointed to be the referendum governing committee. This consisted of the Ganden Throneholder or his appointed representative, the Sharpa Chöjé and Jangtsé Chöjé, a representative from the Religious Affairs department of the government, the six managers of the six colleges of the three monasteries, the representative of the regional people's deputies, and the director of Mundgod settlement.

The following was also unanimously agreed: that specific referendum committees should be formed from the abbots, chant leaders, and administrators of the individual colleges; that on the days of the vote, members from the referendum governing committee would go to the various colleges and the vote would be carried out together with the specific referendum committees of those colleges; that the day of the vote would be decided on by the various colleges; that when the counting sticks were handed out and the votes counted, if more than 90 percent voted not to practice Dölgyal and not to associate with Dölgyal practitioners either communally or religiously, then with the Three Jewels as their witness, it would be necessary to offer a pledge of allegiance to these two declarations. Similarly, it was unanimously agreed that from then on committees made up of the abbots, chant leaders, and administrators of the individual colleges would be needed, and that these committees would see to it that the procedure of pledging not to practice Dölgyal, or to associate with Dölgyal practitioners either communally or religiously, be continued even to include new entrants to the monasteries.

When the referendum was held with these unanimous resolutions as its basis, with the exception of groups within Pomra House of Sera Mé, Dokhang House of Ganden Shartsé, and a few monks from one or two other houses, 97 or 98 percent of the monks freely selected the counting stick that declared they would not practice Dölgyal and not associate with Dölgyal practitioners either communally or religiously. Furthermore, with the Three Jewels as their witness, they pledged allegiance to these declarations. From that time on, in the three monastic seats in India, Gyütö and Gyümé tantric colleges, and the other monasteries mentioned above, no one is permitted to rely upon Dölgyal. As a result, the troubles surrounding Dölgyal have ceased.

The Effect of the Referendum

As described above, for many years the Dölgyal group was engaged in violent and seriously threatening acts, in complete contradiction to the Dharma. As a result, many monks who were not practicing Dölgyal were unwilling to participate in events where Dölgyal practitioners were present. These included the assembly tea, the college tea, monastic house tea, the monthly purification ceremony, the summer retreat, the ceremony of reiterating the monastic rules at the summer retreat, the Great Prayer Festival in the first month, which was initiated by Tsongkhapa and was one of his four great deeds, the monastic examinations, the Jangun debate gathering, and so on, as well as the debate gatherings between the colleges. This meant that communal gatherings of the three monasteries, as well as inter-college assemblies, were becoming fraught with difficulties. The number of monks from other traditions had been dwindling at the annual Jangun gathering, and within our Geluk tradition the numbers attending the gathering had also dramatically decreased. Had the situation been allowed to continue, before long relationships among the religious traditions would have weakened, and moreover the three main Geluk monasteries would have become isolated from each other, with no connections between them at all.

However, the referendum held at the beginning of 2008 settled the matter. Consequently, in December of that year, about five thousand monastics attended the Jangun debate gathering held at Ganden Monastery. Not only had they come from the main and branch monasteries of the Geluk, exemplified by Ganden, Sera, and Drepung monasteries, but there were Bön participants from the monastery of Menri Trizin Rinpoché and Drigung Kagyü participants from the monastery of Drigung Kyapgön Rinpoché in Dehradun who had never been to the Jangun gathering before. For one month, in an atmosphere of harmony and compliance with the rules, they discussed and debated thoroughly the great texts on logic, such Dharmakīrti's *Treatise on Valid Cognition.*

In 2009 the Jangun gathering was held at the great monastic seat of Drepung. As well as the participants from the various traditions that attended the previous year, there were students from the Sakya tradition and the Kamtsang Kagyü tradition, making in total about six thousand participants. Thus it was carried off in an atmosphere of success, free from troublemakers.

From then on, every year, not only students from the Geluk tradition, epitomized by the three monastic seats, but many learned followers of dialectics from across the religious traditions of Tibet flocked to the Jangun debate gathering like swans to a lotus pool, where they studied in an atmosphere of harmony and discipline.

Similarly, many thousands of monks continue to mingle with each other across the three monasteries, and within the individual colleges, and yet unlike before, there is not even a whiff of discord, as harmony and compliance continues to grow. Such an accomplishment is without doubt a vast and peerless offering made in the service of the precious teachings of our founder, the unequaled Lion of the Śākyas (Buddha).

31. The Final Position of the Eight Geluk Monasteries

THE CONTROVERSIAL HISTORY of Dölgyal or Gyalpo Shukden spans nearly four hundred years. In recent years, practitioners of Dölgyal had done all they can to propagate their claim that Dölgyal is an exclusive and qualified protector of the teachings of Tsongkhapa and so on. As a result, we researched and analyzed the following:

- The authentic biographies and accounts of the great masters and practitioners of the past from the Sakya, Geluk, Kagyü, and Nyingma traditions, who cover Tibet like the sky covers the land, which reveal how they mostly regarded Dölgyal, as well as their sources and reasoning for their perceptions.
- In particular, the autobiography *Heavenly Raiment* and other compositions from the collected works of the Great Fifth Dalai Lama, in whose time the Dölgyal controversy arose. The one who lived through that period, and wrote at that time of the actual events as they occurred, often with dates and times, was the Great Fifth.
- The profound, vast, and eye-opening advice given by His Holiness the Fourteenth Dalai Lama—a wish-fulfilling jewel, guide and protector, the destined deity on whom fell the flower of the snow-mountain dwellers of Tibet, whose discourses provide the information on the outer, inner, and secret perceptions of Dölgyal or Gyalpo Shukden from the past to the present day—on whether or not Dölgyal is an exclusive protector of Tsongkhapa's teachings, on the merits and demerits, the gains and the losses, of relying upon Dölgyal, and finally, on what we should and should not do in this connection.
- The works written by Dölgyal practitioners of how Tulku Drakpa Gyaltsen died, and how, according to them, he first arose in the form of a worldly spirit as the protector of Mañjunātha Tsongkhapa's teachings,

how Dölgyal became the exclusive protector of Tsongkhapa's teachings, and so on, together with any sources and references.

With these documents as the main references, we researched and compared both sides. As we did so, we found that the more we examined Dölgyal side, the more it did not to stand up to analysis and the more unpleasant information we uncovered. It became increasingly clear that reliable and untainted scripture and reasoning establishing Dölgyal as the exclusive protector of the teachings of Mañjunātha Tsongkhapa was nothing more than the hair of a turtle and the siblings of a horned rabbit.

On the other hand, the restrictions on Dölgyal put in place by great masters of the past, and especially the advice and discourses given by the Fourteenth Dalai Lama, were well researched by way of perfect reasoning, and it soon became self-evident that the merits and demerits of this issue presented by a guide whose nature is that of compassion, truthfully, openly, and exactly as he understood them, with great compassion and reliability, were an unparalleled kindness for the teachings and living beings in general and specifically for cleaning up the precious teachings of the Riwo Genden tradition. Therefore, as the venerable Tsongkhapa said:

> Having seen the truth as it is, you taught it well.
> Training in your way is to leave all troubles far behind,
> as all error is forever turned away.
>
> Those outside your teachings
> may practice long and with hardship,
> but it will be like calling back the errors,
> because their view of self is firm.[238]

On the basis of the reality of what is right and wrong as presented above, the monks and nuns, from the young to the old, of the main and branch monasteries of the Geluk tradition in their entirety—namely, the six colleges of the three monastic seats, Gyütö and Gyümé tantric colleges, the great monastic seat of Tashi Lhunpo, Ratö Monastery, Namgyal Monastery, and all other affiliated Geluk monasteries who at present are established in exile—have willingly and happily taken the oath, with the Three Jewels as their witness, not to practice Dölgyal or to associate with Dölgyal practitioners either communally or religiously:

1. From now on, the main and branch monasteries of the Geluk tradition as exemplified by the six colleges of the three monastic seats, Gyütö and Gyümé tantric colleges, the great monastic seat of Tashi Lhunpo, Ratö Monastery, and Namgyal Monastery must put in writing as part of their rules and regulations that no one will practice Dölgyal or associate with Dölgyal practitioners communally or religiously. On that basis, from this time onward, with regard to Dölgyal, the above colleges will continue to maintain this position, down to the pledges they have taken.

2. The six colleges of the three great monastic seats, Gyütö and Gyümé tantric colleges, the great monastic seat of Tashi Lhunpo, Ratö Monastery, and Namgyal Monastery, who are at present established in exile in India, and all monasteries affiliated with them both in Tibet and exile must be as one in regard to the above position on Dölgyal.

3. All patrons and sponsors of the teachings, whoever they may be, who have a connection with Dölgyal and yet who possess unwavering faith and belief in the six colleges of three great monastic seats, Gyütö and Gyümé tantric colleges, the great monastic seat of Tashi Lhunpo, Ratö Monastery, and Namgyal Monastery, all of which are at present based in India, must understand that such a connection is in direct contradiction with the position taken by the Geluk tradition as a whole. Therefore, for as long as they maintain that connection, they cannot have any relationship with the above monasteries.

4. The above monasteries and colleges urge the following: As there cannot possibly be anyone who would deliberately throw themselves into the ravine of the dense forests of frightening wrongdoings and take joy in such self-destruction, current Dölgyal practitioners, whoever they may be, who from this moment on clearly comprehend the reality of the emergence of Dölgyal over the years, who have turned away from the mistaken path and the wrong path, and who have genuinely given up the practice of relying on Dölgyal, the monasteries and colleges as a whole will show open support toward such people, provide them assistance, and make prayers and dedications for the sake of increasing all that is good in their present and future lives.

5. Primarily because of His Holiness the Fourteenth Dalai Lama's universally beneficial and extraordinary activities, which have been carried out effectively and skillfully, these days the number of those who show an active interest in Buddhism is spreading daily throughout

the world. At this time, a few Dölgyal followers are deceiving and misleading those Westerners who do not fully understand the tenets of Buddhism. The monastic community, whether old or young, who are objects of refuge, as epitomized by Geluk lamas and officials, will take on this responsibility and make efforts to convey to Westerners the reality of Dölgyal and its history.

6. At this time, under the violent persecution carried out at will by the Chinese Communist regime, enemy of the teachings, and when the Tibetan religious and secular systems, the people, and their culture are in serious danger of annihilation, there are those who are focused on damaging the great deeds undertaken by His Holiness the Fourteenth Dalai Lama across the world, as well as his glorious reputation and name. By doing so, they are destroying the Tibetan people's struggle for freedom, thereby exploiting time and circumstance to deliberately aid the enemy of the teachings. We, the Geluk tradition as a whole, vow to resolutely oppose such people.

7. At this time when the Tibetan religious and secular systems, the people, and their culture are in serious danger of annihilation, in order to successfully fulfill the powerful wishes of His Holiness the Dalai Lama, the Geluk tradition as a whole should not be lax in doing whatever they can, whenever they can, to promote teachings and studies among all the religious traditions of Tibet without bias, to increase the harmony and goodwill among these traditions, and to be of service to all traditions.

8. The Chinese Communist regime took over and controlled the whole of the great land of China, neighbor to Tibet. On October 1, 1951, it announced to the world the formation of the People's Republic of China. Before long the Red Chinese marched in and violently occupied the religious land of Tibet, thereby turning its world upside down. This was a critical time. "A collapsed mountain cannot be tied back together with rope," as we say, and His Holiness the Dalai Lama was not yet sixteen. However, the people of Tibet unanimously petitioned him with great passion, for there was no other option than for him to take on the sovereign responsibility for the religious and secular affairs of Tibet.

Consequently, from that day on, day and night, His Holiness the Dalai Lama took on countless hardships for the sake of the immediate, future, and long term well-being of the religious and secular systems, the Tibetan people, and its culture. Finally, in 1959 the Ganden Phodrang government, headed by the wish-fulfilling jewel, His Holiness the Dalai Lama, and the lawful government of the Tibetan people with a verifiable history of over three hundred years, sought refuge in the noble land of India.

Generally, the ripened fruits of His Holiness's great endeavors to regain freedom for Tibet are evident for all of us to see. In particular, using a host of scriptural references and reasoning, he has separated good practices from bad ones and imposed restrictions on the oath-violating Dölgyal. In doing so he has carried out exemplary work to restore the teachings of the Buddha in general, and the precious teachings of the second Buddha, Tsongkhapa, in particular.

In this regard, for as long as the precious teachings of Mañjunātha Tsongkhapa remain in this world, the Geluk tradition as a whole, keeping in mind the great kindness of the Fourteenth Dalai Lama, will offer him limitless thanks of gratitude. To repay that kindness, we will retain the meaning of the great and effective advice and instruction he has given us and not spare any effort in performing the great offering of practice.

At the same time, so that this great treasure of compassion may continue his wonderful and inconceivable work as the guide and protector of the living beings of this world, we should constantly and fervently make prayers and requests to the unfailing Three Jewels of refuge in their sacred realms, and regularly perform effective and authentic ritual practices, in their outer, inner, and secret formats, so that, for the beings of this world and particularly for the beings of the snowy land of Tibet under the protection of the Holder of the Lotus, a connection formed through the power of past karma and deep prayers, he remains with us for thousands upon thousands of eons, his lotus feet firmly on the immutable high vajra throne, and so that all his profound and untainted wishes are quickly and without obstruction fulfilled.

32. Dedication and Colophon

There are those whose training in the sciences is weak,
who are incapable of researching the facts of history,
and who, beguiled by an oath-breaker born of perverse prayers,
rise up and protest with fearsome weapons.

Nevertheless, here in the twenty-first century,
where the power of science is all-pervading,
the vajra machine of the three means of reasoning,[239]
which separates out the good from the bad,
is a greatness of the teachings of the Śākya conqueror.

The Ganden tradition, as pure as refined gold,
is the supreme guide and protector,
guarding the teachings and living beings,
worthy of the highest veneration
and endowed with the eye of wisdom.
Why would anyone rely on an oath-violator
born of bad karma and perverse prayers?

Therefore the excessive praise lavished on Dölgyal
in the past by the venerable Morchen Kunga Lhundrup
and Sachen Kunga Lodrö of the glorious Sakya tradition
and, later on, by Kyabjé Phabongkha and others
should be compared to the unerring vajra words
separating truth from falsehood, as clearly as the sky from the earth,
written by the conqueror Ngawang Losang Gyatso,
the Great Fifth, protector and guide of gods and men.

They will be seen to be nothing but the waters of a mirage,
boastful and baseless superimpositions,
the calling of a white snow mountain black,
the white conch shell red;
whereas the sun and moon of the truth
in the pure sky will illuminate the three worlds.

This has been a presentation, therefore,
made purely with altruistic intent
and not containing a trace of ill will against others,
ascertained and established with the subtle reasoning
of the great masters of India and Tibet
and not with the lewd coarseness of thoughtless nonsense.
It is built on the basis of authentic teachings,
biographies, and history,
and not on unsourced, made-up falsehoods.
It is clarification of just who is the exclusive protector of the Geluk,
not senseless talk that deprecates and projects.

However, the more the subtleties of phenomena are analyzed,
the more questions and doubts will grow.
Therefore, should there be omissions, contradictions,
repetitions, and lack of connection,
we humbly declare them to the unbiased and the learned.

Whatever good we have amassed through this endeavor,
and by the virtue gathered by ourselves and others in the past, present,
    and future,
may the wish-granting jewel, His Holiness the Dalai Lama,
the central pillar of the religious and secular systems of Tibet,
and all those who preserve the teachings regardless of tradition,
live long and may their beneficial wishes be effortlessly fulfilled.
And may the teachings of the Buddha, and specifically
the noble tradition of Mañjunātha Tsongkhapa,
flourish until the end of samsara.

Sarva mangalam.

Notes

1. Songtsen Gampo, Trisong Detsen, and Tri Ralpachen, three early and influential kings who lived between the seventh and ninth centuries.

2. The Tibetan government.

3. The Geluk tradition.

4. Being learned, compassionate, and ethical; skilled in teaching, debate, and composition; and having mastered learning, contemplation, and meditation.

5. The bold words spell out (but not in the order of the Tibetan) the long ceremonial name of the Fourteenth Dalai Lama, which is Gyalwang Tenzin Gyatso Sisum Wangyur Tsungpa Mepai Dé.

6. The district in southeastern Tibet where the famous Samyé Monastery stands.

7. Renowned Geluk scholar and practitioner of Drepung Monastery who held the abbotship of Drepung, Sera, and Ganden monasteries in his life and who supporters of Dölgyal claim is a past incarnation of Drakpa Gyaltsen.

8. The First Panchen Lama, and tutor to the Fifth Dalai Lama, Losang Chökyi Gyaltsen (1570–1662).

9. 1594–1615. The third incarnation of Panchen Sönam Drakpa, of whom Drakpa Gyaltsen is claiming to be an incarnation. I cannot identify the place where he died, although Trülnang is sometimes used to refer to Lhasa. The following verse would account for the four years between the death of this lama and the birth of Drakpa Gyaltsen in 1619.

10. *Sa ga zla ba.* The fourth month of the lunar calendar, at the full moon of which the Buddha gained enlightenment under the Bodhi Tree.

11. *Puṣya (rgyal)* is the eighth of the twenty-eight lunar mansions and is found in the astrological sign of Cancer.

12. Rulers of the Tsang province, west of Lhasa. *Desi* is a political title meaning administrator, or sometimes ruler. The first Tsangpa Desi was Tseten Dorjé, who according to sources became ruler of Tibet in 1566, having defeated the Rinpung administration.

13. Although the text could read as if he arrived in central Tibet in that year, other sources state that this was the year he set out from Mongolia, where he was born, and that the journey took two to three years.

14. A subsect of the Kagyü religious tradition of Tibet.

15. An area about thirty miles south of Lhasa.

16. *Silnön* means "suppressing," and so the name of the new monastery could be understood to mean the monastery that suppresses the Geluk monastery Tashi Lhunpo.

17. "Ocean of power."

18. A Mongolian governor.

19. An ancient Indian kingdom.

20. By now the Desi was Karma Phuntsok Namgyal (d. 1631), who began his rule in 1611, when he was fourteen.

21. 1595–1657/58. Also known as Sönam Rabten. A major player in this conflict and holder of high office in the Fifth Dalai Lama's government. He is usually known as Treasurer or Desi Sönam Chöphel. Here the title Shalngo (monastic disciplinarian) refers to the time he held that post at Drepung before his political career (*Treasury of Names*, 1070).

22. Monastery built by the Second Dalai Lama.

23. Village below Drepung Monastery.

24. Sangphu Neuthok in Lower Kyishö district was a monastery founded by the early Kadampa master Ngok Lotsāwa Lekpai Sherab in the eleventh century, but it was a Geluk institution by this point.

25. There had been two separate divinations, both placing the birthplace of the incarnation in the Yarlung region. However, the one from the Tsangpa oracle had indicated Chongyé, where the Great Fifth was born, but the Samyé oracle gave the birthplace as Serma Shung.

26. The 35th Ganden Throneholder (1573–1664).

27. Radreng Monastery's most precious statue, a Guhyasamāja image with three faces and six arms presented to the monastery by the Indian master Atiśa.

28. By tradition a child at birth is said to be one year old, or more correctly, in their first year.

29. Beginning from the second day of the lunar month, every five days is a *bhadrā* day.

30. As asserted below, this is Drakpa Gyaltsen.

31. *Ye shes dbyings dpyad.* In other words, an investigation carried out by way of clairvoyance, examining dreams, divinations, omens, and so on.

32. Some include this twelfth-century Kashmiri pandit (1127–1225) who visited Tibet among the past incarnations of Drakpa Gyaltsen.

33. The Kashmiri Panchen is Panchen Śākyaśrī mentioned above. Butön Rinchen Drup (1290–1364) was a famous Sakya master and abbot who composed many influential works.

34. This refers to *History of the Old and New Kadampa: An Ornament of the Mind*, by Panchen Sönam Drakpa, in the colophon of which (1:102b) the words could be taken to mean that Sönam Drakpa was an incarnation of Butön Rinpoché.

35. Famous verses attributed to the Indian master Mitrayogin (twelfth–thirteenth century) and transmitted in Tibet.

36. Desi Sangyé Gyatso (1653–1705) was prime minister of Tibet who ruled as regent after the Fifth Dalai Lama passed away in 1682.

37. Large subgroup of Mongols.

38. Choghtu Khong Taiyiji (1581–1637), Mongolian noble and supporter of the Tsang rulers. Khong Taiyiji is a title for Mongolian nobles.

39. Karma Tenkyong Wangpo (1606–42) was the last Tsangpa Desi. He took over from his father in 1632 and was finally defeated by Gushri Khan in 1642.

40. *Ban bon.* This term can mean Buddhists and Bönpos, but I have been told that here it refers only to Bönpos. In Shakabpa, *Bod kyi srid don rgyal rabs* (p. 146), this sentence has been translated as, "all religious sects, including the Bon: the only exception being the Ge-lug-pa."

41. Cited in Shakabpa, *Bod kyi srid don rgyal rabs*, 412.

42. Gushri Khan (1582–1655), leader of the Khoshut Mongols. The Fifth Dalai Lama granted him the name Tenzin Chögyal.

43. The first text has many spelling mistakes, far more than you would expect from a learned writer. There is a copy of this work in the TBRC library filed under the name of Ngawang Losang Tenpai Gyaltsen. It cannot be a work by this master because he was not born until 1660. Drakpa Gyaltsen clearly identifies himself in the text and, moreover, states that his masters included Panchen Chögyen, who died in 1662.

    Nevertheless, this TBRC text is mercifully free of the spelling mistakes mentioned above by the compilers. It can only be that the text used by the compilers was copied using dictation (nearly all of the spelling mistakes are homophonic) and a scribe. In its colophon it does say, "The text has been revised once." The second text does not say this and therefore seems to be more original.

    I have corrected the mistakes where possible using the second text. There are even more mistakes not picked up by the compilers. Where differences occur and error is not detectable, I have stayed with the compiler's text.

44. As transliterated.

45. "Jewel" (Tib. *nor bu*). This does not match the child's name in the title, which means "festival for the eyes." The TBRC text has "Jewel of the Eye" (*mig gi nor bu*).

46. A lotus that blooms only rarely or, according to some, a kind of fig that has no visible flowers.

47. The text has "a buddha," although the epithet Bhagavan in the next sentence is usually reserved for the historical Buddha Śākyamuni.

48. Drakpa Gyaltsen's name in Sanskrit.

49. First ruler of Tibet, estimated to have ruled in the first century BCE. See next section for more detail.

50. This puts the regnal date for Nyatri Tsenpo at 127 BCE. By extension, Drakgyen's calculation of the passing of Buddha would be in 465 BCE.

51. The system of Phukpa Lhundrup Gyatso, fifteenth-century founder of a system of calendric calculations based on the *Kālacakra Tantra*.

52. There are several other differing assertions for the dates of the Buddha. Most have been made by Tibetan calendrical astrologers.

53. This refers to how Drakpa Gyaltsen claims the ability to be able to remember his own past lives and those of others, as told in the previous story from his collected works, and yet is unable to correctly calculate the dates of the kings.

54. In 1569 he was the tenth Tashi Lhunpo throneholder. Nenying (Gnas snying) is his place of birth. A *shabdrung* is a monk who has spent time with and studied under a high lama.

55. *Dge legs dkyil 'khor gsum*. Auspiciousness ritual marking the end of the initiation.

56. The Mandal Rawa is the mandala enclosure of Lhasa's Jokhang Temple. The deceased king here refers to Gushri Khan.

57. Four statues of Avalokiteśvara, made from the same sandalwood tree, said to have self-arisen during Tibet's imperial period.

58. *Ma sha*. Special type of bean used in a tantric ritual.

59. The Tibetan text notes in brackets that: "Jaisang Depa was Trinlé Gyatso of Lower Town. He was an important official in the Ganden Phodrang and the grandfather of Desi Sangyé Gyatso. This and other details can be found in *Great Dungkar Dictionary*, 1:1180." He was appointed Desi in 1660 and died in 1668.

60. Lingtö Chöjé Losang Gyatso and Jang Ngö Nangso Dargyé, two medical practitioners of the time.

61. Temple in Lhasa dedicated to Nechung.

62. In two parts of this citation, the meaning was not clear, even to the compilers. However, they are minor, and omitting them does not affect the intended message.

63. Epithet of Nechung.

64. Along with Gyaltsap Jé and Khedrup Jé mentioned above, Dulzin Drakpa Gyaltsen (1374–1434) was a main disciple of Tsongkhapa famed for his adherence to monastic discipline. Supporters of Shukden include him among the past incarnations of Drakgyen.

65. Jamyang Gawai Lodrö (1429–1503) was abbot of Loseling College of Drepung and teacher to Gendun Gyatso, the Second Dalai Lama.

66. This refers to a composition of Drakpa Gyaltsen cited at length in Trijang Rinpoché's work, which describes a vision he received.

67. This paragraph is a gloss on Drakpa Gyaltsen's verse description of the vision he had.

68. A compendium of Shukden-related texts compiled by Losang Thupten Trinlé Yarphel. Alongside rituals, it includes biographies such as those of Panchen Sönam Drakpa.

69. The verses in this work are the root text for Trijang Rinpoché's. They were composed by Dakpo Kalsang Khedrup, who appears to be a contemporary of Phabongkha Rinpoché and may have been his teacher. In the English translation of *Commentary on the Praise of Shukden,* his photo, captioned as "Kyabje Dagpo Dorje Chang," appears alongside those of Phabongkha Rinpoché and Trijang Rinpoché.

70. *Nyes 'dod.* This cryptic phrase is clearly understood in one way here, but below this interpretation is challenged.

71. Refers to the story of the silly rabbit that became terrified when he heard the sound of a tree branch dropping in the water, making the sound "*chal*!" He ran off telling all the animals to flee because the chal was coming. It is used to describe someone who relies on hearsay rather than hard facts.

72. Two metaphors of nonexistence.

73. In the text these two are referred to jointly as Gyalpo Chöyön, a title recently awarded to them that refers to the joint enterprise of patron and lama.

74. Having asked many scholars about this saying, I am still unable to come up with a definitive explanation, but the general meaning seems to be that the lama does not attain enlightenment but the attendant does, meaning that those who are expected to make gains do not, while ordinary folk, who are not expected to, in fact do. Angyikpa (*Ang yig pa*) might be a personal name.

75. *Mig mas 'gebs.* One explanation is that this phrase refers to someone whose power is weak but who tries to wield it over those above him. They are "closing their eyes from below," like some birds whose eyelids move from bottom to top. Another explanation is looking at others with head bowed and eyes raised in a frightening manner.

76. Probably Nechung.

77. The verb *sgor ba* means to thresh grain using the hoofs of cattle, but whether it means that here I cannot say with certainty.

78. *Phra lag sbom gsum,* literally "thin, limb, round," a phrase, probably associated with the body, generally reckoned to mean cleverly exhibiting differing personalities to suit the occasion. This whole extract is difficult to comprehend.

79. Whenever the Fifth Dalai mentions "the monastic college," he is referring to his own Namgyal Monastery.

80. From a collection of stories known as *Corpse Stories*, sometimes attributed to Nāgārjuna.

81. Dölgyal appeared at Sakya Monastery asking to be enthroned as a Dharma protector, as is described in part 2.

82. For the full passage and citation, see below, page 74.

83. "Not known to any valid perception" is the definition of nonexistence as found in the epistemology texts. So here, the compilers are finishing with a flourish.

84. Originally a club, but in the hands of Padmasambhava, portrayed as a trident and adorned with vajras and skulls.

85. *Mdos.* A thread-cross is a ritual structure designed to repel harm, in which a substitute or effigy of the victim, or ransom substances, are offered within a structure made, in its simplest form, of two crossed sticks woven with colored thread.

86. Sitātapatrā (*gdugs dkar*). A female protector who emanated from the crown of the Buddha and is particularly effective for warding off obstacles. She is usually white, with a thousand arms and faces, and is named after the white parasol that accompanies her.

87. *Ngags rgod log tri.* A practice combining earlier and later revealed treasure transmissions.

88. The Nyingma master Orgyen Tenzin.

89. *Rig 'dzin rdo rje drag po rtsal,* one of Padmasambhava's twelve emanations.

90. An old name for Namgyal Monastery. The list of names of the ritual practitioners varies a little from the one reproduced in his autobiography.

91. *Rnam thos sras.* One of the four great kings and protector of the northern direction. Sometimes he is propitiated as a god of wealth, but he also is the guardian of those who protect their ethics.

92. Dulzin, an epithet for Shukden.

93. Sakya master Morchen Kunga Lhundrup (1654–1728).

94. Third hierarch of the Drukpa Kagyü tradition (d. 1720?).

95. His teacher, Lodrö Wangchuk of Gongkar Dé Monastery.

96. *A sras khyams po,* "the wandering son of A," a reference to Drakgyen's mother, [Lak] Agyal.

97. *Bye tshogs.* It would appear that this is a name of a monastery or place, but this is far from clear.

98. Previously Kunga Lodrö was cited as saying that the lineage of Dölgyal was handed down from Morchen several years earlier. Here he says it began with his father Sönam Rinchen.

99. The day is divided into twelve periods named after the twelve animals of the calendar.

100. Here the title of this work is somewhat reworded.

101. This is not the number five hundred but the time of the five degenerations when the lifespan will be one *hundred* years.

102. Jampal Nyingpo (*'jam dpal snying po*) is the name Tsongkhapa is known by in Tuṣita Heaven after his passing. Dīpaṃkara is the famous Indian master Atiśa, who visited Tibet in the eleventh century.

103. Indian teacher of Atiśa.

104. The era of the Dharma kings Songtsen Gampo and so forth.

105. Tsarchen Losal Gyatso, 1502–66.

106. Tibetan rendering of a Mongolian title. *Achitu* = kind one. *Nominhan* = Dharma king.

107. *Rma chen spom ra.* Machen Pomra is an indigenous Tibetan spirit and protector dwelling on Mount Machen in Kham.

108. This is Tashi Gephel Monastery, which Dharmabhadra attended when he was thirteen.

109. Other sources have 1845 as the year of the passing of this Drukpa Kagyü master.

110. Also known as Yeshé Wangden, he held the post from 1933–39.

111. Composed by Denma Losang Dorjé.

112. He held the post from 1921–26. His dates are said to be 1876–1937/47.

113. As can be seen in his *Praise of Shukden,* and from a citation attributed to him by Phabongkha Rinpoché on page 143, there is a strong case for Dakpo Kalsang Khedrup being the first to declare Dölgyal the exclusive protector of Tsongkhapa's teachings. Phabongkha Rinpoché, however, was the first within the Geluk to compose rituals and to spread the practice.

114. In which each line begins with a succeeding letter of the alphabet.

115. Phabongkha Rinpoché was visiting a meditation place of Padmasambhava.

116. A revealed treasure of seven prayers to Padmasambhava.

117. Author unknown.

118. Hermitage in Khau Kyelhé district inhabited by many great Sakya masters of the past.

119. Stone in which the life essence resides.

120. *Sa skya'i gser chos.* The thirteen restricted texts of the Tsarpa Sakya tradition.

121. Shangpa Kagyü tradition practice deriving from the Kashmiri yogini Niguma, who is said to have lived around the eleventh century.

122. This advice is for Tibetan readers only, as the biography has not been translated into English.

123. Lungshar Dorjé Tsegyal (1881–1940) was a prominent figure and confidant of the Thirteenth Dalai Lama, holding a number of posts, and even accompanying four students to England after they had been selected to study there. His life took a tragic turn after the Dalai Lama passed away. This has been well documented elsewhere.

124. Chensal Thupten Kunphel (d. 1963). Chensal means "favorite," and it is said he was well liked by the Thirteenth Dalai Lama because of his many talents. Like Lungshar he was arrested after the Dalai Lama passed away. He fled to India but returned to serve under the Fourteenth Dalai Lama.

125. Lianyu was the last Qing amban stationed in Lhasa, a position he held from 1906–12. The hostile forces arrived in Lhasa in 1909, and the Dalai Lama left for India in 1910. The story of this turbulent time, including the declaration of independence from China, has been well documented elsewhere.

126. Dasang Dramdul (1885–1959) was a man of humble peasant origin who rose to become a favorite of the Thirteenth Dalai Lama. He eventually married into the influential Tsarong family.

127. Chusang Hermitage is near Sera Monastery in Lhasa. Phabongkha Rinpoché frequently stayed and taught there.

128. Drakri Losang Thupten Namgyal (d. 1902) and Denma Riku Rinpoché were two of Phabongkha Rinpoche's main teachers.

129. This probably refers to Phabongka Rinpoché's main and most inspiring teacher, Dakpo Lama Rinpoché Jampal Lhundrup Gyatso (1845–1919) from Lhoka.

130. *Sgo srung,* literally a "door guardian" or gatekeeper. Used literally for a sentry that protects the house from outside.

131. Shagap (*zhwa sgab*) is the name of a Tibetan aristocratic family. Chözé (*chos mdzad*) is a title given to a monk who, by making large donations, is exempt from ordinary monastic labor.

132. Takphu Padmavajra, Jampal Tenpai Ngödrup (1876–1935), one of Phabongkha Rinpoché's main teachers. The "teachings" refer to those given to Phabongkha after Takphu's visit to the heavenly realm of Tuṣita, of which more will be related below.

133. Teaching, debating, and composing.

134. Shidé Monastery is in Lhasa. Tāsur seems to be the title of a former official. Sur (*zur*) is a suffix meaning emeritus, and Tā (*tā*) is an abbreviated form of a Mongolian or Chinese rank. In the oral retelling of this story, the Fourteenth Dalai Lama refers to this person as a student of Phabongkha Rinpoché.

135. *Dgu rdzogs gnam gang yin.* Other recent publications on the Shukden issue have

cited this phrase and have focused on the form of the verb "to be" (*yin*) that is used, stating that this form is used primarily for first person use and for making a commitment or decision to do something, thereby positing grave implications of the utterance.

136. *Chos dbyings.* Here, an honorific way of saying that an advanced spiritual practitioner has passed away.

137. This is a deliberate and contrived vocal style often used in ritual chanting to denote joy.

138. Both places are in Kham in eastern Tibet.

139. More commonly known as the *Yellow Book.*

140. The story of the Panchen Lama leaving Tashi Lhunpo for China in 1924 and not returning is well documented elsewhere.

141. The journey of Phabongkha Rinpoché to Kham and back to Lhasa covers a period from the summer of 1934 to the winter of 1937. Although it seems that 1936 is missing, no events connected with meeting the Panchen Lama occurred that year.

142. The old capital of the Republic of China.

143. Chaksam is in Karzé province, in present day Sichuan, and was originally part of Kham.

144. Geluk monastery in Yushu County.

145. A slate or wooden board on which messages were written in chalk to be delivered back and forth by messenger.

146. Losang Palden Chökyi Wangchuk, thirty-sixth holder of the throne of Tashi Lhunpo Tantric College. He was also visiting the Panchen Lama at this time.

147. This is a verse in which the parts of name are embedded in the words, and the fulfillment of the wishes is entrusted to the protector.

148. On the way back to Lhasa.

149. The English translation of Shakabpa's *Tibet: A Political History* says that the Panchen Lama died on December 1, 1937. This corresponds to the twenty-ninth of the first tenth month.

150. Tibetan author living in China.

151. Birth name of the Tenth Panchen Lama Trinlé Lhundrup Chökyi Gyaltsen (1938–89).

152. The names given to the Tibetan months come from the *Kālacakra Tantra.* Both naming and numbering systems are used in Tibetan literature.

153. The implication of there being only a few months between these two events, such that the tenth would have already been conceived before the ninth's passing, is either that one of the dates is wrong or that the tenth is not the incarnation of the

ninth. The problems with the recognition of the tenth are well documented else-where, and this is a longstanding inconsistency found across many sources.

154. Lhalu was a well-known estate near Lhasa whose family was that of the Twelfth Dalai Lama. Lady Yangzom Tsering (1880–1963) was Phabongkha's chief aristo-cratic disciple and a benefactor of his Shukden activities.

155. Dzasak Lama Losang Rinchen of Kyabying. Dzasak Lama is the title of a high monastic official, often a treasurer.

156. This is an annotation following the inclusion of this short work composed by the Ninth Panchen Lama Chökyi Nyima in a Shukden propitiation ritual supposedly composed by Losang Trinlé Lhundrup Chökyi Gyaltsen, the Tenth Panchen Lama.

157. Sikgyap Rinpoché from Trehor Karzé, who lived in Tashi Lhunpo and, according to the *Yellow Book*, was punished by Shukden for his Nyingma practices.

158. That is, Dzasak Lama Losang Rinchen of Kyabying.

159. This rendering of the title is not the one found in the edition of his collected works published in Delhi. There it reads, *Jeweled Chariot of Faith Carrying the Gems of Great Blessings: The Way to Confer the Profound Life-Entrustment Initiation of Gyalchen Dorjé Shukden Tsal, Manifested Doctrine Protector.*

160. That is, they do not exist.

161. In the sense that it is not possible to know who the father is.

162. This is four sets of different-colored annotations that are woven into the *Great Treatise on the Stages of the Path* by Tsongkhapa: *Lam rim chen mo mchan bzhi sbrags ma*. The annotations are those of Baso Lhawang Chökyi Gyaltsen (1537–1605), the First Jamyang Shepa (1648–1721), Kharok Khenchen Ngawang Rapten (b. seventeenth century), and Trati Geshé Rinchen Döndrup of Sera Jé (b. seventeenth century).

163. This lama was famous for being able to receive teachings in visions.

164. The palace in Tuṣita celestial realm of Maitreya where Tsongkhapa resides.

165. Here the Tibetan text annotates this person as being Dulzin Drakpa Gyaltsen, direct disciple ("born from his speech") of Tsongkhapa.

166. Padmavajra, i.e., Takphu Rinpoché.

167. A monastery in Kham; the latter-day Dragom Tulku of Drepung Gomang monas-tery was one of those who refused to give up the Shukden practice.

168. The lamas, meditational deities, and ḍākinīs.

169. A revealed treasure documenting the lives of Padmasambhava.

170. The Geluk tradition, sometimes known as the Yellow Hat tradition.

171. The Sera Monastery monk (b. 1931) who is a fierce defender of Shukden and who founded the global New Kadampa Tradition, headquartered in the U.K.

172. Padmasambhava, Great Ācārya, and Precious Ācārya are here synonyms.

173. Purification rites compiled by Sönam Bum.

174. A place several miles north of Lhasa.

175. Protector deity propitiated in Sera Monastery.

176. Probably the eighth incarnation, Thupten Ngawang Kalsang Tenzin.

177. Monastery in the area northeast of Lhasa known as Sokdé or Sokgu; an area that was previously a Bön stronghold and whose natives claim they are descended from Mongolians (Sok). The account from a different perspective was described above in a citation from Phabongkha Rinpoché's biography.

178. This is from the foreword of a book on Dölgyal written by Lama Zöpa for Mongolians. I am grateful to Nick Ribush of Lama Yeshé Archives for this information.

179. Written *Dgon pa sa*, but possibly Dgon pa gsar, referring to the incarnation lineage from the Sera hermitage of the same name, now in ruins.

180. Although the text makes no mention of an accident, Lama Zopa's oral retelling of this story mentions an accident.

181. A district whose full name is Gyalmo Tsawa Rong. Tsenlha is one of its eighteen sub-districts.

182. Prophecy made by Padmasambhava in relation to signs of the degeneration of the Dharma.

183. Dulzin, as in "Vinaya holder," an epithet Shukden was known by at the monastery.

184. High government rank.

185. This is the famous document referred to by Mao Zedong as "a poisoned arrow" and that led to the imprisonment, or house arrest, of the Panchen for fourteen years.

186. Founded by the Panchen Lama himself in 1987.

187. In this monastery there was an oracle for both the peaceful and wrathful forms of Shukden.

188. Trijang Rinpoché, *A Deceiving and Illusory Play*. See the translation by Sharpa Tulku Tenzin Trinley, *The Magical Play of Illusion* (Somerville, MA: Wisdom Publications, 2018), 197.

189. There was a Shukden oracle at this monastery that was often consulted.

190. Swarg Ashram, often referred to as "the old palace," was the residence just above McLeod Ganj, Dharamsala, where His Holiness moved to in 1960. The move to his present Thekchen Chöling residence occurred in 1968.

191. The famous mantra of Avalokiteśvara, deity of compassion, constantly on the lips of devout Tibetans.

192. Mantra of goddess Palden Lhamo, in which the seed syllable *bhyoḥ* occurs seven times.

193. The three protectors are Vaiśravaṇa, Mahākāla, and Dharmarāja.

194. The lamas, meditational deities, and ḍākinīs.

195. The Tibetan Buddhist tradition, founded by the Indian master Atiśa in the early eleventh century, that was a forerunner to the Geluk tradition.

196. By Losang Tsultrim Gyatso (1845–1915).

197. The three scopes, or three types of practitioner—lowest, intermediate, and advanced—are the three main stages of the graded path to enlightenment as taught in the stages of the path literature.

198. Protector no longer bound by worldly or samsaric constraints, where one takes birth again and again through the force of karma.

199. *Bslab pa gsum*. Training in ethics, wisdom, and concentration.

200. This letter appeared above on page <?>.

201. *Rgyal 'gong*. Often refers to demon or ghost with the appearance of a monk.

202. Collection of Nyingma deity practices compiled by Terdak Lingpa and Minling Dharmaśrī.

203. Venerable Losang Gyatso, principal of the Institute of Buddhist Dialectics, Dharamsala, who was murdered by assailants in 1997.

204. The Tibetan has bracketed text here that reads, "The Ganden chant leader is Geshé Norsang from Hardong House of Ganden Shartsé College, who was born in Maldro Gungkar, near Lhasa."

205. *Stong bzhi pa*. The fourth of the four empty states These are names given to the arising of the three appearances and the clear light at the time of death and during advanced tantric practice. The other three are empty state (stong pa), the very empty state (*shin tu stong pa*), and the greatly empty state (stong pa chen po).

206. The Dorjé Shugden Devotees' Charitable and Religious Society, founded in 1996. See chapter 28 below.

207. A method of divination using the Tengyur text *Arising Letters (Svarodaya)*, D 4322.

208. See full invocation above, page <?>.

209. A popular work, often translated as the *Advice of Khaché Phalu*, whose authorship is ascribed to an Islamic Tibetan scholar.

210. Both sayings mean separating the good from the bad.

211. *Gdan sa gsum*. The three main Geluk monasteries of Drepung, Ganden, and Sera.

212. *Sku zhabs*. In the 1978 telling of this declaration above, Nechung referred to Pha-

bongkha as "great knowledge holder" (*rig 'dzin chen po*). Other details are a little different too.

213. Dragom Tulku Losang Khyenrab Tenpai Wangchuk (1953–2006), a contemporary follower of Shukden who wrote a book criticizing the Fourteenth Dalai Lama.

214. Throneholder Losang Nyima (1928–2008) published his refutation of Dragom in 2002.

215. *Entrance to the Middle Way*, 6.119. I have fleshed out the verse a little with the commentary from Tsongkhapa.

216. Yangteng Rinpoché (b. 1978) is a lharampa geshé from Sera Mé who now works in the Private Office of His Holiness the Dalai Lama.

217. This is the Central Institute of Higher Tibetan Studies in Sarnath, of which Samdhong Rinpoché was principal from 1971–88.

218. A work that is short but contains the essence.

219. See translation in *Magical Play of Illusion*, 156.

220. English translation of the full prayer appears on pages 284–86 of *Magical Play of Illusion*. The words in bold in the first stanza spell out the name of His Holiness the Fourteenth Dalai Lama.

221. Denma Gönsar was a student of Trijang Rinpoché and Phabongkha Rinpoché as well as a practitioner of Shukden. He passed away in Tibet in 2005, and in 2013 his incarnation was recognized in Chatreng, in eastern Tibet, by the Chinese-controlled Panchen Lama.

222. A pure perception initiation transmitted from the Kadampa master Atiśa.

223. *Zur bltas leb mthong.*

224. Not the Denma Gönsar mentioned above but the student of Geshé Rabten who lives in Switzerland.

225. Location of an old fort where the main monasteries were given sanctuary after first coming into exile in 1959.

226. Founded in Delhi and commonly translated by the society itself as the Dorje Shugden Devotees' Charitable and Religious Society.

227. Now called Institute of Buddhist Dialectics.

228. The main monastic assembly in Ganden Monastery.

229. Composed by His Holiness the Fourteenth Dalai Lama in 1979. It is a lament and prayer for the sufferings of the world in general and specifically for the people of Tibet.

230. Present-day supporter of Shukden who sought and failed to obtain recognition of himself as the incarnation of Kundeling Rinpoché. Tibetans mockingly call him Nga Lama ("I am a lama"), which is something he often repeats.

231. On March 10, 1959, the people of Lhasa protested peacefully against the invasion by the Chinese Communists. This event is commemorated each year in exile.

232. These are methods found in the monastic discipline scriptures for restoring order among the monastic community.

233. There is some doubt about the meaning of this sentence. The original sentence from the *Spotless Mirror* has "If the protector is genuine," and the compilers have suggested "not" has been omitted. However, I have come across a translation of this whole speech, which includes more than what is reproduced here and in *Spotless Mirror*. There the translation runs, "If we invoke protectors with a mind focusing on the nine types of pride as the center of our practice, it is said that if the protector is genuine..." I do not as yet have access to the Tibetan source of this alternate translation, and so I have stuck with the suggestion of the compilers of this Tibetan text.

234. *Dga' rab dbang phyug*, a cupid-like māra from the higher levels of the desire realm who holds the five arrows of desire and is also the personification of hindrance.

235. Ga Lotsāwa Namgyal Dorjé (1203–1282).

236. A deity who, like Nechung, appeared through oracles and made predictions concerning the affairs of Tibet.

237. *Liberation in the Palm of Your Hand* by Phabongkha Rinpoché.

238. From Tsongkhapa's *Praise to Dependent Arising* (*Rten 'brel bstod pa*).

239. *Tshul gsum*. The three logical processes employed to arrive at an unfailing inferential cognition.

Glossary

ārya beings (*'phags pa*). Strictly speaking, Buddhist practitioners who have reached the path of seeing by gaining a direct and nonconceptual perception of no-self.

birth deity (*skyes lha*). A worldly god or spirit assigned to a person at birth, determined by way of locality or date of birth.

bodhicitta (*byang chub kyi sems*). The mental state that desires to attain the highest state of enlightenment for the sake of all beings and is essential to both sutra and tantra.

Bön (*bon*). The religious culture prevalent in Tibet before the arrival of Buddhism in the seventh century.

Central Tibet (*dbus*). Central region of Tibet dominated by the capital city of Lhasa and encompassing the Kyichu, Yarlung, and Chongyé valleys. It is often joined with the region of Tsang to its west to form Ü-Tsang.

Chamsing. (*lcam sring*). Fierce red protector also known as Bektsé (*beg tse*).

clear light (*'od gsal*). The very subtle or primordial mind activated by advanced tantra practice and by natural means at death. It can also refer to the object of this mind and sometimes to the luminous nature of mind itself.

ḍākinī (*mkha' 'gro ma*). A nonhuman female practitioner or yoginī who has gained high spiritual realizations or is able to perform supernatural feats. The name means "sky goer," thereby indicating her supernatural powers.

Dispelling All Obstacles (*bar chad kun sel*). An initiation granting permission to rely upon the protector Mahākāla, as an emanation of Avalokiteśvara, in order to reduce obstacles to life and practice.

Dorjé Drakden (*rdo rje grags ldan*). Another name for the protector Pehar.

Drok Riwo Ganden Namgyal Ling Monastery. Ganden Monastery, founded by Tsongkhapa in 1409.

Dulzin (*'dul 'dzin*). Literally, "Vinaya Holder," an honorific term applied to the names of certain lamas renowned for their adherence to monastic discipline. It is also an epithet for Shukden.

Dzokchen (*rdzogs chen*). The naked and clear entity of primordial awareness in its present state free of all mental contamination.

effigy torma (*glud gtor*). Torma given to appease demons and ghosts that cause illnesses and so on. Sometimes it is an effigy of the affected person.

fire-offering ritual (*sbyin sreg, homaḥ*). Tantric ritual involving the pouring of substances, such as grains, into a ritual fire. It is performed to accomplish the four activities and also at the end of a retreat to compensate for any omission or deviation.

five degenerations (*snyigs ma lnga*). The five degenerations characterizing a given era as degenerate, in which (1) lifespan reduces, (2) the times are beset with wars and strife, (3) mental afflictions increase and are more entrenched, (4) views degenerate, and (5) living beings are more difficult to aid by spiritual means.

five-emanation protector (*rgyal po sku lnga*). Or the five gyalpo emanations. The five body, speech, mind, activities, and qualities emanations of a protector of Samyé Monastery. The five emanations are Pehar, Gyajin, Mönbuputra, Shingjachen, and Dralha Kyechikbu.

four activities (*las bzhi*). Powers of pacifying, increasing, controlling, and destroying gained through tantric practice and used to remove obstacles and hindrances for self and others.

Gadong (*dga' gdong*). Protector who along with Nechung appears by way of an oracle to give predictions for the Tibetan government. He is said to be a minister of the Samyé Monastery protector Pehar, and in later times was oath-bound and assigned to Gadong Monastery as its protector.

Ganden Phodrang (*dga' ldan pho brang*). The official title of the Tibetan government instituted by the Fifth Dalai Lama in 1642. It was originally the name of a residence in Drepung Monastery where the Fifth and previous Dalai Lamas lived.

Guru Puja (*bla ma mchod pa*). Rite of offering and praise focused on the guru as the personification of all the buddhas, meditation deities, ḍākinīs, and so on.

gyalpo (*rgyal po*). Usually "king" or "ruler," but also is the name for a type of a powerful spirit with its own entourage.

Hayagrīva (*rta mgrin*). Horse-headed meditational deity and protector whose origins are in ancient India.

Hundred Deities of Tuṣita (*dga' ldan lha brgya ma*). A guru-yoga practice focused on Tsongkhapa.

imperious spirit (*dregs*). The term literally means "arrogant" or "haughty." Like terms for nonhumans in English, such as ghost, spirit, demon, and so on, similar terms in Tibetan are difficult to classify with clear distinction. However *dregs* appears to be a general term for any worldly spirit, although it has been suggested that it specifically refers to those nonhumans who appear in human form and take on a wrathful stance.

Jangtsé Chöjé (*byang rtse chos rje*). Literally "Jangtsé Dharma master." Along with the Sharpa Chöjé, these two positions are the second highest in the Geluk order. They alternate in the succession to become Ganden throneholder.

Jangun debate gathering (*jang dgun chos chen mo*). A traditional winter debate gathering held at Jangpu Monastery, west of Lhasa, consisting primarily of the three main Geluk monasteries.

Jinasāgara Avalokiteśvara (*span ras gzigs rgyal ba rgya mtsho*). A red, four-armed form of Avalokiteśvara.

Kadam tradition. The Tibetan Buddhist tradition founded by the Indian master Atiśa in the early eleventh century.

kuśa grass (*rtswa mchog, dharba*). A species of tussock grass long regarded as sacred and used to form a ritual meditation seat. Its pairs of leaves are so sharp that it symbolizes discriminating wisdom.

labrang (*bla brang*). The monastic household of an incarnated lama.

life-entrustment rite and practice (*srog gtad*). Often taken to mean a ritual whereby the practitioner entrusts their life to a protector, but according to His Holiness the Dalai Lama should be the practice of the protector entrusting itself to the practitioner.

Mahākāla (*mgon po*). A protector whose origins are in India and who takes many distinct forms, such as the seventeen aspects of Four-Faced Mahākāla.

mahāmudrā (*phyag rgya chen mo*). A multivalent word that most commonly refers to a style of meditation on the emptiness of the mind. It is especially common in the Kagyü tradition but is found in the Geluk tradition as well.

Mañjunātha Lama (*'jam mgon bla ma*). Epithet of Tsongkhapa reflecting the belief that he was a manifestation of Mañjuśrī.

Māra/māras (*bdud*). Personification of hindrances and obstructions to spiritual practice.

mind training (*blo sbyong*). Special meditation and behavioral techniques to develop and transform the mind toward the achievement of positive qualities, such as compassion.

nāgas (*klu*). Beings dwelling somewhere between the animal and the spirit realm, sometimes taking on the form of snakes, and with a fondness for water.

Nechung/Pehar (*gnas chung / pe har*). There are varying accounts of the identities of Nechung and Pehar, but generally, along with Dorjé Drakden, they are treated as synonyms of the same protector. In this book, for example, Nechung calls himself "I, the Pehar Gyalpo." Also, Nechung is often referred to as Nechung Dorjé Drakden. At first, he was appointed by Padmasambhava as protector of Samyé Monastery and was known as Pehar. It seems that before that time he was a harmful spirit. Later he became known as Nechung ("little place"), after his physical abode, and served as protector of Drepung Monastery and counsel, by way of oracle, for the Ganden Phodrang Tibetan government and the Dalai Lamas. Some accounts describe him as one of five ministers appointed alongside others as protectors of Samyé and having the name Dorjé Drakden. *See also* five-emanation protector.

oath-breaking spirit (*dam sri*). Strictly speaking, this is applied to a malevolent, nonhuman spirit that is a rebirth of a practitioner who has broken the sacred bond with his or her master.

Orgyen (*o rgyan*). A fabled land to the west of India. Said to be the birthplace of the tantric master Padmasambhava, the name has come to be synonymous with him.

Padmasambhava (*padma 'byung gnas*). Tantric master who visited Tibet in the eighth century and is credited with taming unruly local sprits and committing them to pledges to work for the good of the people. He is especially venerated in the Nyingma tradition, which holds him to be a second Buddha.

Palden Lhamo (*dpal ldan lha mo*). Female protector deity of Tibet with a close connection to the Dalai Lamas. She is wrathful in appearance, dark blue, and rides a mule.

Pehar (*pe har / pe dkar*). *See* five-emanation protector; Nechung.

Pehar Chok (*pe har lcog*). Temple in Lhasa dedicated to Nechung.

phurba/phurbu (*phur ba, phur bu*). Generally, a ritual dagger used in tantric ceremony, but here personified as a tantric meditational deity.

Riwo Genden tradition (*ri bo dge ldan*). The Geluk tradition.

Setrap (*bse khrab*). Protector associated with Ganden Shartsé and Sangphu Monastery. He is said to be an emanation of Buddha Amitābha.

Sharpa Chöjé (*shar pa chos rje*). *See under* Jangsé Chöje.

Shukden Society. Founded in Delhi in 1996, the full title translated from Tibetan is Society for the Protection of Men and Gods by the Power of Unwavering Faith in Dorjé Shukden, Protector of the Teachings of Mañjunātha Tsongkhapa, but commonly translated by the society itself as the Dorje Shugden Devotees' Charitable and Religious Society.

Sitātapatrā (*gdugs dkar*). A female protector who emanated from the crown of the Buddha and is particularly effective for warding off obstacles. She is usually white, with a thousand arms and faces, and is named after the white parasol that accompanies her.

torma (*gtor ma*). "That which is thrown," an edible-substance offering for deities, protectors, nāgas, sprits, and so forth. It is cast away at the end of the ritual in order to reduce attachment. In Tibet tormas were usually made of roasted barley flour, or tsampa, then shaped and decorated according to the description laid down for that particular object of offering.

Vajra Guardian of the Tent (*gur gyi mgon po*), a two-faced form of Mahākāla that is a central protector of the Sakya tradition.

vajra guru mantra. The mantra of Padmasambhava, *Oṃ aḥ hūṃ vajra guru padma siddhi hūṃ*.

Vajradhara (*rdo rje 'chang*). The Buddha as the teacher of tantra. Commonly affixed to a lama's name to indicate his prowess in tantra.

Bibliography

Aśvaghoṣa (first century). *Fifty Verses on Guru Devotion. Gurupancāśikā. Bla ma lnga bcu pa.*

Changkya Rölpa Dorjé (Lcang skya rol pa'i rdo rje, 1717–86). *Biography of the Achitu Nomin Han Precious Ganden Throne Holder: The Great Drum of the Gods, Beautiful Words to Gain a Ḍākinī Form. Dge ldan khri rin po che a chi thu no min han gyi rnam thar mkha spyod 'grub pa'i gtam snyan lha'i rngo bo che.* Woodblock edition.

Chinese-Tibetan Institute of Higher Buddhist Studies. *Opening the Doors to a Hundred Fields of Knowledge in the Land of Snow. Gangs can rig brgya'i sgo 'byed.* Beijing: People's Printing Press, 1988.

Chökyi Nyinjé (Chos kyi nyin rje, nineteenth century). *Treasure Pot of Supreme Blessings: A Brief Biography of the All-Knowing Yongzin Lama. Kun mkhyen bla ma'i zhabs kyi rnam par thar pa cha tsam brjod pa byin rlabs mchog gi gter bum.* Dergé woodblock edition.

Compendium of Compassionate Advice. Rjes brtse'i lam ston bka' slob phyog bsdus. Dharamsala: Namgyal Monastery Educational Association, 2010.

Dakpo Kalsang Khedrup (Dvags po skal bzang mkhas grub, nineteenth century). *Praise of Shukden.* Presented as the root text in Trijang's *Commentary on the Praise of Shukden,* where its full title is not recorded. Moreover, it was modified by Phabongkha Rinpoché.

Dalai Lama Jampal Gyatso, Eighth ('Jam dpal rgya mtsho, 1758–1804). *Lotus that Beautifies the Teachings of the Buddha: A Prayer Composed by Way of a Biography of the Venerable and Supreme Lama, Whose Nature Is That of the All-Pervading Master Vajrasattva, the Tutor, Dharma King, and Great Pandit, Yeshé Gyaltsen. Rje btsun bla dam pa khyab bdag rdo rje sems dpa'i ngo bo yongs 'dzin chos kyi rgyal po paṇḍi ta chen po ye shes rgyal mtshan dpal bzang po la rnam thar gyi sgo nas gsol ba 'debs pa thub bstan mdzes pa'i padmo.* Kyishö Kumbum Thang woodblock edition.

Dalai Lama Kalsang Gyatso, Seventh (Skal bzang rgya mtsho, 1708–57). *Enthronement of Dharma Protectors. Chos skyong spyi'i mnga' gsol.*

Dalai Lama Ngawang Losang Gyatso, Fifth (Ngag dbang blo bzang rgya mtsho, 1617–82). *Heavenly Raiment: An Illusory Play of the Appearances in the Life of the Zahor Monk Ngawang Losang Gyatso Presented as a Biography. Za hor gyi ban de ngag dbang blo bzang rgya mtsho'i 'di snang 'khrul pa'i rol rtsed rtogs brjod kyi tshul du bkod pa du kū la'i gos bzang.* Woodblock edition, Lhasa edition, 3 vols. Volume 1 has been translated by Samten G. Karmay as *The Illusive Play.* Chicago, Serindia, 2014.

———. *Precious Garland: The Life of the Lord of the World, the All-Knowing and Glorious Yönten Gyatso. 'Jig rten dbang phyug thams cad mkhyen pa yon tan rgya mtsho dpal bzang po'i rnam par thar pa nor bu 'phreng ba.* Lhasa woodblock edition.

———. *Secret Sealed Teachings on Pure Perception. Dag snang gsang ba rgya can.* Collected works.

———. *Secret Teachings Sealed by a Pot Marked by Hayagrīva and a Lotus. Gsang ba rgya can rta mgrin padmas mtshan pa'i bum pa'i rgya can.* Collected works, old handwritten edition.

———. *Secret Teachings Sealed by a Sword and a Skull. Gsang ba rgya can gri thod rgya can.* Collected works, old handwritten edition.

———. *Spontaneous Evocation of the Four Actions: The Insights, Offerings, Supplication, Praises, and So Forth of the Myriad Oath-Bound Dharma Protectors Possessed of Unimpeded and Wrathful Power. Thogs med drag rtsal nus stobs ldan pa'i dam can chos srung rgya mtsho'i mngon rtogs mchod 'bul bskang bshags bstod tshogs sogs 'phrin las rnam bzhi lhun grub.* Lhasa woodblock edition of his collected works housed at the Potala, vol. *da.*

Dalai Lama Tenzin Gyatso, Fourteenth (Bstan 'dzin rgya mtsho, 1935–). *Discourses on Dölgyal. Dol rgyal skor gyi lam ston bka' slob,* 2 vols. Dharamsala: Namgyal Monastery, 2010.

Denma Losang Dorjé (Ldan ma blo bzang rdo rje, 1908–75). *Meaningful and Melodious Speech of Brahma: A Biography of Phabongkha Dechen Nyingpo, Heruka Performing the Dance of the Orange-Robed Monk, the Sole Refuge and All-Pervading Master of a Myriad Buddha Families and Mandalas. Rigs dang dkyil 'khor rgya mtsho'i khyab bdag he ru ka dpal ngur smig gar rol skyabs gcig pha bong kha bde chen snying po'i rnam par thar pa don ldan tshangs pa'i dbyangs snyan.* Woodblock edition.

Desi Sangyé Gyatso (De srid sangs rgyas rgya mtsho, 1653–1705). *Yellow Vaidūrya: A History of the Ganden Tradition. Dga' ldan chos 'byung vai dūrya ser po.* Qinghai Peoples' Printing Press, 1989.

Dodrup Jikmé Tenpai Nyima (Rdo grub 'jigs med bstan pa'i nyi ma, 1865–1929). *Treasure of All-Pervading Joy without Fear: A Brief Account of the Life of Mañjuśrī Dharma Mitra, Great Master of the Land of Bhoṭa (Tibet). Bho ṭa'i yul gyi slob dpon chen po mañju śri dharma mi tra'i zhabs kyi rtogs pa mdo tsam du brjod pa 'jigs med kun tu dga' ba'i gter.* Collected works, vol. 5. Chengdu: Sichuan People's Publications, 2003.

Domé Dölgyal Research Committee, ed. *Spotless Mirror: An Examination of the Coming of Dölgyal and the Ensuing Controversy. Dol rgyal gyi byung rim dang rnyog gleng la dpyad pa g.ya' sel me long.* Central Domé General Standing Committee, 2006.

Drakpa Gyaltsen (Grags pa rgyal mtshan, 1619–56). *Dreams at a Young Age. Na tshod phra mo'i rnal ltas.* Secret autobiography, volume *kha.*

———. *Jewel Casket: A Special Life-Story. Thun mong ma yin pa'i rtogs brjod rin chen za ma tog.* Handwritten autobiography, volume *ka*.

———. *Precious Garland Life Story: Taking Birth as the Youth Nayanotsava in Ancient India. Ngon rgya gar du khye'u mig gi dga' ston tu skye ba bzhes pa'i rtogs brjod rin po che'i 'phreng ba.* Collected works, volume *kha*.

———. *Prophecies. Ma 'ongs lung bstan.*

———. *Vaidūrya Garland: A History of the Written Word. Sngon byung yi ge'i byung tshul gyi lo rgyus bai dūrya'i 'phreng ba.* Collected works, volume *ga*.

Dreu Lhepa and Morchen Kunga Lhundrup (Dre'u lhas pa / Rmor chen kun dga' lhun grub). *Propitiation of Dölgyal: Activities That Fulfill All Wishes. Shugs ldan gyi gsol kha 'phrin las 'dod 'jo.*

Dzemé Rinpoché (Dze smad rin po che, 1927–96). *Oral Transmission of the Brave Father-Like Lama* (a.k.a. *Yellow Book*). *Pha rgod bla ma'i zhal lung.*

Dzongsar Khyentsé Jamyang Chökyi Lodrö (Rdzongs sar mkhyen rtse 'jam dbyangs chos kyi blo gros, 1893–1959). *Dedicating an Effigy Torma to Wealth-Keepers and Oath Breakers.* Collected works, 4:359ff.

Encyclopedia of Past Tibetan Masters. Gangs can mkhas grub rim byon gyi ming mdzod. Compiled by Koshul Drakpa Jungné and Gyalwa Losang Khedrup. Lanzhou: People's Publishing House, 1992.

Haribhadra (eighth century). *Clarification of the Meaning of the Ornament of Realization. Prajñāpāramitā-upadeśa Abhisamayālaṃkāea-vṛtti. Shes rab kyi pha rol tu phyin pa'i man ngag gi bstan bcos mngon par togs pa'i rgyan zhes bya ba'i 'grel pa. 'Grel pa don gsal.*

Jamgön Kongtrul Lodrö Tayé ('Jam mgon kong sprul blo gros mtha' yas, 1813–99). *Precious Treasure Collection. Rin chen gter mdzod.*

Jampal Gyatso ('Jam dpal rgya mtsho, twentieth century). *Panchen Rinpoché the Great Master. Slob dpon chen po paṇ chen rin po che.* Translated from the Chinese into Tibetan by Tsering Lhamo of the Department of Information and International Relations of the Tibetan Government. Dharamsala: Research and Analysis Centre of the Tibetan Security Department, printed by the Tibetan Educational Printing Press, March 23, 1997.

Jhado Rinpoché (Bya do rin po che, b. 1954). *Miscellaneous Comments on What Has Been Seen, Heard, and Experienced Concerning Dölgyal, or Gyalpo Shukden. Dol rgyal lam rgyal po shugs ldan skor gyi mthong thos myong tshor gyi dpyad gtam thor bu.*

Khyenrab Jampa Ngawang Lhundrup Tenpai Gyaltsen (Mkhyen rab byams pa ngag dbang lhun grub bstan pa'i rgyal mtshan, 1633–1703). *Ambrosia for the Ears of the Fortunate. Skal ldan rna ba'i bdud rtsi*, part 1. In *Sa skya Lam 'bras Literature Series*, vol. 5. Dehradun: Sakya Centre, 1983.

———. *A Crystal Garland: The Spiritual Achievements of the Chetsun Master of Speech. Lce btsun ngag gi dbang phyug gi rtogs brjod shel dkar kyi 'phreng ba*, part 2. In *Sa skya Lam 'bras Literature Series*, vol. 5. Dehradun: Sakya Centre, 1983.

Losal Gyatso (Blo gsal rgya mtsho, seventeenth century). *Historical Accounts: Dispelling the Darkness of Torment. Byung ba brjod pa gdung ba'i mun sel.* Compiled by Lelung Shepa Dorjé (1697–1740).

Losang Nyima (Blo bzang nyi ma, 1929–2008). *Dra sgom pa'i chos skyong rtog bzo'i rtogs brjod pha lam dkar po zhes par cung zad dpyad pa lung rigs thog mda'.* Mundgod: Author, 2002.

Losang Tenzin Wangyal (Blo bzang bstan 'dzin dbang rgyal, nineteenth century). *Sunlight that Brings to Bloom the Lotus Grove Minds of the Faithful: Biography of the Venerable Losang Palden Chökyi Drakpa Tenpai Wangchuk. Rje btsun blo bzang dpal ldan chos kyi grags pa bstan pa'i dbang phyug dpal bzang po'i rnam thar dad ldan pad tshal bzhad pa'i nyin byed snang ba.* Tashi Lhunpo woodblock edition.

Losang Thupten Trinlé Yarphel and Losang Tayang (Blo bzang thub bstan 'phrin las yar 'phel, b. 1941 / Blo bzang rta dbyangs), compilers. *Shukden Compendium. Shugs ldan be'u bum.* 2 vols. Lhasa edition, 1991.

Losang Tsultrim Gyatso (Blo bzang tshul khrims rgya mtsho, 1845–1915). *Extensive Prayer for the Excellent Geluk Tradition. Dge ldan lugs bzang rgyas pa'i smon lam.*

Minling Lochen Dharmaśrī (Smin gling lo chen dharma shri, 1654–1717). *Chariot of Faith: The Life Story of Terdak Lingpa Gyurmé Dorjé. Gter bdag gling pa 'gyur med rdo rje'i rnam thar dad pa'i shing rta.* Woodblock edition.

Mitrayogin (twelfth–thirteenth century). *Three Essential Points. Snying po don gsum.*

Morchen Kunga Lhundrup (Rmor chen kun dga' lhun grub, 1654–1728). *Mirror for the Beautiful Woman of Intelligence: A Biography of Morchen Kunga Lhundrup. Rmor chen kun dga' lhun grub zhabs kyi rnam thar blo gsal sgeg mo'i me long.* In *Sa skya Lam 'bras Literature Series*, vol. 5. Dehradun: Sakya Centre, 1983.

———. *The Three Activities: Presentation of the Gyalpo Spirit. Las gsum rgyal po'i rnam bzhag.*

Ngawang Khetsun (Ngag dbang mkhas btsun, twentieth century). *Brief Account of the Authentic Origins of the Conflict between Palden Lhamo and Dölgyal. Dpal ldan lha mo dang dol rgyal gnyis mi mthun pa'i sngon byung khungs ldan lo rgyus mdor bsdus.*

Paljor Jikmé (Dpal 'byor 'jigs med, twentieth century). *Various Events Connected with My Life. Mi tshe'i lo rgyus dang 'brel yod sna tshogs.* Supplemented and annotated by Tashi Tsering. Dharamsala: Tibetan Library of Works and Archives, 1988.

Panchen Lama Tenpai Wangchuk, Eighth (Paṇ chen bla ma bstan pa'i dbang phyug, 1855–82). *Strict Directive for the Great Monastic Seat of Tashi Lhunpo* (a.k.a. *Strict Directive for Tashi Lhunpo Monastery*), a.k.a. *Yoke of the Shining Golden Vajra Bringing Back the Life of the Two Laws: A Decree Applying to All Monks of All Ranks, and Those Who Share in the Monastery Food, Such as the Staff of the Labrangs, within the*

Tashi Lhunpo Monastic Seat That Is the Glory of Great Bliss and Victorious Every-where. Bkra shis lhun po dpal gyi bde chen phyogs thams cad las rnam par rgyal ba'i gling gi dge 'dun dbu dmangs dang bla brang nang ma sogs lto zan khongs gtogs dang bcas pa spyi khyab tu nges dgos pa'i yi ge khrims gnyis srog gi chad mthud rab brjid gser gyi rdo rje'i gnya' shing. Foreword by the Editorial Committee for the Preparation of Educational Materials from the Sino-Tibetan Institute of Buddhist Studies. Beijing: People's Printing Press, 1989. Also appears in *Opening the Doors to a Hundred Fields of Knowledge in the Land of Snow,* 11:35–158. Beijing: Peoples' Printing Press, 1988.

Panchen Losang Chökyi Gyaltsen (Paṇ chen blo bzang chos kyi rgyal mtshan, 1570–1662). *Precious Rosary: A Clear Account of the Deeds of the Dharma Proponent the Monk Losang Chögyen. Chos smra ba'i dge slong blo bzang chos rgyan gyi spyod tshul gsal bar ston pa nor bu 'phreng ba.* Collected works, vol. *ka.*

———. *Pure Gold Propitiation of Protectors. Bskang gso gser zhun.*

———. *Supplication Prayer to the Past Incarnations of Tulku Drakpa Gyaltsen. Sprul sku grags pa rgyal mtshan gyi skyes rabs gsol 'debs.* Miscellaneous works, woodblock edition, vol. *ca.*

Panchen Sönam Drakpa (Paṇ chen bsod nams grags pa, 1478–1554). *History of the Old and New Kadampa: An Ornament of the Mind. Bka' gdams gsar rnying gi chos 'byung yid kyi mdzes rgyan.* Gangtok: Gonpo Tseten, 1977.

Phabongkha Jampa Tenzin Trinlé Gyatso / Phabongkha Dechen Nyingpo (Pha bong kha byams pa bstan 'dzin 'phrin las rgya mtsho / Pha bong kha bde chen snying po, 1878–1941). *Extensive Libation Offerings, Feast Offerings, and so on for the Propitiation of Various Powerful Doctrine Protectors, and Compilation of Some of the Yakṣa Wealth Deities Rituals. Mthu ldan bstan srung khag gi 'phrin bskul gser skyems tshogs mchod sogs dang gnod sbyin nor lha'i skor 'ga' zhig phyogs gcig tu bkod pa.* Collected works, 7:451ff. Delhi: 1973.

———. *Invocation Speedily Summoning All Fulfillment of Wishes. 'Phrin bskul 'dod don myur 'gugs.*

———. *Jeweled Chariot of Faith Carrying the Gems of Great Blessings: The Way to Confer the Profound Life-Entrustment Initiation of Gyalchen Dorjé Shukden Tsal, Manifested Doctrine Protector. Rgyal chen rdo rje shugs ldan rtsal gyi srog dbang zab mo bskur tshul gyi byin rlabs rin chen nor bu'i yid ches 'dren pa'i shing rta.* Collected works, 7:500ff. Delhi: 1973.

———. *Melodious Drum of the Conqueror, Glorious in All Directions, an Extensive Exclusive Propitiation Rite of the Wrathful Five-Family Gyalchen Dorjé Shukden. Rgyal chen rdo rje shugs ldan rtsal gyi bskang chog rgyas pa phyogs las rnam par rgyal ba'i rnga dbyangs.* Collected works, 7:655ff. Delhi: 1973.

———. Supplement to the Eighth Dalai Lama's *Enthronement of Dharma Protectors. Chos skyong spyi'i mnga' gsol.* Collected works, 7:478. Delhi: 1973.

———. Supplement to Panchen Losang Chögyen's *Pure Gold Propitiation of Protectors. Bskang gso gser zhun.* Collected works, 7:477. Delhi: 1973.

Phurchok Ngawang Jampa (Phur lcog ngag dbang byams pa, 1682–1762). *Garland of White Lotuses: The Formation of the Four Great Monasteries and the Upper and Lower Tantric Colleges. Grva sa chen po bzhi dang rgyud pa stod smad chags tshul pad dkar 'phreng ba.* Woodblock edition.

Sachen [Ngawang] Kunga Lodrö (Sa chen [ngag dbang] kun dga' blo gros, 1729–83). *Amazing Storehouse of the Sakya Dynasty. Sa skya'i gdung rabs ngo mtshar bang mdzod kyi kha skong.* Beijing: People's Printing Press, 1991.

———. *Offerings Made to the Jetsok Dharma Protector. Bye tshogs chos skyong la phul ba.* Collected works, vol. *śrī,* 1988ff.

———. *A Timely Thunderbolt: The Great Wrathful Torma of Dharma Protector Gyalpo Dorjé Shukden Tsal. Chos skyong rgyal po chen po rdo rje shugs ldan rtsal kyi drag po'i gtor chen dus bab thog mda'.* In *Shukden Compendium,* 1:265ff.

———. *Whirl of Perfect Wishes Fulfilled: A Ritual Offering to the Dharma King and Monastic Discipline Holder. 'Dul 'dzin chos kyi rgyal po mchod pa'i cho ga phun tshogs 'dod rgu yongs 'khyil.* In *Shukden Compendium,* 1:206ff.

Sakya Kunga Tashi (Sa skya kun dga' bkra shis, 1654–1711). *Amazing Magical Play and Source of the Four Classes of Perfection: The Biography of Sachen Kunga Lodrö. Sa chen kun blo'i rnam thar ngo mtshar 'phrul gyi rol rtsed sde bzhi'i 'byung gnas.* In *Sa skya Lam 'bras Literature Series,* vol. 6. Dehradun: Sakya Centre, 1983.

Sakya Paṇḍita (Sa skya paṇḍi ta, 1182–1251). *Jewel Treasury of Wise Sayings. Legs bshad rin po che'i gter.*

Shakabpa, Tsepon W. D. (Zhwa sgab pa, 1907–89). *Bod kyi srid don rgyal rabs (A Political History of Tibet).* Delhi: T Tsepal Taikhang, 1976.

Sönam Bum (Bsod nams 'bum), compiler. *Pure Dharmakāya Incense Purification Rites. Lha bsang rnam dag chos sku ma.*

Sönam Rinchen, Dakchen (Bdag chen bsod nams rin chen, 1704–41). A.k.a. Ngawang Kunga Sönam Rinchen Tashi Drakpa Gyaltsen Palsangpo (*Ngag dbang kun dga' bsod nams rin chen bkra shis grags pa rgyal mtshan dpal bzang po*). *Request to the Gyalpo: Destroying the Beguilers. Rgyal gsol log 'dren tshar gcod.* In *Shukden Compendium,* 1:197ff.

Tenpa Tenzin Rinpoché (Bstan pa bstan 'dzin rin po che, 1917–2007). "Advice to Kalsang Gyatso in England." *Dbyin yul skal bzang rgya mtsho la gdam pa.* In *Garland of Pearls Compilation. Gsung rtsom phyogs bsgrigs mu tig do shal,* vol. 2.

Terdak Lingpa and Minling Dharmaśrī (Gter bdag gling pa, 1646–1714) / Smin gling dharma shri, 1654–1717), compilers. *Excellent Wish-Fulfilling Vase. 'Dod 'jo bum bzang.*

Thuken Chökyi Nyima (Thu'u bkwan chos kyi nyi ma, 1737–1802). *An Adornment to the Ganden Teachings: A Brief Biography of the Glorious and Supreme Lama, Yeshé Tenpai Drönmé, Whose Nature Is That of the All-Pervading Vajrasattva. Khyab bdag rdo rje sems dpa'i ngo bo dpal ldan bla ma dam pa ye shes bstan pa'i sgron me dpal bzang po'i rnam par thar pa mdo rtsam brjod pa dge ldan bstan pa'i mdzes rgyan.* Lhasa woodblock edition.

Trijang Rinpoché Losang Yeshé Tenzin Gyatso (Khri byang rin po che blo bzang ye shes bstan 'dzin rgya mtsho, 1901–81). *Commentary on the Praise of Shukden,* a.k.a. *Music to Delight the Oath-Bound Protectors: A Biographical Account of the Wonderful Three Secrets of Dorjé Shukden Tsel, Great Deity Guarding the Geluk Doctrine and Emanated Great Dharma King. Shugs ldan bstod 'grel / Dge ldan bstan pa bsrung ba'i lha mchog sprul pa'i chos rgyal chen po rdo rje shugs ldan rtsal gyi gsang gsum rmad du byung ba'i rtogs brjod pa'i gtam du bya ba dam can brgya mtsho dgyes pa'i rol mo.* Collected works, vol. *ca.* Translated as *Music Delighting the Ocean of Protectors,* pdf, no further data.

———. *A Deceiving and Illusory Play: The Candid and Natural Presentation of My Life Told by Myself, an Inferior Person Supposedly an Incarnation of the Ganden Throne Holder Jangchup Chöphel. Dga' ldan khri chen byang chub chos 'phel gyi skye gral du rlom pa'i gyi na pa zhig gis rang gi ngang tshul ma bcos pa lhug par bkod pa 'khrul snang sgyu ma'i zlos gar.* Collected works, 4:3–557. New Delhi: Mongolian Lama Gurudeva, 1978–85. Translated into English by Sharpa Tulku Tenzin Trinley as *The Magical Play of Illusion* (Somerville, MA: Wisdom Publications, 2018).

———. *Supplemental Explanation as a Preliminary to the Gyalchen Life-Entrustment. Rgyal chen srog gtad kyi sngon 'gro bshad pa'i mtshams sbyor kha skong.* In volume 7 of the collected works of Phabongkha.

Tseten Shabdrung Jikmé Rikpai Lodrö (Tshe tan zhabs drung rje btsun 'jigs med rigs pa'i blo gros, 1910–85). *Medicine Tree Dispelling All Pain: A Biography Detailing the Extraordinary Three Mysteries of Venerable Jikmé Damchö Gyatso (1898–1947), Immeasurably Kind and of One Nature with the All-Pervading Vajrasattva. Khyab bdag rdo rje sems dpa'i ngo bo bka drin mtshungs smed rje btsun 'jigs med dam chos rgya mtsho dpal bzang po'i gsang gsum rmad du byung ba'i rtogs brjod pa gdung sel sman gyi ljon pa.* Collected works, vol. 2. Beijing: People's Printing Press, 2007.

Tsongkhapa (Tsong kha pa, 1357–1419). *Essence of Excellent Explanation: Differentiating the Definitive and the Provisional. Drang nges legs bshad snying po.*

———. *Praise of Dependent Arising. Rten 'brel bstod pa.*

Yangchen Drupai Dorjé (Dbyangs can grub pa'i rdo rje, 1801–87). *Ornament of the Yellow Hat Doctrine: A Biography of the All-Knowing Dharmabhadra, Venerable Lama Possessed of the Three Kindnesses and Embodiment of the Buddhas of the Past, Present, and Future. Dus gsum rgyal ba kun gyi spyi gzugs bka' drin gsum ldan rje btsun bla ma thams cad mkhyen pa dharma bha dra dpal bzang po'i rnam par thar pa zhva gser bstan pa'i mdzes rgyan.* New Delhi: Ngawang Gelek Demo, 1970.

Yeshé Dönyö (Ye shes don yod, twentieth century). *Document on the Position Held by Ganden Dönyi Ling Monastery of Lhodrak, as Presented by Yeshé Dönyö. Lho brag dga' ldan don gnyis gling grwa tshang gi gnas 'dzin ye shes don yod nas phul ba'i tshig tho.*

Index

About Wisdom Publications

Wisdom Publications is the leading publisher of classic and contemporary Buddhist books and practical works on mindfulness. To learn more about us or to explore our other books, please visit our website at wisdompubs.org or contact us at the address below.

Wisdom Publications
199 Elm Street
Somerville, MA 02144 USA

We are a 501(c)(3) organization, and donations in support of our mission are tax deductible.

Wisdom Publications is affiliated with the Foundation for the Preservation of the Mahayana Tradition (FPMT).